A CALLING
IN QUESTION

A Calling in Question
A Memoir

Peter Walther

iUniverse, Inc.
Bloomington

A CALLING IN QUESTION
A Memoir

iUniverse books may be ordered through booksellers or by contacting:

iUniverse
1663 Liberty Drive
Bloomington, IN 47403
www.iuniverse.com
1-800-Authors (1-800-288-4677)

ISBN: 978-1-4759-5681-8 (sc)
ISBN: 978-1-4759-5683-2 (hc)
ISBN: 978-1-4759-5682-5 (ebk)

Library of Congress Control Number: 2012920029

Printed in the United States of America

iUniverse rev. date: 10/24/2012

CONTENTS

Sabah, North Borneo

PREFACE

This book owes its origin to a casual conversation in a Toronto pub. When I retired from teaching a few years ago, I joined a group of ex-teachers who still meet regularly, every Thursday, as a way of keeping in touch. Like the others, I often spoke about my experiences in Toronto. But occasionally I would talk about the years I taught in North Borneo. One day I told the story of a buffalo that fell off a steep jungle mountainside, crushing a friend's car as he drove home at night. There were mixed reactions to the story, but after concern for the buffalo had subsided, I was told, "Peter, you should write a book." The seed was planted.

I came to Canada in 1970 as a Catholic priest. I was thirty-three years old. I had just completed a six-year appointment teaching at a school in the jungles of Borneo. I arrived in Toronto with serious doubts about my vocation and quickly discovered I was not alone. In the sixties and seventies, priests were abandoning the Catholic Church in droves. Their reasons for doing so were, on the surface at least, quite similar. However, my pub friends were convinced that my own story was unique. Every Thursday they would urge me to start writing. One of them, Michael Forster, even threatened to do so himself if I did not.

This memoir is the result of all that urging. It is not just one story but a collage of several stories, weaving in and out like patterns in a fabric. It is the story of a small boy, growing up in the midst of a world war. It is the story of a family caught in the disintegration of the British class system. It is the story of a Catholic Church, toying with the challenge of change and failing to accept that challenge. But, most of all, it is the story of a young man struggling to be authentic while breaking from the embrace of a Catholic culture that had become a substitute for family.

Many people do not know that the Catholic Church, until quite recently, had an established policy of recruiting pre-pubescent boys as candidates for priesthood. The rationale for this policy was formulated by the Church at the Council of Trent, 400 years ago. It stated:

> "Whereas a young boy, unless he be rightly trained, is prone to follow after the pleasures of the world; and unless he be formed from his tender years unto piety and religion, before habits of vice have taken possession of the whole man, never will he perfectly, and without the greatest and well-nigh extraordinary help of God, persevere in ecclesiastical discipline" (Session 23, Chapter 18).

In 1948, when I was eleven years old, this was the rationale that formed the basis for my induction into a junior seminary. The seminary was an all-male boarding school, geared to avoiding the distraction of females. It was an artificial, purely academic society that overtly discouraged particular friendships. Human love was to be excluded. The love of Christ and his Church had to suffice. That was a rather grim outlook for someone like me who had grown up largely separated from family and deprived of human affection.

My story is not one of total doom and gloom. In my days as a seminarian and a priest there were many moments of "laughter and apple-blossom floating on the water," as T. S. Eliot so luminously expressed it. Without such moments, those of us who believed we were called to the priesthood would not have survived.

My hope is that this memoir will be of interest to readers who, while not necessarily Catholic, wonder what persuaded men of my generation to become priests. Perhaps, also, it will help skeptical Catholics understand why so many of their priests have either given up or sought other substitutes for the emptiness in their lives.

PROLOGUE

The railcar pounded along a single track, snaking through sago swamps and rubber plantations. It pushed aside overhanging palm leaves and trailing *kesidang* vines. Inside, fourteen tightly packed bodies bounced and swayed on hard, wooden benches. Hot, humid air blasted through the open windows.

It was January 1967. I was travelling to a mission station in Sabah, North Borneo, the "land below the wind." Seventeen years earlier, as an eleven-year-old Catholic boy, I had believed I was called by God to be a missionary priest. After twelve years of seminary training and three years of university, I was now on my way to a remote little jungle town deep in the interior of Sabah. It had been named Beaufort by early British colonizers. I was to be the principal of its new Catholic secondary school.

A Kadazan family sat across from me. Their traditional black costumes sparkled with silver buckles and medallions. The berry-brown children gazed wide-eyed at the *orang puthi*, the white man. They reached out to stroke the hair on my bare arms. The grandmother pulled their hands away, her wrinkled face split by a wide grin. A bright red wad of betel nut remained firmly stuck in the corner of her mouth.

The railcar slowed slightly, negotiating a steeper incline. Then, it swung precariously along the rocky bank of a tumbling river. The town of Beaufort appeared around a long curve. It was little more than a row of shop-houses raised above ground level for protection from frequent river floods. At the end of the row was a large *padang*, or village green, dominated by a grey, weather-beaten wooden building, the local government district office.

"Welcome to Beaufort!"

Father Tobias Chi held out his hand to me as I lugged my suitcase out of the railcar. He was a slightly built Chinese priest with thinning hair, twinkling brown eyes, and a Sherlock Holmes pipe. Taking my bag, he threw it into the back of a dilapidated Land Rover. I pulled myself up onto the passenger seat beside him.

"It's only a short ride to the mission," he said, "but you don't want to carry anything very far in this heat."

We bumped along a dusty track beside the railway line. It led to a square compound formed by a whitewashed, tin-roofed church, a two-story concrete school building, and a wooden house built on stilts. A young girl was sitting on the steps that led up to the veranda of the house.

"Jenny, this is your new principal," Father Chi said as we climbed out of the Land Rover.

Jenny got up with a shy smile and shook my hand. She was a slim girl, about fifteen years old, with long dark hair hanging loosely below her shoulders. She wore a brown skirt and white blouse that I realized was her school uniform.

"Jenny is our housekeeper's daughter," Father Chi told me as we climbed the stairs to the veranda. "Her mother is Chinese, but Jenny was born and raised here. She's fluent in Malay so she can help you with your sermons."

"I'll certainly need the help," I said.

I had landed in Kota Kinabalu, the capital of Sabah, Malaysia, two years earlier. During the six-week voyage from England, on a small merchant ship, I had tried to learn the rudiments of the Malay language. But I had been sent immediately to teach English at a high school. There, everyone, teachers as well as students, wanted me to speak English and I lost much of what I had learned. Now, here in Beaufort, I was expected to preach a sermon in Malay every Sunday.

I quickly established a routine with Jenny. On Saturday evenings, I would sit down with her and explain what I wanted to say. She would help me write out the sermon in Malay and the next morning I would try to deliver it without making too many mistakes.

Fortunately for me, the congregation was quite racially diverse. There were Kadazan people from the interior, Chinese merchants from the town, and Timorese immigrants who worked in the rubber plantations. Malay was not the first language for any of them.

One Sunday, a small group of Timorese gathered outside the church, waiting to see me. They seemed very excited, talking so fast that I could not understand them. Luckily, I saw Jenny out of the corner of my eye.

"Jenny, come over here," I called. "I don't know what they're talking about."

It was a strange story.

"They say that a fire broke out in their sleeping quarters yesterday," Jenny told me. "They were terrified. All their belongings were about to go up in flames. But then you appeared. You knelt down with them and prayed and immediately the skies opened in a downpour, putting out the fire."

Jenny was looking at me in awe.

"It's not true, Jenny. I never went to their camp. I never prayed with them or put out a fire. Tell them."

Well Jenny tried, but the more she spoke the more they insisted that I had really been there. In the end, we could not persuade them otherwise. I was forced to accept the fact that I had performed my first-ever miracle of bilocation. When I got back to the house, I told the story to Father Chi. He took his pipe from his mouth and chuckled.

"You're in trouble now," he said. "We're all going to expect miracles from you. By the way, we get tropical downpours here every afternoon, regular as clockwork."

PART ONE

A WARTIME CHILDHOOD

1937-1949

CHAPTER 1

I was born in London, England, in 1937.

With my very first breath, I sucked in the culture of the Catholic Church. My mother had entered a convent as a teenager, but the nuns turfed her out when they discovered holy obedience was not her strong point. Her first boyfriend became a Dominican priest when she rejected his offer of marriage. I was baptized in the hospital by Father Bruno Scott-James, a charismatic cleric whom my mother much admired. My second name, Bruno, was a tribute to him.

My mother, Betty Rita Connell-McDowell, was Irish Catholic. She had been raised from the age of six by the Sisters of Christian Instruction, an order of Catholic nuns who ran a boarding school for girls in Sherborne, Dorset. She hardly knew her parents. Her father had fought with the British army in South Africa during the Boer War and spent the rest of his life working for the British government in India. He rose to become an Inspector General of Police and was awarded the title Companion of the British Empire. He died in 1944, of cirrhosis of the liver, while traveling in his own private train. My mother was unaccountably proud of her absent father.

My own father, Malcolm Walther, met my mother in 1934, when he was a young law student in London. He was playing trumpet in a dance band at the time, to help pay for his tuition. It was the beginning of the swing era when young people flocked to the Astoria Ballroom in Charing Cross Road. He was immediately attracted to the bright-eyed Irish girl who became a fan. "He was so handsome," my mother told me, "but he wasn't a Catholic." She wouldn't agree to marry him unless he converted. When he did so, his father, a bigoted Protestant, was furious. He was immediately disinherited and the rest of his family ordered to ostracize him.

My father, of course, later resented being pressured to become a Catholic. It had cost him a substantial inheritance. His father, Dr. David Walther, was a wealthy veterinarian who owned a large estate in Norfolk. He had added to his wealth by marrying the sister of Lord Blackford, a lady by the name of Miriam Holt-Mason. She was the only member of my father's family to attend my parents' wedding. When she too became a Catholic, her husband promptly threw her out of his house and divorced her. I grew up convinced that self-sacrifice was intrinsic to Catholicism.

At first, things seemed to go well for the newlyweds. In 1934, my father was offered a partnership in a London law firm. My elder brother, Michael, was born a year later and my sister, Elizabeth, in 1938. We occupied a large rented house in a suburb of South London called Redhill.

My earliest memories are of that house. It was the summer of 1940. World War II had just broken out across the Channel, but the fields and towns of England still basked in peaceful sunshine. I was barely three years old. We children had the run of the big, three-story stone building. Sunlight streamed through tall windows as we chased each other from room to room.

The garden seemed huge. It was a magical place. The old man who was our gardener loved us. He shared slices of cheese from his lunch as he sat in the shade of the potting shed. On long summer days we played hide-and-seek among the bushes until the cool evening mist came creeping across the lawn. Then, out of breath, we leaned our backs against the stone walls of the house, still warm from the afternoon sun.

In the evenings after supper, while waiting for bath time, we played in the sand-box by the kitchen door. We built roads and tunnels and bridges until we were called indoors. Then, the three of us sat happily in the tub together, shrieking with delight when my mother's face and hair were soaked with our splashing. I always wanted to be the last one out of the bath. I loved standing up to be toweled dry, watching the water drain away from between my toes, leaving little trails of dark, wet sand in the bottom of the tub.

But the peacefulness of that summer did not last. In September, my father disappeared.

"Your daddy has volunteered to fight Hitler," my mother told us. "He has gone to India to train with a regiment of Gurkhas."

I did not know about Gurkhas or India. But I did know what war meant. Hitler had begun his blitz to bomb England into submission. The house that had been so bright and cheerful was now dark and gloomy. Heavy blackout curtains hung over the windows. Every night, German planes droned above our heads. Every night, the crash of bombs shook the walls and rattled the windows.

Startled awake by the long wailing sound of air-raid sirens, Michael and I would poke our heads under the blackout drapes covering the nursery windows. We watched, fascinated, as pencil-thin searchlight beams groped around the dark sky looking for enemy planes.

One morning Michael ran back from school early.

"It's all gone!" he shouted gleefully. "The Germans bombed the school! It's all gone!"

Now the house was no longer our own. The garden and ground floor were crowded with strangers. Soldiers, snatched from the beaches of Dunkirk, were temporarily billeted with us. Later, the Home Guard requisitioned the top floor to use as an observation post, as our house was perched high on a hill. My mother was away all day working in a munitions factory. She was up before we awoke and did not get home until long after our bedtime. It seemed to us that we scarcely ever saw her. My grandmother, Miriam, came to take care of us for a while.

We must have been quite a handful. I clearly remember the weekend when, with my baby sister, I invaded my mother's bedroom. She was out shopping. We pulled open the draws of her bureau and threw all her clothes out the window. Peering impishly over the sill, we watched as she walked up the hill to the house, her underwear festooned over the shrubs below. We did not understand why she dissolved into tears.

My mother's world was falling apart. The romance of an idyllic marriage, full of promise, was shattered by the war. With her new husband gone and her home overrun with strangers, her only refuge was the factory. There, surrounded by all the other women workers, she could almost feel young and single again. That winter she gave up the house. She sent Michael to a boarding school for boys run by Dominican nuns in Sussex. She took Elizabeth and me to be cared for by the nuns at her old boarding school in Dorset. Then, she drove back to London, convinced that she had done the best thing for us.

I was terrified of the nuns. Their long black robes and white, wimpled faces made them look really scary. Apparently, my enraged screams at being abandoned carried on so long that I fell ill. In desperation, the nuns summoned a doctor.

"There's nothing wrong with the boy," the doctor told them. "Call his mother. Tell her to come and take him back."

Fortunately, my father had only just then landed in Scotland with a regiment of Gurkhas. He was stationed at an army training camp in Cultybraggan. My mother went back down to the convent to pick up Elizabeth and me. She took us by train to the little village of Comrie which was close to the camp. There, she rented a house where my father was able to stay over occasionally. My only memory of this time is running beside him as he strode through the highland heather to shoot rabbits; then afterwards, being surrounded by cheerful Gurkhas at the camp and treated to sweet semolina pudding.

The following year, I turned five and was banished to the boarding school to which my brother Michael had already been sent.

CHAPTER 2

"You boys, be good now," my mother said as she handed us over to two black-draped Sisters of St. Dominic.

Paddington station was crowded with disheveled, anxious mothers giving their little boys a final hug. Khaki-clad soldiers, lugging huge canvas kit-bags, pushed past us. Porters, wheeling carts piled high with luggage, yelled out, "Watch yer back."

"I'll see you at Christmas time," my mother shouted frantically, while Michael dragged me onto the train.

In the compartment, Michael pushed my forlorn little suitcase up onto the webbed luggage rack. I sat down next to the window and looked out at my mother standing amid the chaos on the platform. She was pressing her open hand against the glass, her fingers spread wide, and her mouth forming words I couldn't hear. The train slowly started to pull away. She ran alongside at first. Then it picked up speed. She stopped, turning away quickly to hide her face. I watched until her head disappeared in the crowd. I was miserable. But I refused to cry. Not in front of all those other boys.

St. Dominic's Preparatory School was run by Dominican nuns. It was originally located on the south coast of England, close to the site of the battle of Hastings where the British had been defeated by invading Normans in AD 1066. With the Germans threatening their own invasion, the nuns decided to retreat inland to another of their boarding schools. It was near the town of Stroud, in Gloucestershire, and had been, until then, an all-girls school.

Sister Benedict was the nun appointed to be in charge of us boys. She was tall and thin, with a bleached-white face. To me, it seemed that she seldom smiled. Her eyes, a steely grey-blue, glinted behind gold wire-framed spectacles. She carried a bamboo cane to deal with any evil we might get up to. At one time or another, every one of us felt the sting of that cane across our hands.

The girls had their own boarding house, but we boys were put up in the nuns' convent, a long, lovely, two-storey Georgian manor house. We only saw the girls on rare occasions when they came out to play field hockey. Their playing field was separated from ours by an iron rail fence. Whenever we saw them, we would hoist ourselves up to the top rail and watch as they chased around in their short, blue, hockey skirts. Then, Sister Benedict would come running, her long robes flying. "Get down from there," she would shriek, and we climbed down sheepishly, not knowing why we five-year-old boys were not allowed to watch the girls play.

Fortunately the other nuns did their best to keep us happy with games and play. We ducked for apples on Guy Fawkes Day and searched for conkers with which to fight in the fall. Conkers, the nuts of a horse chestnut tree, were threaded on a short string and used in a game where the objective was to smash an opponent's conker with your own.

I don't remember my brother Michael being at the school. He was all of seven years old. He must have played with the older boys and slept in a different dormitory. I was not aware that he was even there.

One pretty young nun, Sister Mary Vincent, would read adventure stories to us while we sat on the floor at her feet. She had bright, laughing eyes and a mesmerizing reading voice. I liked her. I would sit as close to her as I could. I played with the big, wooden beads of the long rosary that hung from her leather belt. Sometimes she would read us letters from her brother who was a missionary in Borneo. He belonged to an order of priests called the Mill Hill Missionaries. The name came from the location of their seminary in Mill Hill, a suburb of North London. His letters were full of stories about headhunters and orangutans and adventures in the jungle.

Then one day Sister Mary Vincent told us there would be no more letters. She looked as if she had been crying.

"You must all help me pray for my brother. Borneo has been invaded by the Japanese. All the missionaries have been put in a prison camp."

I was upset for her. I didn't know what she meant by the Japanese invasion. But it was obvious that something bad had happened to her brother. I missed his stories.

The war was never very far away from our lives. Most of us were at the boarding school because our fathers were fighting in the army and our mothers were working in factories or in the land army. I made friends with a red-haired boy called Rory whose father was with General Montgomery in North Africa. He was a cheerful little lad who always had a mischievous gleam in his eye, always ready for a dare.

One day the Mother Superior of the nuns came to our classroom door. "Rory, come here," she said. She was a large woman whom we only saw occasionally as she swept along a hallway or down the stairs. She looked strange because she always kept her hands hidden under her long black robe.

Rory got up and walked over to her, hesitating, apprehensive. She withdrew one hand and placed it on Rory's shoulder as she led him out of the room.

He's in trouble, I thought.

When Rory came back into the classroom he was looking pale.

"What's up? What did she want?" I whispered as he sat down.

Rory just looked straight ahead and said nothing.

"Go on. Tell us! Tell us!" whispered some of the other boys, grinning.

But Rory just sat there, a glazed look on his face.

After class, Rory and I managed to escape from the other boys. We made for a huge beech tree in the playground where we often spent time together. We would sit with our backs pressed against the firm, smooth, grey trunk, enjoying the feel of its solid strength. Rory sat silently for a while, looking down at his crossed feet, picking at a loose strand of wool at the top of his knee socks.

"It's my dad," he said finally. "He's dead. He got blown up by a mine."

He didn't cry. There were no tears. He just sat there with his head down.

It didn't feel strange to me that he wouldn't cry. The only time we ever cried was on the first night back at school after holidays. Then it was hard not to, listening to all the other boys sobbing into their pillows. I would cry too. But I made sure the other boys didn't hear me.

A few weeks later we were all eating lunch at the long tables in the room the nuns called the refectory. Unexpectedly, the Mother Superior came into the room. She beckoned to Michael and me to come outside. She was holding a telegram in her hand. "It's from your mother," she said. "Your granddad just died in India." She looked at us sympathetically. It felt odd because I had never even met him.

Although we were safe from bombs at Stroud, we were very aware of the war. Our games were always about killing Germans. We would run around with arms outstretched, pretending to be fighter planes attacking German bombers. Sometimes, high in the sky, we saw the tangled contrails of planes weaving in and out. One day a burning Spitfire came low over our playground. I saw the pilot's white face looking down at us as he tried to avoid the school. His plane crashed just beyond the trees at the edge of the hockey field. A huge column of black smoke rose into the air. The nuns hustled us back into the school as fire trucks raced across the field. I knew that the pilot probably died, but we were never told.

It was a long time before I stopped seeing his white face in my dreams.

CHAPTER 3

In spite of the war, we still went home for school holidays. It was always an adventure. We were put on a train at the station in Stroud, with our names and addresses printed on pieces of paper pinned to our coats. We imagined the tags were to identify us if the train were to be blown up by a bomb. Two of the nuns accompanied us to London where we were met by one of our parents.

The first time Michael and I travelled home for Christmas was very strange. It was December, 1942. The train was constantly stopping and starting as we got closer to London. Sometimes it would stand for ten or fifteen minutes until another train, crammed with soldiers, went thundering by.

While waiting, we stared out of the windows at a devastated city. Whole streets were blocked with rubble that had once been houses. Sandbags were piled high in front of doors and shop windows. Huge silver-grey barrage balloons swung above rooftops like great floating whales.

When the train finally reached Paddington station, we were herded out onto the platform. Parents gathered around, picking out the boys who belonged to them. A pretty lady in a green winter coat came up to Michael and me.

"Hello, Peter dear," she said, giving me a hug.

"Hello," I said tentatively. She looked like my mother, but I wasn't quite sure. She took my hand and we started to walk down the platform to the exit.

"Where are we going, Mummy?" I finally asked her.

She stopped and turned to me, shaking with laughter.

"I'm not your Mummy," she said. "I'm your Aunt Doreen!"

I was mortified. I felt she was laughing at me for being so stupid.

"Your mother has rented a house on the Isle of Wight," she explained. "There's a thick fog over the Channel, so the ferries aren't running. She phoned and asked me to pick you up. You, Michael, and Elizabeth are going to stay with me in London until the fog lifts."

I don't remember very much of that Christmas holiday. But the following summer of 1943 was unforgettable. The house that my mother had rented was just a few hundred yards from a sandy beach in the little town of Bembridge, on the east coast of the Isle of Wight.

One morning in mid-July we woke to a particularly gorgeous, sunny day. It was the kind of day when time seems to stand still. No breath of wind stirred the leaves on the trees that lined the road outside our house. The sky was an infinity of blue. Summer holidays stretched endlessly before us, memories of school obliterated. I had just turned six years old.

That morning I could hardly wait to finish breakfast and scamper out into the sunshine with Michael and Elizabeth. It was already so hot on the road that the soft, black tar squelched between our toes as we ran barefoot down to the beach. There, a couple of soldiers slouched lazily against the sandbags surrounding an anti-aircraft gun, smoking cigarettes. They grinned at us as we ran past, a little wistful, perhaps, at seeing our excitement.

Standing on top of the lifeboat ramp that led down to the water, I could just make out the long, thin strip of hazy contour that was the mainland. Out in the Channel, there was the distinctive, three-funnel silhouette of the Queen Mary. Other smaller ships were forming into a convoy. And stretching along the sand, half submerged by the incoming tide, was the rusty iron scaffolding erected to block the landing craft and gliders of Hitler's impending invasion.

The beach was littered with crates of rotting fruit and the flotsam from supply ships sunk by German U-boats. But that did not stop us from playing among them and risking our mother's wrath when we came home with hands and feet black from oil tar.

We had taught ourselves to swim by hanging on to the satchel-like life vests that washed ashore. We were completely oblivious to the fate of the sailors who had drowned because they had no time to put them on.

As we ran into the waves that morning, there seemed to be more debris than usual. There were boots and tin mugs and pieces of clothing rising and falling on the surge of the incoming tide.

"Look there," Michael shouted.

He was wading through the water towards a wisp of smoke that was coming from a bright orange can. He scooped it up and threw it onto the beach. The smoke started to get thicker.

"Quick," he yelled, "let's make a volcano."

Awed by the brilliance of the idea, Elizabeth and I splashed our way to the shore and began to shovel sand onto the can. Soon we had a substantial mound. Michael took a stick and dug a hole all the way down the middle, rotating it to make a crater. Almost immediately, black smoke billowed up with a hissing sound. Then a splendid spear of bright, white flame shot skywards. It was perfect.

We capered gleefully around our volcano. Michael poked at it with his stick. I flapped a soggy rag over it to make smoke signals like the Indians in the movies.

Suddenly, a loud yell came from the top of the beach. "Oy, you lot! Get away from that thing!" The two soldiers from the gun were pounding down the sand towards us. "Get out of there. What do you think you're doing?" The soldiers grabbed our arms and dragged us up to the top of the beach. They pushed us behind the sandbags and started to wind down the barrel of their gun until it was pointing at our volcano.

Kaboom!

The shock wave thumped against our bodies. A huge blast of flame and smoke mushroomed into the air. Sand and bits of metal rained down on the beach. Then the plume of black smoke began to drift slowly out across the water. The incendiary bomb and our volcano had completely disappeared.

The soldiers were waving their arms at us and making strange shapes with their mouths. We couldn't hear a word they said, our ears still ringing from the blast of the explosion.

Slowly the ringing faded into silence.

The sun still shone. The sky was still blue. The waves still lapped gently against the shore.

We turned and raced each other up the road, wanting to be the first to tell of our adventure.

Chapter 4

I often felt confused and uncertain of myself during those school holidays. I was never quite sure about what was going on around me.

I was too young to question why my mother chose to live on the Isle of Wight during the war. It was one of the closest parts of England to occupied France, and directly in the flight path of German bombers attacking Portsmouth harbour. Years later Michael told me that he thought she was having an affair with one of the officers at the nearby naval base.

It was entirely possible. My mother was still a vibrant young woman and was quite capable of flirting with the young servicemen who flocked around her at the local pub. My father came home so rarely that I hardly recognized him when he did. Once, when he was home on leave for a few days, a woman came to the door asking for him. Apparently I answered the door and told her, "Mummy's upstairs in the bathroom with a man." My mother thought it hilarious that I didn't know the man was my father.

Another day I found my mother in the kitchen reading a letter. "Daddy has some leave and may be coming home for a visit," she said. I felt enormously excited and ran out of the house determined to be the first to meet him. I went up the street to the crossroads where I could see him coming from any direction. I sat on the sidewalk and waited. Occasionally I would see a figure in the distance and jump up expectantly. But it was never my father. All afternoon I sat there. When the daylight started to fade I gave up. I walked home, hardly able to hold back tears. My mother just seemed surprised that I had waited that long.

Going back to school after a holiday was always painful and very strange. On the train I would deliberately try not to think about home. School was a different world. I was a different Peter in the school world. I erased my family from my consciousness. Instead, I did everything I could to please the nuns, especially Sister Benedict.

In 1944 I turned seven. According to the Catholic Church, I had attained the age of reason. With the other boys in my class, I was prepped by Sister Benedict to make my First Communion.

I think that most Catholic children never forget the day of their First Communion. I clearly remember kneeling in my place at Mass, praying desperately for God to help me be good and do everything right. When the time came for communion, I went up to the altar and knelt at the railing, looking straight ahead. I felt someone pushing in beside me, but the priest was there offering me the host.

At the end of the Mass, we all filed out of the church. As I came out into the sunlight, a woman rushed up to me and enveloped me in a hug. It was my mother. I knew it was her, but at the same time she felt like a stranger. She was not supposed to be there. She did not exist in my school life.

"Didn't you see me kneeling next to you at communion?" she asked, almost in tears. "Your daddy's here and we're all going out to breakfast."

I saw a tall man standing back from us, smiling. He wore the army uniform that I remembered and he looked very smart. But he too felt like a stranger. The woman took my hand and I kept looking up at her, trying hard to recognize her, to connect with her. I was completely disoriented. I knew they were my parents, but at the same time they were strangers. They could not really exist in my school space. School was one world. Home was another, different world. You had to take a train to get across from one to the other.

As the three of us walked over to a car that was parked next to the church, I looked around at the other boys. They were all surrounded by people I didn't know, chattering and laughing. And then I saw Rory. He was standing alone, just outside the church door, blinking in the sunlight.

"Can Rory come with us?" I asked, pointing at him. "He hasn't got anyone to go with."

My mother looked down at me doubtfully. "We'll have to see if Sister Benedict will let him," she said. I desperately wanted Rory to come. I didn't want to be alone with these people. But Sister Benedict would not allow it. As we drove away I looked back to see Rory walking into the school with Sister Benedict holding his hand.

Driving to the restaurant, my parents were having fun together in the front seat. They had stopped to buy a few groceries and my father teased my mother by repeatedly reaching out of the window and balancing a cereal box on the hood of the car. Every time he caught it as it almost fell off, my mother screamed, thinking it would drop onto the road.

When we arrived at the restaurant, I was relieved to see that some other boys from the communion class were there. People fussed over us, serving different kinds of food that we had never seen before. When my plate arrived, I could not eat most of it. I sat there looking at the food while everyone else was eating.

"Eat up, Peter," my father said.

"I can't. I don't like it."

"Nonsense, my boy. You've got black pudding there and artichokes. You can't waste it. That's good food. There's a war on. Think of the starving Russians!"

"But I don't like it," I insisted.

I could feel things getting tense.

"Now look here," he said loudly, leaning across the table at me, as the rest of the room went suddenly quiet. "Just you eat that food, or we're going straight back to the school, right now!"

"No," I said. "I can't."

His face turned a nasty purple colour.

"Malcolm, please don't," my mother pleaded. But it was no use.

"That's it," he yelled, pushing his chair back and grabbing my arm. "Let's go!"

We marched out of the restaurant. He pushed me into the car and we drove back to the school. My mother was in tears. She tried to hug me as I got out of the car, but I twisted away and ran for the front door. It was good to get away from the nightmare, good to be back in my school space. I didn't turn to look as they drove off.

CHAPTER 5

War meant being permanently hungry.

"We can't just buy food any time we want," my mother explained when we arrived back home for the summer holidays. She showed us our ration books. "We have to tear out stamps to give to the shopkeeper whenever we buy groceries. No stamps, no food."

In some strange way, after the train and ferry ride to the Isle of Wight, my mother was my real mother again.

I constantly craved food. We kids foraged for blackberries and raided apple orchards. More than once, I was up a tree throwing apples down to my sister when the farmer saw us. He scared us with his yelling but we were able to run fast enough not to be caught. The apples were still green but we ate them anyway, risking fearsome stomach aches.

We shared our house with a young American woman called Susan. Her husband was involved in the preparations for the D-Day invasion. They had a small baby girl, only one year old. Susan was able to buy tins of powdered glucose for her baby and foolishly left the can in a low cupboard in the kitchen. I got into the habit of sneaking spoonfuls of glucose when no one was around.

We were all sitting at the kitchen table one day when Susan discovered the half-empty tin.

"Your children are stealing the baby's glucose!" she shouted at my mother.

"Nonsense," my mother said, tossing her head. She had never really liked Susan. She resented having to share the house with her. "My children would never do anything like that!"

"Well, who else is around here to take it?" yelled Susan, "unless it's you!" She glared at my mother.

I could feel my face getting hot.

But my mother was up for a fight. There was no way that she was letting a foreigner get the better of her.

17

"How dare you accuse me of stealing!" she said, stepping up to Susan. "You Americans come here thinking you can take over the country. We'd be much better off without you. Mr. Churchill must be mad to let you come here."

My Irish mother had no high opinion of the British government or Americans. Susan was taken aback. She had no idea that my mother harboured such resentment. The two of them launched into a slanging match about who needed whom to win the war. I was able to slip away without owning up to being the thief.

For days afterwards, I felt horribly guilty and ashamed. But I couldn't confess without shattering the good-boy image that I so carefully cultivated. I did not know my mother well enough. How could she possibly love me if she knew I was a thief?

And then one day in the summer of 1945, when I was eight, we heard the most exciting news. Japan had surrendered. The war was over.

The whole town poured out onto the street. Everyone was yelling and screaming and dancing. There was a general movement down to the beach. People were carrying old pieces of furniture, wooden crates, anything that would burn. It was all thrown into a huge pile on the sand. All day they came, until the pile grew as tall as a house.

By the time the sun had sunk into the sea and the sky had dimmed to a dusty purple, the entire population of Bembridge was there. Old people, young people, shopkeepers, even the little old lady from the post office, they all milled around the monster pile.

In the gathering darkness, we three children managed to squirm our way to the front. Two soldiers were splashing petrol around the edge of the bonfire. Then they stepped back and one of them set fire to the end of an old broom. He reached out with it and a line of flame flickered along the sand. With a whoosh, the fire shot skywards in one great sheet of flame. People were shouting, singing, hugging each other, their faces lit by the roaring inferno.

Everyone seemed giddy with joy. The intensity was almost scary. People started holding hands. I grabbed at Michael and Elizabeth. A huge circle formed. It swayed from side to side, everyone laughing and yelling and crying. Sparks and smoke billowed up into the night sky. The bonfire became a gigantic candle in celebration of peace.

CHAPTER 6

The end of the war meant that St. Dominic's Preparatory School for Boys could return to its original home near Hastings.

The school was a mess. It had been used to billet soldiers. Graffiti and garbage were everywhere. The wooden blocks that formed the parquet floor of the chapel had been torn up for firewood. Smashed windows were covered with cardboard. The soccer field had been ploughed to grow potatoes.

At first, it was fun because classes could not start right away. Sister Benedict organized us into work crews to help clean up. We were given buckets of soapy water to scrub the walls. We wandered through the building collecting the trash that was strewn everywhere.

The nuns had decided to bring in some lay people to help manage us. There was a Mr. O'Gorman who became our gym teacher, and a delightful old gentleman called Mr. Groves who taught us music.

I liked Mr. Groves. He gave us a singing lesson every Thursday afternoon. He was an elderly man with long, silver-white hair and a ruddy complexion. He dressed very elegantly in a dark formal suit, starched white shirt, and little red bow tie. It was obvious that music was his passion. I did not particularly like the songs he wanted us to sing, but I enjoyed listening to him play the piano. He was always kind and patient with us.

"Here, hold this," he would say, giving us a lighted candle. "Hold it in front of your mouth. Control your breath from your stomach. I don't want to see the flame flicker when you sing."

I loved to sing. I had a particularly strong soprano voice. Mr. Groves decided to enter three of us in the town music competition that was held each year. We had to learn a seventeenth-century song called "Nymphs and Shepherds" by Henry Purcell. It was hardly a song that appealed to nine-year-old boys in 1946. Mr. Groves must have assumed we were too young to appreciate the lively, playful mood of the song. He was content if we just stayed in tune without going flat.

As the day of the competition approached, Sister Benedict started to fret because my voice was beginning to break. She made me swallow two raw eggs. "They will keep your vocal chords lubricated," she said. I was proud that I was able to swallow them down, especially when Rory screwed up his face and said it was gross when I told him.

The eggs must have worked because I got through my song without my voice breaking. However, the judges, having sat through some 40 desperately dreary renditions, decided not to award a prize. They felt that none of us had captured the spirit of the piece. I was hugely disappointed, mostly because I had endured the egg torture for nothing.

I had never been particularly athletic, so it was hard for me to impress our new gym teacher, Mr. O'Gorman. He was among the first merchant marine sailors to come home after the war. He had huge, muscular arms like Popeye, complete with an anchor tattoo. His tight T-shirt always seemed about to split over his enormous chest.

The one experience I had in his gym class that scares me to this day was boxing. Boxing was taught in most English boys' schools. It was considered a manly sport, but was also used to settle differences.

I had been particularly aggravated by one boy in my class called Archie. He delighted in mocking the fact that I had started to wear glasses. Catcalls of "Hey four-eyes," "Hey sissy," and "Hey softy," started to get to me. So I exercised my right in gym class to challenge him to a fight.

Mr. O'Gorman acted as referee. He laced us into boxing gloves and took my glasses. Then we went at it. Archie landed a few punches to my head and I felt myself getting furious. I could only see a white blur where his face was. So I ignored his punches and simply threw myself at him, pounding away at his face. He started to back off but I wouldn't let up. I kept pounding and pounding and pounding until I felt Mr. O'Gorman pulling me away. I was in a blind rage. I would never have stopped if I had not been pulled off him. The two of us just stood there, Archie sobbing, me still trembling with fury.

"Shake hands, now," Mr. O'Gormon said.

We touched gloves briefly and I turned away. I was shocked at the intensity of my anger. It had erupted from somewhere deep, deep inside me. I felt frightened and ashamed. How could I possibly have had so much rage? I had wanted to obliterate that white face.

CHAPTER 7

The Christmas of 1945 was the first without a war that any of us could remember. We impatiently counted down the days to the holiday. By the time we boarded the train to London we were a noisy, boisterous bunch.

But then we began to notice the passengers around us. Everyone looked so tired and anxious. They didn't seem to have enough energy to even tell us to be quiet. They just sat there with unseeing, vacant eyes, bodies swaying listlessly with the rocking of the train. For the first time, I think, we began to understand what the war had done to people. So many homes destroyed, so many families deprived of mums or dads or children.

At school I had been shocked when the nuns told us that our hero, Winston Churchill, had been defeated in the election. We hated the new Prime Minister, Clement Atlee, mostly because he had a little black moustache just like Hitler. The nuns had told us how happy we would be when the war was over. Happiness, for small boys, translated into plenty of food and sticky sweets. But food was still rationed, even more than it had been during the war. Even basic foods, like bread and potatoes, were rationed.

When my mother met me in London, I was surprised that we headed for the Underground instead of boarding a regular train.

"Where are we going?" I asked. "Aren't we going to the Isle of Wight?"

My mother looked at me with sad eyes.

"No, we won't be going back there anymore."

I was immensely disappointed. I looked up at her, wanting to make her smile. Her face looked so thin and pale in the flickering lights of the Tube as it rattled and roared through the dark tunnels.

We got out at a station that had the name TOOTING-BEC written on the blue stripe across the bright red circle that was the London Underground symbol.

"Hold onto my hand, Peter. We have to walk. We have a flat in Streatham that we're renting until your daddy gets a better job."

It seemed as if we walked for miles. Most of the shops were boarded up. The streets were wide and empty, with only an occasional rickety red bus or taxi cab passing by. There were great gaps in the row houses. Walls that were once the inside of someone's private home lay exposed to public view. Bits of torn, faded wallpaper hung loose from the brickwork, flapping forlornly in the wind.

We came to Streatham Common, its trees black skeletons wreathed in wisps of winter fog. A few little children in grubby clothes sat on some swings, idly twisting in endless, dispirited circles. They gazed at us with wide solemn eyes as we passed, strangely silent.

The flat turned out to be on the second floor of a rundown row house. The front door hung open from a broken hinge. It had been blasted by the bomb that demolished the house across the street. We had to climb a set of narrow wooden stairs leading to another, only slightly more secure, door. It had four cracked glass panes, covered on the inside by a frayed lace curtain.

As we walked in, Michael and Elizabeth jumped up from the kitchen table directly in front of us.

"What took you so long?" Elizabeth asked, hanging on to my mother's arm.

"Come with me," Michael said, grabbing my suitcase. "I'll show you your bed." He pushed aside a curtain that hung across a small archway. "This was really meant to be a dining room," he said, "but it's our bedroom for now."

It was a windowless little room painted a dull green like the rest of the flat. A bare light bulb hung from a wire in the ceiling. Two wood and canvas camp beds had been set against opposite walls. Michael's suitcase lay open on one of them, with his clothes spilling out onto the floor.

"That's yours," he said, pointing to the other bed. "There's not much room in here but this will do for the next two weeks."

I sat down on the camp bed and it immediately tipped over. Michael grinned. "You can't sit on them," he said, pulling me up. "It takes a bit of practice to even lie down on them."

It was good to be with Michael again. I had not seen him for a while as we were no longer at the same school. He had been removed from St.

Dominic's because of his hatred for Sister Benedict. Her predilection for administering corporal punishment with a bamboo cane had only served to stimulate his frequent acts of rebellion. My mother sent him to Laxton Hall, a school administered by Dominican priests. She must have assumed that male authority figures would have a more salutary effect on his behaviour.

"Daddy's going to be late," my mother said as we came back into the kitchen. "We'll have supper without him."

My father had survived the war, but it had taken its toll. He had been particularly traumatized when, as a lawyer, he was ordered to collate evidence of the Holocaust for the Nuremberg trials.

My mother was still dressed in her winter coat as she stood peeling potatoes at a large porcelain sink. Elizabeth was struggling to open a can of baked beans.

"We don't have very much to eat. The schools kept your ration books," she said.

Somehow I felt it was my fault that the school had kept my ration book.

After supper we all decided to go to bed early. The flat was cold and damp as there was no central heating. The only warmth came from the gas stove in the kitchen. I piled whatever extra clothes I had on top of my blanket and was soon fast asleep.

I woke up suddenly.

In the blackness I heard someone stumbling up the stairs. The kitchen door crashed open just as a light came on. Through the crack between the curtains in our doorway, I could see my mother standing by the light switch in her pink terry cloth robe. She was looking down at my dad sprawled across the kitchen table.

"Where's supper?" he asked loudly, slurring his words.

"Shush, the children are asleep." my mother said. "I left your supper to warm in the oven."

There was the sound of scraping chairs and banging plates.

"Is this all there is? Just baked beans?"

"I don't have the children's ration books. I couldn't buy anything else."

"That's no excuse. Harry's wife buys all their stuff on the black market. Why can't you do that?"

"Because we don't have enough money," she said. "You're spending it all on beer. You really need to get a better job."

"I've got a great job," he exploded. "Damn it, woman, you just don't know how to use the money I give you."

I shut my eyes tight and pulled the pillow around my ears. I was beginning to get a hollow feeing in my stomach. Why did they have to quarrel? I had only just got home. It shouldn't be like this.

On weekdays my father left early for work and came home from the pub late at night. But on Saturday he would sleep in. Then, in the afternoon, he was transformed into a different person, charming and cheerful.

I found myself looking forward to weekends; each one was a new adventure. There was the time he found a rusty old bicycle and took us up to Streatham Common where we took turns learning to ride. The next week he took us to the British Museum and showed us world famous objects like the Rosetta Stone and sculptures from the Parthenon.

Another week, we stood in awe looking up at Foucault's massive pendulum at the Science Museum. He explained how it demonstrated the rotation of the earth as the slowly swinging bob gradually changed direction. I was fascinated by all the mechanical inventions, the craftsmanship with which they were built, and the amazing ingenuity of the inventors.

With all the visits to the museums and galleries, I quickly learned to navigate the London Underground. Travelling on the Tube was cheap and admission to the museums was free. After a while, I was able to get around on my own.

And I learned the use of money. We were only given a few shillings to go places, but I soon realized I could actually buy things with the change. To a food-deprived child, this was a significant discovery.

There was a small grocery shop at the end of our street, next to Streatham Common. On my way to and from excursions, I would pause to salivate over the displays of rosy apples, yellow bananas, and juicy pears in the window. They were far too expensive to purchase with the meager number of pennies I had in my pocket. Then one day I noticed a tray of grapes; huge bunches of exotic purple grapes; grapes

25

that I had only ever seen in baroque paintings at the National Gallery. By the time I arrived home, those grapes had become an obsession. I had to have some.

As luck, or fate, would have it, my mother had left her purse on the kitchen table. A purse had money. Money could buy grapes. I quietly tore out a stamp from her ration book. Perhaps I could get away with it, in spite of my guardian angel. Elizabeth was the only one at home to witness the crime.

"How would you like to go with me and buy some grapes?" I asked her as I slipped a half crown coin out of the purse.

She looked at me with a curious smile. "OK," she said and the two of us went skipping off down the stairs and along the street to Joe's Fruit and Vegetable shop.

That half crown bought a lot of grapes. We walked out of the shop carrying two great bunches. We crossed the street into the common and found a park bench conveniently obscured by shrubbery. It was paradise regained. Bacchus had nothing on us. We gorged ourselves on those grapes.

When we got back to the house, my mother was frantically going through her purse. She took one look at us and she knew. Guilt and grape juice were spread all over our faces. It was then that I realized I had reversed the biblical story of Eve.

"Peter made me do it," Elizabeth shrieked, dissolving into tears. "He took the money from your purse. He made me go with him. He used the money to buy grapes."

I stood betrayed.

"You bad child, Peter; you bad, wicked child; stealing is a sin. Wait till your father hears about this. How could you do it? How could you take all that money?"

When my father got home, it was much the same; except that he yelled louder and longer. Then he grabbed me by the arm and marched me down the stairs into the street.

"We're going straight to church," he said. "You've committed a mortal sin. You're going to confession."

I was terrified; a mortal sin! I could go to hell, forever. Shame and guilt seared my soul. My dad strode into the church, found a priest, and proclaimed my guilt in ringing tones for all to hear.

Strangely, by the time I left the confessional with a whole rosary to pray as a penance, my dad's anger seemed to have dissipated. He took my hand. As we walked back home, I could have sworn he was smiling quietly to himself.

That Christmas in Streatham was bleak. My gifts turned out to be Michael's old clothes that he had outgrown. Food was so scarce that my mother couldn't make our traditional Christmas dinner. The government had just removed the restrictions on fraternizing with the prisoners of war who were cleaning the rubble from the streets. Families were allowed to invite them over for Christmas dinner but we could not even do that.

CHAPTER 8

After Christmas, back at St. Dominic's, things were no better. The nuns were doing everything to economize. They decided that we did not need hot water. Once a week, we were herded, naked, into a communal shower to shiver and shriek under the ice-cold deluge. Sister Benedict would stand guard and thwack our nine-year-old bare bottoms with a cane if we tried to escape. I was more aware of the sudden, sharp pain than the inappropriateness of what she was doing.

Every day we had to go out into the playground, no matter how cold the weather might be. "You need fresh air," Sister Benedict insisted. We would stand around in the playground, our hands deep in our pockets to keep them warm.

"The devil finds work for idle hands," Sister Benedict would say when she saw us. She was convinced we were playing with our penises in the cold. She took our pants and sewed up the pockets.

Because food rationing was still in effect, the nuns decided we should all help create a vegetable garden. It was down at the bottom end of the soccer field. In the first few weeks of autumn, Sister Benedict had taken us down there to prepare the soil. Now, with the coming of spring, we were each given a section to plant.

I enjoyed working in the vegetable garden. There was something reassuring about the warm, moist soil. I liked marking out the rows where the seeds were to be planted. We tied binder twine to sticks to keep the rows straight and dug a little trough under them for the seeds. When Sister Benedict had given her approval, we would pat down the soil over the seeds and go back to the school to get water. Later, during play time, we'd run down to see if the seeds were growing. For a few days, we'd forget. But when we remembered, we'd go racing back down to find neat little rows of bright green shoots springing up from the dark earth.

Sometimes two of the nuns would take us for walks in the nearby woods. In May, the clearings between the trees were carpeted with bluebells. We'd pick huge armfuls of them to bring back to school. Along the paths, daffodils and primroses grew wild and the hedges were white with hawthorn blossoms. Beyond the school were the gently rolling hills of the Sussex Downs stretching as far as my eyes could see, pastures for the imagination.

I think that the beauty of the countryside around the school helped soothe the ache in my heart for human affection. Strangely, the cold, clinical aloofness with which Sister Benedict treated us only made me try harder to win her attention. Instead of rebelling, I desperately struggled to please her.

One day, an American soldier with an officer next to him drove a Jeep into the middle of our playground. The officer got out and unloaded a big cardboard box labeled Action Rations. We all crowded around as he started to hand out little khaki-coloured tins. Each tin contained small packages of gum and candy.

Instantly, Sister Benedict appeared.

"You boys, hand those over to me at once, do you hear?"

Frantically, we tried to hide the tins behind our backs, under sweaters, in any unsown pocket.

The officer removed his cap. "Aw, Sister, don't be such a party pooper. It's time to celebrate. Today's the first anniversary of VE day."

He turned back to the Jeep and lifted out another box. It was crammed full of fireworks.

"You guys need to have a show. You've got a nice big field here. You could set these up tonight and invite all the neighbours. It'll be fun." He grinned naively.

Sister Benedict drew herself up like a cobra preparing to strike.

"Young man, this is a school, not a circus," she hissed. "Just take that . . . that stuff, and get off our property."

"Aw shucks, Sister, don't be like that. I talked to Monsignor Hennessey at the church and he said it would be okay. In fact, he said he would come over here to watch the show himself."

Sister Benedict flinched. The appeal to Monsignor Hennessy trumped her authority. If there is one thing that is unassailable in the

Catholic Church, it is the hierarchical pecking order. But she would not easily give in.

"In that case, I shall go and consult with Reverend Mother. You! Come along with me." She turned on her heel and strode back to the school.

We had been watching this exchange with considerable interest. As the officer followed across the playground, he turned and gave us a broad wink. "Enjoy the candy," he said.

We did.

This was one of the rare battles that Sister Benedict lost. Monsignor Hennessey approved the fireworks. Ecclesiastical authority triumphed.

After supper we gathered outside the school. It was a dark, cold night. There was no moon. A few stars glimmered between scudding clouds. Occasionally a gust of wind made us huddle together, jacket collars pulled up around our ears. Our excited anticipation of the imminent spectacle rendered the cold insignificant.

Monsignor Hennessy had organized some men from the parish to set up the fireworks. The first rocket went up with a whoosh and a bang. A splendid canopy of blue and red light mushroomed over our heads. It was followed by two more in quick succession. In between, we could see the little yellow sparks of spent rockets falling back to earth. And then, of course, one landed right in the middle of the box of fireworks. The men scattered in panic. The box exploded into a fiercely bright fireball. Coloured tracers shot out in every direction. The nuns screamed. Everyone was running. From the shelter of the school, we watched sadly as all those fantastic fireworks burned themselves out.

Chapter 9

At the end of June I got a rare letter from my mother. "Your dad was very ill after Christmas," she wrote. "He had to go to a hospital for soldiers who had a bad time in the war. When he got better, I took him over to our family home in Ireland. You will be spending the summer here with us."

I was immensely excited. Ireland was famous for not having any food rationing.

On the last day of school, I could hardly contain myself. The train ride to London seemed to take forever. My mother was waiting on the platform with Elizabeth and Michael. I would have kissed her if my friends hadn't been watching.

Soon, we were on the train to Holyhead and from there we took the ferry across to Dublin. My father was waiting for us with a rented car. We were all a little shy of him at first, but he was in a good mood. He packed us into the little Morris Minor and we headed off to Limerick and the West Coast.

He talked all the way. He pointed out peat bogs and donkey carts. He explained the myth of how donkeys got a cross marked on their backs after carrying Christ into Jerusalem on the first Palm Sunday. He told us how, centuries ago, St. Patrick had driven all the snakes out of Ireland and how everyone was now Catholic because of that.

In County Clare, we stopped at a farm just outside Ennis. A little old man came out of the farmhouse to meet us.

"This is your Great Uncle Alfie," my mother said. "Alfie Finucane." My mother was very proud of the Finucane name.

I liked Uncle Alfie immediately. His face was all brown and wrinkled, like a withered potato. He lived alone and managed the farm by himself. He had never been married. When he ushered us into the tiny, thatched-roof farmhouse, everything was as clean and neat as a new pin. The walls were whitewashed and the stone floor covered with rush mats. He had a couple of sheep dogs that followed him wherever he went.

I was fascinated by the blocks of peat that he burned for fuel in the kitchen stove, and by the little wooden whistles he whittled out of hazel wood. He used them for directing the dogs. He showed us how he practised willow witching, finding underground water by using a willow stick, shaped like a Y.

Uncle Alfie treated us to steaming mugs of strong tea. In his delightful Irish brogue, he told us stories about our mother as a little girl. He made her laugh and blush in a way I had never seen before. I was sad when we had to leave. My mother gave him a big hug. He stood in the doorway waving goodbye as we drove off. For some reason, we were never taken back to visit him again.

It was an amazing summer. Ireland had escaped semi-starvation by remaining neutral during the war. There was no rationing. For us, it was a land flowing with milk and honey. We were treated to ice cream and tropical fruits, bananas and oranges, things we had only dreamed about.

My mother had rented a house in a lovely little seaside town called Kilkee. The town was nestled in a horseshoe bay, with high, headland cliffs reaching out into the ocean on each side. The cliffs on the south side were called Diamond Head, the granite seamed with quartz crystals that sparkled in the sunlight. At low tide there was a broad, flat band of firm sand where the locals raced their horses on weekends. Elizabeth, Michael, and I would sit on the seawall and watch the horses pounding past while their owners roared and yelled, waving their betting slips. It was all very exciting. That holiday was the first time I ever felt really happy.

We were a real family. My father was a real dad, tall and handsome and kind, not just an imaginary person we prayed about. He was fun. He took us out in the old Morris car he had rented and we drove around the countryside to various parties with other children whose parents he had somehow met. He was a gregarious man, quick to make friends.

He took us out for picnics on the rocks at the far end of the beach. He would sit watching us as we ran back from the huge Atlantic waves that came crashing onto the cliffs. When we found prawns left behind in the tidal pools among the rocks, he would come down to help us fish them out with our buckets.

Once, I waded out into a shallow pool only to have my bare feet pierced by the thorny spines of sea urchins. My father carried me screaming up to the car and drove me to the doctor to have them removed. He held me as the black thorns were pulled out one by one. I can still feel the comfort of his strong arms pressing me to his chest, the musty smell of his jacket all wet from seawater. The thorns had gone in very deep. I yelled every time the doctor dug into my foot. I could feel my father flinch. He tried to make a game of it, promising me sixpence for every thorn.

That summer, too, my mother was a different person. She seemed younger and prettier than before. There was something about the way she looked at my father. It seemed she couldn't take her eyes off him. She was always laughing and flirting with him. When there were other women around she was almost too vivacious, as if she was afraid of losing his attention. Because she was so focused on him, she ignored what was happening with us. As a result, most days we were left to our own devices.

But I didn't mind. It felt good that my father and my mother were so absorbed with each other. It freed me from the anxiety and wariness that I usually carried around with me. We kids had time to get to know each other again and enjoy each other's company.

I was particularly intrigued by my sister, Elizabeth. She was eight years old now and as tall as me, even though I was a year older. We both had the same golden-red hair. Once, when we were walking along holding hands, some people stopped us and asked if we were twins. I felt proud to be seen with her and enjoyed the fact that she was my sister.

One day we were given some money to go and buy an ice cream at our favourite little store on the beach front. As we were waiting in line to be served, we heard a squeal from behind us. Two girls grabbed my sister as she turned around.

"Lizzie!" they shrieked, jumping up and down with excitement. "What are you doing here?"

It turned out that they were both from her boarding school at Sherbourne; one of them, Annie, was actually in the same class as Elizabeth. She was a pretty little girl with short, dark-black hair and a creamy complexion. She had a wonderful smile. It lit up her eyes, as bright and blue as forget-me-nots. I stood back shyly and watched her as she explained that their parents had a horse farm up behind Diamond Head. After Elizabeth introduced me to Annie and her older sister, Grace, the two girls dragged us outside.

"You can see our house from here," Annie said, pointing at the hillside south of the town. It looked tiny from where we were standing, but we could see half a dozen ponies grazing in the field next to the house.

"You must come up and visit," Annie insisted. "We can ride the ponies. It'll be fun!"

The very next day, we walked up the road out of town to the farmhouse. The girls must have been watching for us. They came tumbling out of the house before we even got to the front yard.

"Come and see the ponies," they shouted.

We went over to the paddock and climbed onto the fence. The horses trotted over to where we sat on the top rail. They looked at us sideways and nuzzled their noses against our hands as we stroked them. Close up, they seemed very big and a little scary.

"They want some apples," Annie said. She jumped down and ran off to the barn, returning with an armful of green apples.

"Here," she said, giving me one. "Hold it flat on your hand so he doesn't bite you."

I watched as she held out an apple to the pony in front of her. His lips curled back and his huge teeth crunched into the apple. When I held out mine my hand shook so much that the apple fell off.

"Don't worry. You'll get used to it," Annie laughed.

I didn't mind, because I could see the kindness in her eyes.

"Would you like to ride him?" she asked me.

"I don't know how," I said.

"That's OK. I'll show you." Annie stood up on the top rail. She grabbed at the rope around the pony's head, swung her leg over his back, and straightened up.

"Now you, Peter," she said. She reached out her hand.

I took it and swung my leg up and over the pony. Suddenly there I was, sitting up close behind her. "Hold on," she said, and the pony began to walk slowly alongside the fence. Its hips dipped and swayed with each stride, and ours did too.

But my legs weren't strong enough to grip his sides. Slowly, I began to slip. Because I was holding on to Annie, she began to slip as well. Then, shrieking, we both fell off into the long grass. We scrambled to our feet and she was laughing.

"Are you OK?" she asked. "You know it's very hard to stay on without a saddle and stirrups."

"I'm all right," I said. "Let's try one more time!"

The five of us spent the rest of the morning riding the ponies bareback, with Elizabeth and I having many falls. In the end we both learned how to hang on by ourselves.

Annie's mother called us in at lunch time. She had been watching us from the kitchen window. I thought she was a splendid mother for not rushing out to fuss over us whenever we fell. We were ravenous and wolfed down the soup and sandwiches she had made, chattering away non-stop. Afterwards, we all went back down to our house, picked up our swim suits, and ran down to the beach where the tide was just coming in.

Unlike us, the two girls could not swim, so the rest of the day was spent trying to teach them. I stood in the water with my hands under Annie's stomach while she kicked her legs and pushed out with her arms. She was fearless. She kept her head down in the water and before long could swim a few strokes towards me, grabbing me when she felt she might sink.

That night, lying in bed, I went over and over the day in my mind, recalling the feel of Annie's body against mine as we rode the pony, the feel of her arms around my neck when she swam to me. I just didn't want that day to end.

There was only one more week of the holidays left before we all had to head back to our boarding schools. Annie and Grace spent as much time with us as they could. We played for hours on the beach, building cities in the sand and digging complicated channels and moats. We explored the headland where huge Atlantic waves crashed through caves in the rocks, creating gigantic water spouts. And we went back to the farm to improve our horse-riding skills.

On our last evening together, we arranged to meet after supper. We went down to the beach and sat on the seawall, unusually quiet, sad that the summer was over. Annie and I sat next to each other, kicking our heels against the rough stones.

"You'll write to me, won't you?" she said, head down, face hidden by her falling hair.

"Okay," I said, "although there's not much that happens at school to write about."

She looked at me sideways. "I don't care," she said. "It's just fun to get letters."

Chapter 10

That golden summer of 1946 was all too brief.

Back at St. Dominic's, a third person had been added to our constellation of lay staff. Her name was, appropriately, Miss Sergeant. She had been hired as the school nurse.

A tall, thin spinster, she was particularly chummy with Sister Benedict. All of her free time seemed to be spent gossiping in Sister Benedict's office, where she chain-smoked cigarettes and drank endless cups of tea.

Miss Sergeant did not live at the school but showed up for breakfast every morning and left after supper. She and Sister Benedict were always exchanging strange looks and secret smiles when they thought we were not looking. I acquired an intense personal dislike for her after a particularly unfortunate incident.

Our meals were held in a large room called the refectory. We were assigned places at long tables that ran the length of the room. At the head of each table a place was set for a nun, or, as at my table, for Miss Sergeant. Before every meal we had to stand at attention waiting for Miss Sergeant and the nuns to come in and say grace.

This particular morning I noticed that there was a birthday card standing open on Miss Sergeant's plate. On the inside was written, "Happy Birthday, Stella, all my love, Sister Benedict." I turned and whispered to the boy next to me, "It's Miss Sergeant's birthday today." Soon, the whisper had gone all round the room and everyone knew. As Miss Sergeant walked in with Sister Benedict, everyone was smiling and we all started singing "Happy Birthday to you, Happy Birthday to you, Happy . . . ."

The song faltered and then petered out as we noticed the look on Sister Benedict's face. Clearly, she was not pleased. There was an uncomfortable silence.

"And which of you boys dared read my card?" Sister Benedict finally spat out.

Another silence.

"Whoever it was, own up."

I looked down, but I could feel my face starting to flush.

"There will be no breakfast for anyone until I find out who it was."

I felt the whole room looking at me. There was an even longer silence. Finally, the boy next to me moved uncomfortably.

"It was Peter," he mumbled.

"So!" Sister Benedict hissed. "Go and wait for me outside my office."

Head down, I walked out slowly past all the rows of boys at the tables and shut the heavy wooden door behind me.

There was a bench outside Sister Benedict's office where we sat when awaiting punishment. It felt strange sitting there alone, excluded from the familiar noise of clashing plates and chattering boys that I could hear from the other side of the door.

Breakfast over, the boys came out of the refectory in a rush and poured past me down the stairs to the playroom. I kept my head down, not wanting to look at them. Sister Benedict and Miss Sergeant swept past into the office. Then I was summoned.

Sister Benedict was standing in front of her desk, her shiny yellow bamboo cane in her right hand. Miss Sergeant gave her a smirk. I felt intimidated and guilty. It never even occurred to me to question what was about to happen. The two of them were oblivious to any good intentions I might have had. Instead, they chose to focus on the crime of reading a private birthday card set open in full view.

Trapped by my own frantic need to please, I was incapable of feeling anger or resentment and was completely unaware of the bizarre nature of Sister Benedict's behavior. I felt utterly destroyed. The cut of the bamboo across my hands was nothing compared to the hurt inside. I was a criminal, an outcast. When I got back downstairs to the playroom, I was surrounded by my buddies. I showed them the welts across my hands in order to recover some self-esteem.

We were a close group of friends, Rory and three other boys, Jim, Colin, and Liam. We shared everything. Their parents, unlike mine, regularly sent them care packages of candies which they hoarded in their lockers for special occasions. My thrashing was rated a special occasion. Before long we were ensconced in a little basement storage room near the janitor's office enjoying a sugar feast.

The room was dark because it was used to store root vegetables. It smelled thickly of earth and carrots and was an ideal place to escape from the noisy crowd of boys in the playroom. It was in this den that I was first introduced to sex and smoking.

Our cigarettes were made from discarded butts that we picked up from the streets when we went for walks. Rory would expertly roll them all together into one cigarette and pass it around. I was the most inexperienced of the group. The first time I tried to smoke, I blew instead of inhaling. Afterwards Rory teased me mercilessly, to the huge delight of the others.

And, of course, it was Rory who introduced us to sex. One day as we huddled together in the dark, he told us that in the summer his mother had started dating another man.

"I saw them humping each other in my mother's bed," he said laconically.

We all looked at him blankly.

"What do you mean, humping?"

"Well, you know. That's when you stick your cock into a girl's crack."

There was a shocked silence. I don't think any of us had even had an erection yet.

"Go on! I don't believe you," I said. "My mother would never do a thing like that."

Rory nearly fell off the vegetable crate he was sitting on.

"Oh no? How do you suppose you got here? Don't you know how babies get made?"

He proceeded to demonstrate how he could get his penis to go hard. We all tried to copy him but somehow it didn't work for us. So we gave up and went to play a pick-up game of cricket.

Chapter 11

When Christmas came that year, my father seemed to have retained the warmth and optimism generated by our summer in Ireland. He had found a new job in London. So he rented a little cottage for us in the village of Earnley, close to Bracklesham Bay, in West Sussex.

His cheerfulness was surprising because the winter of 1946 - 1947 was particularly harsh. A thick, grey fog kept us trapped inside the house on Christmas Eve. We tried to drive to Midnight Mass but it was impossible to see more than a few feet in front of the car. This particularly upset my mother, who had never before missed a Midnight Mass.

The fog was followed by a series of heavy snow falls. Huge drifts blocked the roads and the whole of England crawled to a stop. Electricity was cut off when the power stations shut down from lack of coal, still in short supply after the war. Newspapers had to be reduced in size and radio broadcasts were restricted to a few hours a day. Vegetables froze in the fields and everyone was scrambling to find food.

But in our little snowbound cottage, my father refused to let things get him down. He took over the kitchen and made an elaborate production of cooking our meals, which consisted mostly of bangers and mash. He insisted that we all pitch in with the washing-up, encouraging each of us to take turns starting a song to make it less of a chore. Afterwards, he had us sit down and play card games. Though the house was freezing, he somehow managed to make it feel warm and cozy. His being there was the best of all Christmas presents.

The following summer was very different. In spite of my father's new job, there was a distinct feeling in the house that there was no money. We kids spent our days playing and swimming off the beaches of Bracklesham Bay. But my father was never there and my mother seemed angry and depressed.

"He's off on one of his wild schemes to make a quick buck," was all that she said.

We imagined he was involved in the black market, smuggling food across from Ireland, something illegal but vaguely romantic. We never discovered what he was really up to.

By the summer of 1948, we had moved again. We were in another rented cottage, this time no longer close to the sea. It was in the village of Churt, near where my mother's sister, Doreen, lived. My father was absent for most of the summer, back to his mysterious business meetings in London. His absence left a big hole in the family.

For the first time I began to notice how isolated we all were. Michael, Elizabeth, and I had become used to summers by the sea. We had always been able to roam free, play on the beach, and swim endlessly. Now I felt that we were becoming as much strangers to each other as we were to the rest of the world. We had separate friends at school, none of whom knew each other. As a family we were never in one place long enough to make any local friends. Whenever we walked to the village, the children who hung around the grocery store looked at us curiously.

"Stay away from them," my mother warned. "They're rough children, not the sort you should be playing with," and she would walk us quickly back to the house.

I was too young to realize my mother was being a snob. She really felt that somehow we were superior to the local kids. She would never have dreamt of sending us to the village school. It would have been beneath her to do that. She had to send her kids to private boarding schools even if it meant she had to starve to do it.

Both she and my father had grown up in upper-middle-class English society before the war, with all its semi-aristocratic traditions. She could never forget that her mother-in-law was the sister of a Peer in the House of Lords, and that her father was the Inspector General of Police in India and a Companion of the India Empire. Unfortunately, my father no longer earned enough money to support such pretentiousness. It never occurred to my mother that she should get a job herself.

Even though my mother never talked about it, there was always a feeling around the house that there was not enough money. I felt like the boy in D.H. Lawrence's story, *The Rocking-Horse Winner.* I desperately wanted my mother to be happy. But I had no rocking horse I could ride to rescue her. Only my father could do that, and it seemed less and less likely that he ever would.

CHAPTER 12

"Here, Peter, I think you will like this."
Sister Vincent pushed a glossy pamphlet into my hand.
"You remember how I told you about my brother in Borneo? How he'd been freed by the Australians? Well, he's written a story about it in this pamphlet. I thought you'd like to read it. You can give it back to me when you're finished."

"Thanks, Sister," I said, stuffing the pamphlet down the front of my sweater. Later I found a quiet corner of the playground where I read it.

Sister Vincent's brother had been dying of starvation when he was rescued. He had spent a long time in hospital recovering. Then, he was sent back into the jungle to persuade the natives to give up headhunting. Apparently, the British had encouraged the revival of the practice while fighting the Japanese. He had trekked through the jungle visiting mountain villages to talk about it. Once he was bitten by a snake. He was saved by a native woman who sucked the poison out of the wound. It all sounded very romantic.

I went to find Sister Vincent to give back her pamphlet.

"When I grow up," I announced, "I want to be a missionary like your brother."

Sister Vincent positively glowed.

"Why Peter, that would be wonderful!" She gave me a quick hug. "You must pray to Jesus to guide you. It's not easy to be a priest and you must make sure that's what you really want."

The reaction of the nuns to the news of my 'calling' was very satisfying. Now, in their eyes, I could do no wrong. I was God's chosen one. I was not like the other little ruffians in the school. I was special. I basked in the warmth of their new smiles.

I wrote to my mother. "I know it will be hard for you," I said, relishing the high drama of my heroic decision. I would be giving up my family for the service of God.

My mother's letter back was like a slap in the face. She completely ignored what I had written.

"Your dad and I are leaving for Africa," she wrote. "He has a new job as a Queen's Counsel to the circuit court in Uganda. You will stay with your grandmother for the holidays from now on."

It took a while to sink in.

I was being orphaned!

I couldn't believe it. I had imagined my mother being distraught at my proposal to become a missionary. She should have been begging me to change my mind. Instead, it was she who was abandoning me, and not just me, but Michael and Elizabeth too. The happy family life we had so briefly experienced in Ireland would now be unattainable.

That night I cried hot, angry tears into my pillow. How could my mother do this? How could she?

After a while the anger turned into resentment. If my mother did not want me, then I would become God's hero. I would go off and save souls in distant lands. When she wanted me back, it would be too late. She would regret abandoning me. But I wouldn't care. I wouldn't belong to her any more. I would belong to God.

Of course I did not write anything of this to my mother. My letters were full of stories from Sister Vincent: stories about her brother's adventures in Borneo, about head hunters and orangutans. I even pretended to be excited about spending holidays with my grandmother.

In fact, the Christmas Michael and I spent with my grandmother was far from exciting. She lived in a tiny isolated village in Norfolk called Walsingham. We did not know anyone there and we spent two miserable weeks missing Elizabeth who was staying with one of her school friends.

Shortly after I returned to St. Dominic's, Sister Benedict summoned me to her office. She was holding in her hand the latest letter I had written to my mother. Our letters were never private. They were always censored before being sent.

"Now Peter, what's all this about you wanting to become a Mill Hill missionary?" she asked with a strange, twisted smile.

I was surprised she asked. She had obviously known about it from my weekly letters home.

"It's what I want to be," I said to her. "Sister Vincent has told me all about the Mill Hill Missionaries, and . . . and . . . that's what I want to be."

"Are you sure?" Sister Benedict wasn't smiling any more. "You know, they have a very hard life. They make you go to a special school with lots of foreigners. You will have to learn a foreign language. You know how much you hate French!"

She paused.

"And you will never get to see your parents again."

She paused to let it sink in.

"No more holidays. No more drinking tea. For the rest of your life!"

The horror of permanently giving up tea seemed to be a decisive argument. She leaned across the desk and fixed me with a forceful stare.

"You should become a Dominican priest, not a Mill Hill missionary."

Dutifully, I wrote to my mother that I had now decided to become a Dominican priest, not a Mill Hill missionary.

Suspecting that I had been unduly influenced by Sister Benedict, my mother did not even reply. Instead, she wrote to my grandmother in Walsingham. "Find out what Peter really wants when he's with you for the Easter holidays," she told her.

Chapter 13

The tiny village of Walsingham was an ideal spot for an eleven-year-old to decide how to give himself to God. In mediaeval times, long before the Reformation, it had become a place of pilgrimage. The Virgin Mary was said to have appeared there in 1061 and a shrine had been built in her honour. Supplicants flocked to it from all over England and Europe. Many miraculous events were ascribed to Mary's intervention. In 1150 a magnificent gothic abbey church was built over the shrine. Thereafter, every king and queen of England visited it until Henry VIII, in 1511, came seeking Mary's help to produce an heir to his throne.

Unfortunately for Walsingham, Henry's pilgrim prayers remained unanswered. Disgusted at the Pope's lack of co-operation in approving his divorce, King Henry declared himself Head of the Church. He seized the abbey, removed its valuables, and melted down the lead roof for bullets. The villagers were summoned to witness monks being dragged out to a neighbouring field and executed in the fearsome manner fashionable at the time. Today, only the blackened main gatehouse and gothic ruins of the abbey survive.

My grandmother was an elegant, Victorian lady. She had enough money from her own family trust that she was able to live independently after being divorced. She had retired to Walsingham and joined a group of aristocratic Catholic ladies who were scheming to restore the village to its former glory as a centre of Catholic pilgrimage.

A mile outside the village was a small building called The Slipper Chapel. In mediaeval times it was a place where pilgrims removed their shoes and walked the last mile to the shrine barefoot. The ladies got together and bought the building, which had been used by a local farmer for housing cattle. They restored it as a chapel, and a priest was appointed to set up a temporary shrine. But this was only the first step

45

in a grander strategy. They wanted to re-establish the original shrine in Walsingham itself.

Soon after she became a Catholic, my grandmother bought a small house in Walsingham. It overlooked an open area in the middle of the village known as Friday Market. In the spring of 1949, Michael and I arrived for the Easter holidays. She put us up in two tiny bedrooms on the third floor. Elizabeth had been sent to spend Easter with one of her school friends.

Since there was no Catholic church in Walsingham, my grandmother invited a priest to say Sunday Mass in her dining room. To me it all seemed part of her nefarious scheme to restore the village to the 'true faith.' Word soon leaked out, via the neighbours, that a popish priest was performing secret rituals in her house. And indeed, at the Masses, there was invariably a prayer for Walsingham to be restored to the Catholic fold.

After a few days Michael and I became aware of the suspicion directed at us by the locals. A young girl at the grocery store, whom Michael much admired, would not even look at him. Children on the street stopped talking as we walked past. Michael was quite unfazed by this social ostracism. He simply took off on my grandmother's antique bicycle and toured the countryside. But I felt increasingly isolated. I spent long hours up in my room reading the novels of Charles Dickens. My grandmother had his collected works in her personal library.

Gradually, I came to think of my grandmother as a female Guy Fawkes, plotting against the Protestants of Walsingham,—not quite as violent, perhaps, but just as romantic. It was as if history had bequeathed her the right to redeem the village from its murderous past. But Satan was not going to let go of his kingdom so easily.

There was a third room, opposite mine, on the top floor of the house. It was occupied by a local farm girl, Emily, whom my grandmother had hired as a maid. She was a Protestant. In spite of that, she cheerfully cooked for us and cleaned and did the laundry. However, when I lay awake at night, I was very aware that there was a Protestant girl sleeping just across the hall. This must surely give the devil a toe-hold in the house, I thought.

And then, one night, all hell actually did break loose. I awoke to hear fearsome shrieks and howls coming from the next room, accompanied by a crashing of glass and banging of furniture. I opened my door a crack. I was just in time to see Emily flinging herself down the stairs, her nightdress streaming behind her. I heard her wrench open the front door. When I ran to my window, I saw her stumbling out into the middle of Friday Market, spinning around wildly, arms flailing, her upturned face white and weird in the light of a full moon.

At breakfast next morning, Emily appeared in her maid's outfit just as if nothing unusual had happened. My grandmother sat at the head of the table in the dining room as she always did, surrounded by her Victorian silver tea set and toast rack, delicately slicing away at her grapefruit.

After breakfast, I asked about Emily.

"Don't worry," my grandmother said. "Emily always has a little trouble when it's a full moon. The devil is just trying to make life uncomfortable for us, to make us move away from Walsingham. The poor girl can't help it. That's why we also have a poltergeist."

"We have what?"

"A poltergeist."

I was shocked. I knew what a poltergeist was, a mischievous ghost-like spirit who startles people by playing pranks.

"We have our own poltergeist?" I asked.

"Yes," she said, "it lives in the china cabinet."

She got up and opened the glass door of the cupboard. All over the middle shelf of the cabinet there were pieces of frosted glass, some large chunks and some smaller ones, scattered in between the china.

"There you are," she said. "He's really quite harmless. I was working in the kitchen one day when I heard an awful crash coming from the dining room. When I looked in the cabinet, I saw all this glass lying around, but none of my china pieces were broken. Here, you can have some."

She scooped up a handful of the supernatural glass and put it in a tea cup. I was more than a little awestruck as I gazed at the glass, but even more so as I looked at my grandmother. How could she be so phlegmatic about a poltergeist? How could anyone be phlegmatic about a poltergeist?

I retired to my room clutching the cup with sweaty fingers. I set it next to the wash basin by my bed. In my imagination, it glowed with a secret menace. Obviously, the poltergeist would not discriminate between me and my grandmother. I was a party to the exorcism she was inflicting on Walsingham. The blood of the martyrs out there in the field was shrieking for atonement. Wretched orphan that I was, I would have to suffer more than I bargained for.

But I could take it. I could take it and more. I would dedicate my life to fight the devil in all his forms, friendly or otherwise. I would learn the rite of exorcism. I would become a caster-out of demons. I would travel to Africa or India or even Borneo and confront witch doctors with my greater powers. I would hold up a cross and evil spirits would fly before me. I would not be a dull, old Dominican priest. I would become a Mill Hill missionary.

"Well," my grandmother said when I told her of my decision. "There's a Mill Hill priest coming to the village with a pilgrimage next week. Why don't we talk to him and see what he says?"

Every year at Easter time, groups of Catholic university students carrying heavy wooden crosses walk to Walsingham from all over England. That year Father McKee, a Mill Hill priest, was acting as chaplain to a group from Liverpool. When they arrived in Friday Market, the students set down their crosses and sat around on the sidewalk pulling off their boots and proudly comparing blisters. Granny set up a little table outside her front door and offered them tea and sandwiches and rubbing alcohol. She introduced me to Father McKee. He was a darkly handsome priest, dressed in a black cassock and a bright red sash that made him look very dashing.

"Peter is interested in becoming a Mill Hill missionary," said my grandmother as she served him a mug of tea.

"Is that so?" said the priest, eyeing me with a grin. "And what made you want to do that?"

I looked at him, suddenly feeling shy.

"It's just that I've read a lot about the Mill Hill missionaries in your pamphlets, and . . . and . . . I guess I just liked the idea of being a missionary."

"Come over here," Father McKee said, putting his hand on my shoulder. "Let's talk about it."

We sat down on the edge of the sidewalk, and he took out a pipe and began to stuff it with tobacco.

"Tell me about yourself," he said, pulling out a box of matches and striking one. He protected the flame with his cupped hand to stop it from blowing out in the breeze.

I told him about St. Dominic's and Sister Vincent and how I was afraid of Sister Benedict and how she wanted me to become a Dominican. It seemed a long story.

When I finished, he sat there for a moment looking across the square at the students milling about. Then he turned to me.

"How old are you?" he asked.

"Eleven," I said. "I'll be twelve this May."

He took a couple of puffs on his pipe. I liked the smell of his tobacco and watched the blue smoke as it curled up before being snatched away by the breeze.

"You know what?" he said finally. "I don't think you should go back to St. Dominic's. I'll phone St. Peter's. That's our junior seminary near Liverpool. I'll see if they'll let you join right away. We don't usually take boys at eleven years old, but you will be twelve in a few months."

He turned and looked at me. "What do you think?" he asked.

I gaped at him.

"Not go back to St. Dominic's? Wow!" I yelled, jumping up. "That's brilliant!"

I sprinted back to my grandmother, bursting with excitement.

"He says I can go! He says I can go!" I shouted as I galloped around her little tea stall. "I won't have to go back to St. Dominic's ever, ever again! No more Sister Benedict! No more Miss Sergeant! Thank you, God! Thank you! Thank you! Thank you!"

EARLY DAYS

My parents' wedding, Our Lady of Victory, Kensington, 1934

My mother and Elizabeth at Stone House, 1941

Michael (left), Elizabeth (centre), and me (right) at Stone House, Redhill. Summer, 1940

St. Dominic's Convent School, St. Leonards-on-sea, Sussex

The beach at Bembridge, Isle of Wight, where we built our volcano

The house at Bembridge

PART TWO

TEEN TROUBLES AND A TRIP TO AFRICA

1949-1953

Chapter 14

" Hello," she said as the Liverpool Express pulled out of London. "My name's Mrs. Lily. What's yours?" Surprised, I turned my head away from the window and looked across at her.

"Peter," I said cautiously.

I turned back to the window. I wasn't used to people talking to me on trains. In fact, even now I prefer to keep my thoughts to myself when I'm travelling. But there were just the two of us in the six-person compartment, and Mrs. Lily was persistent.

"Where are you off to, dear?" she asked in the fake voice that adults sometimes use with children. I turned away from the window again and looked at her.

She was a large woman. Her breasts were impressive. They were contained, with some difficulty, by a brown cardigan stretched tightly over a plain yellow blouse. She was leaning back, her permed hair against the white antimacassar which, in those days, was used to protect the plush railway upholstery. Bright red lipstick outlined a cupid-bow mouth and her cheeks were heavily rouged. But her blue eyes were bright and perhaps a little mischievous. She had a large tapestry carrier bag with circular bamboo handles strategically placed on the seat next to her.

"I'm going to a school in a place called Freshfield, just north of Liverpool," I told her.

I suppose her curiosity was understandable. Here was this small boy sitting across from her, red hair sprouting from under a schoolboy cap, round wire-rimmed spectacles on a freckled nose, wearing a brand new school uniform: grey shorts, grey shirt, grey socks, grey blazer with a black and white school tie. It must have seemed a little odd to see me sitting there all alone.

"How old are you, luv?" she asked. "And how come you're travelling all by yourself?"

I hesitated.

"My parents are in Africa," I said somewhat reluctantly. "And I'm eleven."

"Goodness gracious!" she said, sitting up. "In Africa? What are they doing in Africa?"

"I don't know," I said. "My dad just works there."

Mrs. Lily's smile had begun to fade.

"So they're sending you to a boarding school?"

"Well, I'm used to it," I answered. "I've always been in a boarding school. It's just that this is a new one."

I was beginning to wish I hadn't told her anything. She seemed to be getting upset.

"You poor dear," she said, leaning across and touching my bare knee with her hand. "Come and sit next to me and tell me all about it."

I stiffened and pressed back in my seat, acutely aware that we were alone in the compartment. It was going to be a while before the train stopped at another station. I was trapped.

"It's not just another boarding school," I said. "It's a Catholic seminary. I want to become a priest."

"A priest?" She looked shocked.

"Yes," I said. "A missionary priest."

She sat there for a moment as if turning this idea over in her head.

"So what makes you think you want to be a missionary?"

"Well," I said, with a little more enthusiasm. "A nun at my last school told me all about it. Her brother's a missionary. He treks through the jungles of Borneo and meets head hunters and has lots of adventures. That's what I want to do. I think it'll be fun."

"I suppose it could be," Mrs. Lily said doubtfully. "But why do you think you have to become a priest? Why couldn't you just be an explorer or something? You don't have to be a missionary to go on adventures."

I turned back to the window. I didn't know quite how to answer that one. The train rocked rhythmically as it clattered over switch-points and sped past the grimy red-brick suburbs of London. I looked down at the dingy row houses backing onto the railway tracks: all those unknown lives behind all those grimy windows; dispirited laundry hanging in dispirited back yards; the upturned white faces of small kids, eyes wide, arms lifted to wave, frozen in the moment as our express train thundered by. Why *did* I want to be a priest?

I had absorbed religion unquestioningly from the nuns at St. Dominic's. I had been taught to believe in a loving God. The love that this God had for people had nothing to do with physical affection; you prayed to him in your head. If you listened hard enough, and if you were good, you might just hear him talking back to you.

"The nuns at my last school told me that lots of people don't know about God," I told her. "They said that if people don't know about God their lives are meaningless. Sister Vincent told us that we have a special responsibility for people living in the British colonies. So it makes sense for me to be a missionary; and besides, it'll be fun traveling through jungles and things."

Mrs. Lily stared at me. And then she started fumbling around in her carrier bag. In a minute or so she found what she was looking for, a package wrapped in grease-proof paper.

"Here," she said. "I made some egg sandwiches for the trip, help yourself," and she reached over and offered me one.

"Thank you," I said politely as I took the sandwich.

I was always polite. I knew that ladies liked small boys who were polite.

"And where are you going?" I asked after a mouthful of sandwich.

"Oh," she said, "I'm going to visit my nephew and his girl in Birmingham. I don't suppose you've ever been there, have you? That's where my mum and dad were living when I was born. Then we moved to London when I was six. They bought a fish and chip shop. My brother and I lived on fish and chips when we were kids. Fish and chips! Day in, day out!" and she shook with laughter.

"Wow!" I said. "That must have been great; fish and chips every day!"

"Don't kid yourself," she chuckled. "I've never wanted to eat fish and chips since! But that was a long time ago. My brother got married and moved back to Birmingham. He was working down in a coal mine so he never got called up to fight in the war. Then last year, there was an explosion. The tunnel collapsed and he was killed, along with a lot of his buddies. It was in all the papers, you know."

She paused and looked out at the fields and hills sliding past the window. Then, she turned back and went on.

"But they gave him a beautiful funeral. His mates in the colliery band all showed up. They played *Abide With Me*. The fire brigade carried his coffin on one of their trucks. And the Home Guard shot off their rifles into the air. The vicar was all dressed up in a long white robe with a purple thing around his neck. It was ever so beautiful."

Mrs. Lily reached for a hanky and dabbed her eyes for a minute. Then she said, "Jake, my nephew, had to leave school after his dad died. He's working down in the mine now. He's a grand lad, takes after his dad like you wouldn't believe. His girl, Polly, has just left school too. They're about to have a baby. I'm going to stay with them for a couple of weeks to help out."

Mrs. Lily stuffed her hanky back into her carrier bag. Her face looked a bit weird where her mascara had run. But she seemed to have recovered and was smiling again.

"So there you are. It's a rum world, ain't it?" she said. "One minute a person dies, and the next another one's born."

I finished my sandwich.

I wasn't feeling so uncomfortable with her now. She was real; a real person with real feelings. I didn't need my barrier of reserve anymore, at least not with her. I started telling her about my parents and how I missed them; that missing them was like having a heavy stone in my stomach.

"I know," Mrs. Lily said. "That's how I feel about my brother. We were real mates when we were growing up. It was bad enough when he moved away, but now he's gone for good. I kind of feel angry at him for leaving me. That's so silly, isn't it?"

For a while we both sat gazing out the window. I was hypnotized by the telephone wires at the side of the track, how they curved up and down as each post flashed past, mile after mile. I wondered how many people were chattering away to each other along those wires as we sped past, their voices travelling so much faster than the train. And I could feel the stone in my stomach.

"You know," Mrs. Lily said, interrupting my thoughts, "it must be scary going to a new school. You won't know anyone."

"Maybe," I said, "but I'm excited about it, too. I don't have to go back to St. Dominic's. And I've never been to Lancashire. I read a book of Wordsworth's poems once. About the Lake District. Ever since I've wanted to go there."

"Poems!" Mrs. Lily was astonished. "You read poems?"

"Well, yes," I said. "My granny has a whole collection of books. There was this poem Wordsworth wrote, about when he was a boy; how he stole a rowboat and went out on a lake at night, and how he got scared when the moon came up from behind a dark mountain; it kind of made him feel all guilty. It reminded me of how I felt one time when I stole candy from my friends."

"I can't say as how I've ever read a poem that I understood," Mrs. Lily said. "The only poems I ever read were in school and I didn't understand a thing. The teacher kept talking about rhyme schemes and feet and stuff, and I had no clue what she was on about."

As the train sped north, past fields, farm houses, and little villages, Mrs. Lily told stories of her childhood in London. She talked about how she had begun to work in her parents' shop serving fish and chips; about all the different people she got to know. It was obvious that she had enjoyed chatting with the customers.

The time passed quickly. Before I knew it the train began to slow down. We were pulling into Birmingham station.

"Here we are," Mrs. Lily said, as she got up and smoothed the wrinkles from her skirt. She reached up to the luggage rack and pulled down a straw-coloured suitcase with brown leather triangles at the corners.

"It's been lovely talking to you," she said. "You take care of yourself at that new school and all. And don't let on to the other boys that you like poetry; they might beat up on you."

I stood to open the carriage door for her. She picked up her bag and transferred it to the hand carrying her suitcase. Then, suddenly, she reached out with her other arm and pulled me against her chest, one large breast knocking my cap sideways in the process. Giving my shoulders a hard squeeze she said, "You're a good lad, Peter. Just you take care, now. I'm sure your mum and dad will be back to see you soon." She let me go and stepped down from the carriage, swinging the door shut.

I leaned out of the window and watched as she turned and joined the other passengers streaming along the platform. Then I saw a girl struggling towards her against the flow of the crowd, a very pregnant girl. She ran up to Mrs. Lily and threw her arms around her. The train began to pull away. I saw Mrs. Lily say something to the girl and they turned to look at me. "Goodbye, Peter," I heard them shout, and they both waved.

"Goodbye," I yelled back and then sat down.

The train gathered speed. I looked across at the empty seat in front of me. I could feel that stone in my stomach again.

I had the compartment all to myself from Birmingham to Liverpool. There was plenty of time to think about what Mrs. Lily had said. I sat there, repeating with the rhythm of the train, "It's going to be good, it's going to be good, it's going to be good."

In spite of myself, I was starting to feel anxious. Mrs. Lily was right. The other boys in my class would have already been together for seven months; what would they think of me, being parachuted in among them in the middle of April? There would be so much school work to catch up on. What if I couldn't do it? What if the teachers were mean? What if it turned out to be another St. Dominic's?

CHAPTER 15

At Liverpool I had to catch a local train to a little town called Freshfield where I had been told to get off. I didn't know how many stops there were and I anxiously scanned the names of each station we passed until I saw it.

As the train creaked to a stop, I opened the carriage door and jumped out, pulling my suitcase behind me. Looking down the platform, I could see a few other passengers slamming the carriage doors shut and heading to the exit. Then I noticed a cheerful-looking priest walking towards me, a little Yorkshire terrier trotting behind him on a leash. The priest was dressed in a rather worn black suit with frayed arm cuffs that made him appear comfortably casual.

"You must be Peter," he said as he came up to me. "I'm Father Heweston, the rector at St. Peter's College. Here, give me your bag."

"It's OK," I said, "I can manage it."

"Give it to me," the priest insisted, smiling. "I'll never carry a bag for you again, so make the most of it!"

It was only a three minute walk from the station to the college.

"You'll be just in time for supper," Father Heweston said. It was already dusk and I could hardly make out the shape of the huge building that was to be my home for the next four years. "I'll get one of the boys to take your bag upstairs. They'll show you around after supper. Right now we'll go and eat."

We went in through a side entrance leading to a long, brightly lit corridor that formed one side of a large quadrangle. At the end of the corridor was a pair of great yellow oak doors. Behind them I could hear the muffled noise and clatter of a meal in progress. Father Heweston opened one of the doors and there was a sudden hush. The room was huge but somehow familiar. It was the refectory, long tables with rows of boys on each side, a priest at the head of each one, and 150 pairs of eyes staring at me. I felt enormously self-conscious. Then, thankfully, everyone turned back to eat and the hubbub rose again.

Father Heweston led me to the top end of one of the tables where there was an empty place.

"This is Peter, the new boy I was telling you about," he said to the priest at the head of the table. "And this is Father Vincent McCann," he said to me. "He'll take care of you."

Vince McCann was a tall, lanky priest with wiry, red hair. Little did I know that he was eventually to become hugely significant in my life. He was a genuinely good man who cared about the boys in his charge. He looked at me that evening with his characteristic lopsided grin as I sat down.

"Well now, Peter," he said, "You're a bit late but there's still plenty of food left."

He introduced me to the boy sitting across the table from me.

"This is Frank Monaghan," he said. "For some strange reason, everyone calls him Rinty."

"Rinty Monaghan is a world flyweight boxing champion," said Rinty with a wide smile. "*That's* why they call me Rinty."

"OK, OK. Just teasing," said Father McCann. "After supper, take Peter up to the dorm. Explain the rules to him. He's to have the empty cubicle next to yours."

Before going up to the dormitory, Rinty took me down a corridor to a set of stairs leading to a large room with rows and rows of desks.

"This is the study hall," he explained. "We have a half-hour recreation period after supper. Then we do two hours of homework here."

At the far end, was a raised stage with an oak pulpit to one side.

"That's where Johnny gives his pep talk once a week." Rinty explained. Johnny is our name for Father Heweston. He's the priest who met you at the station. He's the big boss."

The dormitory was another large room divided into little cubicles by wooden partitions. There was just enough space in the cubicle for an enamel wash basin with a jug of water, a small closet, and a narrow plank shelf with a thin mattress for a bed. A curtain could be drawn across the entrance for privacy.

Rinty sat on the edge of the bed and watched as I unpacked my suitcase.

"There's no talking allowed from the beginning of study hall in the evening until after breakfast next morning," he told me. "They call it the *magnum silentium*, something monks did in mediaeval times. We're supposed to be thinking of God and stuff. Really, I think it's just a way to stop us getting rowdy." He laughed. "They're pretty strict about it. You're not allowed to visit anyone else's cubicle, either. In fact, I shouldn't really be sitting in here with you now."

Rinty got up.

"Somebody will walk through the dorm in the morning to wake everyone up. They yell out a Latin phrase, *Laudate Dominum*. It means *Praise the Lord*. Personally, I never feel like praising anyone when I wake up. You're supposed to answer *Deo Gratias, Thanks be to God*. You have to throw your bed covers over the partition. It's to show them you're up. Otherwise, they'll come in and drag you out of bed!"

Rinty grinned.

"Think you'll be OK?" he asked.

"I'm OK," I said a little doubtfully. There seemed to be a lot of rules.

"I'll see you in the morning, then," Rinty said, pulling the curtain closed as he left.

That night, as I lay between the cold, unfamiliar sheets, a thousand anxious thoughts came crowding through my head. There was so much to get used to. Everything was new and different. I could feel the hard wooden bed boards beneath the thin mattress. I wondered if I would ever fall asleep. Sister Benedict's warnings of the tough life of a Mill Hill missionary echoed in my brain. But I was determined I would never give up. I would learn to become God's missionary to the world. I would bring the light of His love to the darkest corners of the universe . . .

I was soon fast asleep.

CHAPTER 16

I was startled awake by the sudden glare of an overhead light.
Someone was walking down the length of the dorm banging loudly
on the cubicles. I scrambled to throw my bed clothes over the partition
to show I was up. Ten minutes later I joined the throng of boys clattering
down the concrete stairs to the chapel.

The senior boys were already there, having got up half an hour
earlier for silent meditation. Actually, as I discovered afterwards, most
of them simply sat there and went back to sleep. Formal morning
prayers were read, followed by a Mass. Then we all went back to the
dorm to clean out our washbasins, empty our chamber pots, and make
our beds. Once our cubicles had been checked by a prefect, we rushed
down to the refectory for breakfast.

Breakfast consisted of a bowl of porridge, a slab of cold, salty bacon
fat to spread on slices of thick bread, and a mug of tea. Food was still
being rationed, so I was not surprised by the rather spartan quality of
the meal. But it felt awkward not being able to talk to anyone until after
breakfast. I quickly picked up on the sign language used for requests to
pass things down the table. Waggling a fist with a thumb sticking out
meant 'pass the teapot.'

Rinty met me in the hallway afterwards.

"Most of us go outside until classes start," he said, pushing open
the heavy glass door.

"Hey there, Rinty!" A group of boys were hunched down playing
knucklebones. They looked up at me curiously.

"This is Peter," Rinty said.

"That's my name, too," said one of the boys immediately.

Rinty turned to me. "OK, then what's your second name, Peter?"

"Bruno," I said, reluctantly.

"Bruno!" he grinned.

"Bruno!" they all yelled, hooting gleefully. "Brunoooo, Brunooo,
Brunooo!"

"Well, it's going to be Bruno from now on," Rinty said.

And it was.

That little naming ceremony had served as my initiation. Now I was accepted. They had no curiosity about why I joined them so late in the year, or why I spoke with a posh accent so unlike their mix of Lancashire, Yorkshire, and Geordie dialects. In fact, I was half-disappointed at not being the centre of attention. On the other hand, it was a relief to be considered just another classmate.

A bell clanged and I followed Rinty upstairs to the first-form classroom. He left me at the door as he was in the second-form class, one year ahead of me.

"Here, Nick. You take care of Bruno," he said.

I had noticed Nick Morgan hanging out on the edge of the crowd at my naming ceremony. He was a shy, skinny boy with skimpy fair hair and a pale face. He seemed pleased that Rinty had given him the responsibility of shadowing me through my first day.

"First class is always math," Nick said. "You can sit with me if you want."

I looked around the room. It was filled with rows of double, wooden desks. They had the familiar boy smell that comes from years of contact with sweaty arms and legs. Each had an individual hinged lid attached to a ledge with a hole for inkpots, stained dark blue from numberless ink drops. Ballpoint pens were only a recent invention, considered by teachers to be a threat to traditional penmanship.

"Math's easy," said Nick as we clambered behind one set of desks. "It's just boring. I hate being made to repeat hundreds of sums just to show that you've understood the lesson."

"Me too," I said.

But I was terrified of math. It had all started with Sister Benedict trying to make us memorize our times tables. She would have us stand in a line in front of the class while she fired questions at us, her bamboo cane gripped firmly in her hand.

"What's twelve times eleven"

Panic.

"Er . . ."

"Go to the end of the line! Next."

If you gave the correct answer you were allowed back to your desk. Invariably, I would be the last one standing in front of the class. She would glare at me.

"Stay behind at recess. Study your times tables. I'll test you again next class!"

To this day, I have trouble with numbers. I explained my problem to Nick.

"That's OK," he said. "We'll work together. The teachers never ask us to do things we don't understand, as long as you tell them when you have a problem. They *want* you to ask questions."

Other than math, my anxiety about catching up at St. Peter's was quickly dispelled. I found it easy to make up the two terms I had missed.

Life at St. Peter's was highly organized and always busy.

"You have to check the notice board every week," Nick told me. "There are lists for everything. After lunch there's a half-hour of what they call manual labour. Your name will be on the list for a work station. You will be assigned an area to clean. It's different each week. Prefects come around to check on you. They'll wipe their fingers along ledges to see if you missed any dirt."

He saw me starting to look apprehensive.

"Don't worry," he laughed. "They'll show you what to do and how to do it. Each job has its own routine. The rest of the afternoon we get to play sports."

The sports master was a stocky, older priest called Father Turnbull. He had a permanent tan from having spent years teaching in a mission school in India. He had a large hooked nose through which he constantly snorted, a habit we assumed he had acquired while in India. He wore a biretta all day long to hide his bald head. A biretta is a liturgical hat that most priests only use in church. His long black cassock flowed around him and caught in his legs when he ran for a ball.

Father Turnbull was the first truly sports-crazed priest I had met. He was obsessed with sports. The kids loved him because of it. They would crowd around him in the halls as he teased them about the soccer teams they supported. He was a huge fan of Everton, one of two Liverpool soccer teams. There was an intense rivalry between supporters among the boys at St. Peter's.

As the spring days lengthened into summer, Father Turnbull organized impromptu cricket games after supper. He had the whole school taking turns at bat while he bowled. It was virtually impossible for anyone to stay at bat for very long, surrounded as they were by a crowd of fielders waiting to pounce on the ball. Almost everyone got a turn at bat and everyone strove mightily to blast at least one of his pitches to the boundary in order to gain bragging rights.

As sports master, Father Turnbull's job was to organize soccer, rugby, or cricket games every afternoon. He knew our strengths and weaknesses well. No one was ever always on a winning or a losing team. And the games went on no matter the weather. It was a good way to get rid of all the pent-up energy accumulated during morning classes.

Because I knew nothing about professional sports, I tended to hang back when other kids chatted with Father Turnbull about their favourite teams. He must have noticed because one day he stopped me in the hall.

"Hey there, young man," he said. "How come you don't support a soccer team?"

I squirmed uncomfortably.

I don't know," I said. "I don't know anything about teams or leagues and things."

He crooked his arm around my neck.

"Can't have that," he said brusquely.

He groped around in his cassock pocket.

"Here," he said, handing me a folded magazine. "Read this. It'll give you all the league tables and articles about different teams and players. Find one you like and then you can talk it up with the other kids. You won't feel so left out." He gave my neck a shake. "See if you can find a team better than Everton. It'll be tough, mind you, but give it a try." And he went off chuckling and snorting down the hallway.

"What was all that about?" Nick said, coming up behind me.

"Turnbull just gave me a sports magazine," I said. "Now I'll become a jock."

A few weeks before the term ended, I got a rare letter from my mother.

"You and Michael are to spend the summer holidays with your granny in Walsingham again," she wrote. "It's a lovely, peaceful place.

Granny has lots of great books you can read, and you can help the priest at the Slipper Chapel by serving Masses there."

For me the summer of 1949 in Walsingham was not much different from being at the seminary. I was completely cosseted by the Catholic ladies who clung like bees around the shrine at the Slipper Chapel. There was no possibility of deviating from my role as a pious, dedicated seminarian. I was secretly envious of my fourteen-year-old brother Michael who was quite clearly fancied by many of the local girls.

Michael, however, was oblivious to their wiles. He wallowed in resentment, furious at being incarcerated in "this mediaeval backwater," as he called it.

"Why do we have to stay in this dump?" he raged. "We don't know anyone here! There's nothing to do! I'd rather be back at school." He fired off a stream of protest letters to our parents, threatening to run away unless they agreed to take him with them to Africa.

Fortunately, one of the local farmers offered him a job baling and stooking wheat for the summer. He was able to burn off some of his anger as the work was physically strenuous. In the evenings he would come back completely exhausted. On weekends he would take off on his bicycle and pedal like a maniac, mile after mile. At first I tried to tag along with him, but there was no way I could keep up. And he did not seem to want my company anyway. I was too young to be employed, so there was nothing for me to do but bury myself in my grandmother's books.

My grandmother had an amazing library. Besides Charles Dickens, there were the complete works of Walter Scott, Conan Doyle, and G.H. Henty, as well as the poetry of Keats, Shelley, Byron, and the other romantics. The historical novels of Scott and Henty completely captured my imagination. I identified with all the young heroes who left their families to fight in foreign wars for patriotic causes. I fought with Ivanhoe against the Norman barons, with Drake against the Spanish Armada, and with Wellington against the French armies of Napoleon. It was not much of a stretch to see myself as being just like them, leaving my family to fight the evil empire of the devil in foreign lands.

CHAPTER 17

"Bruno," Father Vince McCann said, "I want you to go out and do some sketches for me."

Vince had discovered that I could draw.

My summer of reading historical novels had not only stimulated my love of history but also of art. I had a knack for representational drawing. I spent hours in history class illustrating the battles we were studying. My very first masterpiece was the battle of Hastings, complete with Norman archers firing arrows high into the air and poor old King Harold being pierced in the eye.

"The Ministry of Education inspectors are coming to the school next week," Vince said. "They will expect to see we're teaching local history. I want you to go and explore Ormskirk."

Ormskirk was a local village first settled by Vikings in Saxon times. Some of the existing houses dated back to before the Reformation.

"There's an old church there with a Saxon font," he said. "Take your sketch book and go draw anything that you think is part of local history. We'll use it in a display on our bulletin board for the inspectors."

I was thrilled. I was to go out on my own. That in itself was exciting. But to spend a whole afternoon drawing instead of freezing my butt in the outfield of a cricket pitch—that was sheer heaven.

Off I went, feeling very important. Ormskirk was a ten-minute bus ride from Freshfield. I jumped off at the first stop in the village and started to wander down the street, gazing at the older houses. I soon noticed a stone window set in the flint wall of a cottage. It was strangely inconsistent with the other windows in that it had a pointed Gothic shape. It had obviously been taken from the ruins of a pre-Reformation priory that was not far away.

I sat down conspicuously on the curb across the street and started to draw, imagining myself to be a distinguished artist. I expected that soon a crowd of admiring spectators would gather round to watch. I had just got started when an old woman in a blue apron opened the front door of the house and came limping across the road.

"What do you think you're doing, young man?" she demanded suspiciously.

"I'm drawing your window for a history project," I said.

She looked back at the window.

"What's that got to do with history?"

"Well, it looks like whoever built your house took it from the ruins of the priory."

"That's not bin stole," she growled. "It's bin there all the time." She glared at me aggressively.

I began to feel uncomfortable.

"I think it must have been a very long time ago," I said. "I don't think anyone's going to want to take it back."

"Just let them try!" she muttered defiantly, stomping back towards her house. Turning around on the doorstep, she gave me a withering look and slammed the door.

I suddenly felt very small and not important at all.

I quickly got up and packed away my sketch book. As I started to walk down the road out of the village, I could see the two towers of the Saxon church that Vince had told me about. They looked slightly weird because one was square and stubby while the other had a round steeple. I hopped over a rail fence thinking to take a shortcut across the field to the church. At the far end I could see a cluster of cows around a drinking trough. There was a pipe coming out of the ground next to it, with a water tap on the end. It was a warm, sunny afternoon and I thought I might be able to get myself a free drink.

As I got closer the cows turned and looked at me suspiciously, much like the old lady back in the village. But they didn't say anything. They just moved ponderously away as I approached. Then I noticed something strange. The trough was circular, with a sloping edge. Suddenly I saw that there was some sort of upside-down lettering around the rim. And then it hit me. This was a giant bronze bell buried in the ground. It had obviously come from the priory ruins too. Some sixteenth-century farmer must have dragged it all the way from the priory after Henry VIII's soldiers had plundered it.

I was so excited at my discovery I could hardly hold my pencil. I hastily sketched what I could see of the bell, and then walked around it with my head sideways trying to read the lettering. It was in Latin. In those days all our church services were in Latin, so it wasn't hard for me to understand it. *Vivos voco, Mortuos plango*, 'I call the living, I cry for the dead'. I ran my hand over the muddy metal edge of that enormous bell, imagining how it had once tolled for the villagers in the surrounding fields. There was something sad about seeing it abandoned and buried. Wordsworth would have sat down and written a poem about it.

As Christmas time approached, my mother wrote that this time we would not be spending the holiday at Walsingham. I later discovered that she had been quite shaken by Michael's angry letters of the previous summer. They must have brought back memories of her own resentment as a little girl when her parents had abandoned her for India.

On the evening before the start of the holidays, Johnny Heweston, the rector, gave us a little pep talk in the study hall. It consisted mostly of warnings about what we would have to contend with on leaving the protective walls of St. Peter's College.

"You are going to see that there are a lot of very attractive girls in the world," he said. "But you have to remember, girls are not for you. You have dedicated your lives to God. You can admire their beauty, there's no sin in that. They are God's creatures. He has made them beautiful. But if you are serious about becoming missionaries, you must avoid them."

But I wasn't paying much attention to his speech. I was going over and over my mother's letter in my head. "You will be spending Christmas with Elizabeth's school friends, Annie and Grace, whom you met in Ireland," she had written.

Apparently, when the girls had found out from Elizabeth that we were homeless, they had begged their parents to let us stay with them. Annie's mother had written and offered to adopt us all for the Christmas holidays, and my mother had agreed.

I was going to see Annie again!

CHAPTER 18

I t was dark when the taxi from the railway station pulled up in front of Annie's house. She came rushing down the steps and flung her arms around my neck before I had a chance to put down my suitcase.

"Imagine! You're going to spend the whole holiday with us!" she shrieked, grabbing my hand and pulling me up to the front door.

"I know," I said shyly. "I'm sorry I never wrote. I didn't think I'd ever see you again."

"That's OK. Neither did I. Besides, I heard you had gone to that seminary place. The nuns at school said I was not supposed to write to you." She looked at me in puzzlement. "I wonder why."

Annie's parents were wealthy. The house was huge. There was a great white marble fireplace in the front hall and a matching staircase that swept up to a long curved gallery with a series of elegant doors leading off to the bedrooms. The hall was decorated with Christmas wreaths and a giant Christmas tree glowing with lights. It reached right up to the balcony on the second floor. The familiar smell of pine needles and Christmas candles made the house feel homey and welcoming. It was bright and cheerful and warm. The air was thick with the smell of baking cookies.

Annie's mother came into the hall from the kitchen wiping her hands on her apron.

"Hey there," she smiled, giving us all a hug. "We're just in the middle of cooking some Christmas goodies. The girls will show you to your rooms. Elizabeth, you'll be sharing with Annie. Michael and Peter, you'll be in the spare bedroom. Take your stuff upstairs and then come down and try some cookies."

It was only a few days before Christmas. Annie's parents were determined to make us feel at home. They gave us money that they said our mother had sent for us, and took us shopping for Christmas presents. Annie's mother helped me buy a necklace that she knew Annie would like and Annie suggested gifts we could buy for her parents. On Christmas Eve we all went off to Midnight Mass. We came back to find stockings tied to the bottom of our beds, stuffed with gifts. Christmas morning was as exciting as if we were with our own parents, except that none of the gifts were from them. But we hardly noticed.

That holiday was a succession of parties. We were invited to go with the girls to all their friends' houses. There were dances with hired bands where Annie taught me how to waltz and do the Palais Glide.

On New Year's Eve, there was to be a big party at Annie's house. Many of the kids we had met at the other Christmas parties were coming with their parents. The huge front hall had been turned into a dance floor, and a band was set up at the top of the balcony stairs. Michael and I were in our bedroom getting dressed. We had plastered our hair down with brilliantine until it shone as slickly as our shoes. We had creased our pants to a sharp edge by laying them out under our mattresses the night before.

"So what about you and Annie?" Michael asked as he fixed his tie in the mirror.

"What do you mean, me and Annie?" I answered.

"Come on, Peter!" Michael laughed, "I thought you were going to be a priest. Aren't you supposed to be avoiding girls?"

"Annie's not . . ."

". . . a girl?" Michael grinned.

"It's not like that," I said hurriedly. "She's a friend. I like her. Besides, I'm not a priest yet!"

"Just teasing," Michael said as he left the room.

I sat down on the bed, suddenly feeling confused. It was true that I had completely forgotten that I was supposed to be God's hero, not Annie's. But God was not nearly as much fun. I enjoyed being with Annie. Besides, we were both going back to our different schools in a few days. The fun times would be over soon. I didn't want to spoil things by thoughts of being a priest in twelve years' time.

Dismissing Michael's question, I headed downstairs to the party. Annie was already there helping her mother set out a punch bowl. She looked up at me with those amazing, laughing eyes of hers and my heart jumped. As the dancing began, we sought each other out more obviously than we had before. I felt impatient when anyone else asked

Annie to dance, and she seemed only too happy when we were together again.

"You must write to me next term," she said. "Ask your mother if you can come and stay with us in Ireland next summer."

"OK," I said, wondering how my mother would react to a request like that from her seminarian son. We were both warm and sweaty from all the dancing. But she was beautiful.

And I didn't want to stop.

Suddenly the lights dimmed and someone was counting down.

"It's almost midnight," Annie said, turning her head to look up at the balcony where the band was on its feet.

"Five . . . Four . . . Three . . . Two . . . One. HAPPY NEW YEAR!" the crowd yelled. The band started to play *Auld Lang Syne*.

And Annie kissed me.

My hands were around her waist. I could feel her back, damp, through her thin satin dress. With her arms around my neck, I kissed her too. And then, embarrassed, I felt a stirring between my legs.

I stepped back, holding her hands in mine, looking into her eyes, not wanting to let go. But other people were rushing up to us, giving us hugs and yelling *Happy New Year*. For a moment she was lost in the crowd and I felt a huge longing, tinged with sadness. We found each other again, but now there was awkwardness between us. I did not know what it was. I did not know what to say.

Then Michael and Gracie came up and dragged us off for another game. Annie was laughing and the awkward moment passed.

CHAPTER 19

L ying awake on the first night back at St. Peter's, I stared up into the darkness.

I missed Annie.

I could still feel the coolness of her arms around my neck, the touch of her cheek against mine when we were saying goodbye. The bare wooden walls of the cubicle rising up around my bed couldn't block out the memory of her shining eyes and carefree laugh.

"That was the greatest Christmas ever!" she had whispered in my ear.

We had promised to write; and I tried. I tried several times. Sitting in the study hall at my desk the next day, I struggled to find words and phrases. But they all seemed so trite. I had no idea how to say what was really in my heart. After a while it was just easier to forget.

Looking back now, it is not really surprising that neither of us followed up on our friendship. In those days, it was too easy to let things slide. We were just two little fish swimming in our own separate streams; streams that happened to flow together for a moment before separating again. We had no control over the direction the streams would take us. I had no freedom to choose. I had been chosen. It seemed that my life had already been planned out for me, not by myself, not by my parents, but by God.

Nevertheless, my friendship with Annie had affected me profoundly. Although we had never talked about how we felt, we had both recognized an excitement that was new to us. She had awakened a spontaneity that I had never felt before. I was happy when I was with her. Before I met her I had never been particularly conscious of my own happiness. She shocked me into seeing that there were parts of myself that were somehow disconnected. For the first time I wondered if being a priest was what I really wanted.

I never told anyone about Annie. As the months went by, she, Michael, Elizabeth, and everyone outside the walls of St. Peter's grew more remote and insubstantial. In contrast, the world of the seminary was up front and very real—a male world, a world with a methodical routine of prayers and classes and sports, a world where the development of any kind of personal relationship was actively discouraged.

"You mustn't form exclusive friendships," Johnny Heweston intoned from his pulpit one day. You all came here for the same reason. God is the one person you should be trying to get close to. You don't need to have particular friends."

He paused, as if searching for the right words.

"Sometimes you might find yourselves spending more time with one of your classmates. There may be something about that person that you find especially attractive. That is quite normal. But it should be a little red flag, a warning that you are being distracted from your main goal. It is something you must guard against. Something you must not let happen. Every one of you must learn to get on with everybody else."

"I suppose that means we should not be spending so much time together," I said to Nick Morgan after Johnny's lecture.

I had been getting together with Nick quite often to work at math. He had been very helpful, but lately I had begun to feel a little uncomfortable in his company. There was something about his pale blue eyes and hang-dog expression that bothered me. I noticed that he was rarely with the other boys.

"Maybe we shouldn't be getting together quite so much," I suggested.

It was a dull morning in late October. We were outside, walking along a path next to the soccer field. It was part of a regular ten-minute exercise break between classes. The shrubs in the hedges beside us had already shed their leaves. The air was full of the pungent smell of dying vegetation.

"I don't think that's what Johnny was talking about," Nick said, kicking at a pebble in the path as we walked along.

"I know," I said. "But the other kids might start to think we're weird. We *do* spend a lot of time together."

"That's true, I suppose," Nick said. "But the others always avoid me. They obviously don't like me being with them."

"I think you should give them a chance. They won't get to know you if you're always hanging around with me."

Nick was looking intently at the path ahead of him. "Well, what will you do about your math?" he asked.

"I'll try and get some of the others to help me," I said. "That shouldn't be a problem."

We walked on in silence for a while. Then Nick looked at me sideways. "Is that what you really want?" he asked quietly.

"Well, no," I said. "But I don't really think it's a matter of what I want; it's more about us mixing in."

Nick turned and looked at me directly.

"Are you sure? I didn't think you were like that. I didn't think you worried about what other people thought."

I felt myself blushing. I knew I was just using Johnny's lecture as a way to avoid Nick. And I was starting to feel ashamed of myself.

"Well, you're wrong." I said angrily. "I *do* care what other people think. In fact that's *all* I care about. I don't want to be different from everyone else; I want to fit in. That's probably a bad thing, but that's what I want."

Nick looked at me. "OK," he said. "If that's how you feel, go ahead."

Nick and I studiously ignored each other after that. I noticed that he still had difficulty relating to the other boys. He always seemed to hang around on the fringes of groups, never really being a part of what was going on. In spite of that, he never gave up. It was as if he felt no other life was possible for him outside the seminary. He persisted quietly at his school work and was one of the few boys in my class who survived to be ordained.

After my conversation with Nick I deliberately went out of my way to mix in with the other boys. Somehow I felt safe with them. They would never talk about anything personal. Rinty Monaghan would occasionally give me a friendly slap on the back and ask how things were going. But he was a whole year ahead of me. It was beneath the dignity of third-form boys to be seen with second-form tykes.

In the late spring of that year, 1950, I turned thirteen. To Michael's dismay, we were both dispatched to Walsingham once again for the summer. My mother had been horrified at the huge bill Annie's parents had sent her for having us at Christmas. Staying with my grandmother would be much cheaper. And Michael could earn his keep working on a farm again.

While Michael went off every day to work in the fields, I had no alternative but to lose myself in my grandmother's library. I read voraciously until my eyes ached. Books were, for me, what video games are for kids today. I would become totally absorbed. By the end of the summer I had read most of Dickens and a great deal of Walter Scott.

My grandmother started to get worried. "Put that book away," she would say. "It's not good to be cooped up indoors all day. Go for a walk, or you'll turn into a mangle-wurzel."

"What's a mangle-wurzel?" I asked, trying to distract her from kicking me out.

"It's a turnip," she said. "That's what you'll turn into if you don't put that book away. Get out of here. Take my bike and go to the chemist's in Fakenham. I need another bottle of paraffin oil."

Fakenham was a little market town about five miles away. Walsingham was too small to have its own pharmacy, so she had to go to Fakenham for prescriptions. She took a spoonful of medicinal paraffin oil every day, insisting that it prevented constipation.

In those days the road to Fakenham was a narrow country lane with very little traffic. It meandered across the countryside past the Slipper Chapel, next to a little stream called the Stiffkey. It wasn't hard for me to imagine the countless colourful pilgrims who walked this road in centuries past. I could see them removing their shoes at the Slipper Chapel and walking the last mile to the shrine in bare feet. And here was I, sharing the same faith that had inspired them, following the same road they had trod, but on a bicycle!

Those pilgrims would have stopped by the stream, as I did, to drink the crystal clear water that sparkled in the sunlight, gurgling over smooth brown pebbles and around flat stepping-stones. They would have rested for a while in the long grass, as I did, looking up at the wide blue sky, listening to the birdsong from the hawthorn bushes and the lazy hum of bees in the warm clover fields. Perhaps they too would have wondered, as I did, about the contradiction in their lives between what they wanted for themselves and what God wanted from them.

CHAPTER 20

In one way it was a relief to return to St. Peter's at the end of the summer. The highly organized life at the college intentionally left little time to think of contradictions. I jumped immediately into the maelstrom of morning classes, afternoon sports, and evening study. New soccer boots had to be greased, leather cleats hammered home, manual labour rosters checked. But gradually, in spite of all this activity, the physical demands of puberty began to intrude.

Waking up in the morning with a huge erection was something not easy to ignore. I worried that the stains on my bed sheets would be noticed by the nuns doing the laundry. What must they think? Who was this boy who wanted to be a priest but who could not control his penis? Not being able to discuss the experience with the other boys made it even more difficult. Involuntary erections became a torture. I was grateful for the long black cassocks that we wore at church. They were perfect for concealing any sudden protuberance.

The enjoyment of accidental orgasm was, we were told, a mortal sin requiring forgiveness in the confessional. I found myself constantly having to acknowledge bad thoughts and impure acts. Fortunately, I began to develop a healthy skepticism towards Catholic sexual morality. It just did not seem logical that a loving God would condemn a boy to eternal punishment for enjoying something which that same God had hot-wired into his body.

Nevertheless, the conflict between what the Church demanded and the physical urges I was experiencing began to create in me a split more radical than my childhood one between home and school. That split had been mutually exclusive. Now I felt as if I was developing an inner self that was in direct contradiction to my outward, public self. There was an inner self, enjoying the physical pleasure of masturbation, co-existing with an outer self, proposing a loyal dedication to the service of the Church.

In the midst of all this confusion, I received a postcard from my father in Uganda.

"Your mother is going to have a baby," he wrote.

She must have already been pregnant for quite a while because in October he sent me another card.

"You now have a beautiful baby brother, with red hair, just like you. We had him baptized Dominic Patrick Caroli Lwanga. We wanted to give him an African name to celebrate his being born here."

I was flummoxed. The news was difficult to absorb. I started to feel angry. Going to Africa was just an excuse for a second honeymoon. How convenient. We three older ones were out of the way. They could have sex day and night without interruption. Why was I supposed to be happy to have a baby brother? They had abandoned me to have him. What was I supposed to feel? How was I supposed to react?

In actual fact, I was to discover that my father's entry into the upper echelons of Ugandan society necessitated patching up his marriage. As a Queen's Counsel, it was required that his wife host elegant cocktail parties for other British officials and their wives. He could not afford to be seen as anything other than monogamous. Reverting to being a good practising Catholic meant that another child was almost inevitable.

At the beginning of December, Johnny Heweston called me into his office. "Your parents wrote to me asking if you could stay here for Christmas," he said. "I'm going to be here myself so I said it would be OK with me." He looked at me over his reading glasses, "How do you feel about that?"

The disappointment hit me like a brick. I had hoped I would be at Annie's again for Christmas.

"I guess it'll be OK," I said doubtfully.

"You can have Father McCann's room. He's going up to Scotland for the holidays. You won't have to be by yourself in a big empty dorm. And you can use his radio and record player."

He could see I was upset. Clearly, he thought it was just because I would miss my brother and sister at Christmas.

As I left, I could feel angry tears stinging my eyes. I went down to the chapel and sat in one of the pews. Obviously, God did not want me to see Annie again. Or was it just my parents? Covering my face with my hands, I sat there, thoroughly miserable. But somehow, youthful resilience broke through. It wasn't going to be *all* bad. At least I would have a room to myself. And I would be able to listen to Vince's radio all day long.

During the school year, we were musically starved. Occasionally we might catch a few lines of a song coming from a radio in one of the priest's rooms. But we were basically ignorant of the rock and roll that was beginning to scandalize parents across the country. Now I would be able to spend the holidays with my ear glued to a radio.

The day the other boys left for the Christmas holidays, Johnny Heweston helped me move my stuff down to Vince McCann's room. As soon as he had gone, I turned on the radio. It was exciting to be able to listen to music any time I wished. I got to know the passionate poetry of puppy love being poured out by pop singers such as Patti Page and Perry Como. But even more exciting were the early rock and roll songs of Roy Brown, Jimmy Preston, and Fats Domino.

Then, best of all, I found that Vince had his own record player with a stack of classical records. The first one I opened was a recording of Fritz Kreisler playing Beethoven's violin concerto. I set it up on the turntable and was immediately entranced. I had never heard anything like it. I played it over and over again. I opened the door to my room so that the glorious, soaring sound poured down the empty hallways. Then Father Heweston appeared at the door.

"Turn it down," he yelled. "You'll go deaf."

But he was smiling. He stood at the door with his thumbs stuck in the red sash that all the priests wore.

"I didn't know you liked classical music," he observed.

"Neither did I. It's the first time I've ever heard it," I said. "It's gorgeous."

He looked quizzically at me for a moment. "Would you like to go to a real concert?" he asked. "The Liverpool Philharmonic is performing Handel's Messiah next week. Would you like to go?"

"Yes, definitely!"

"OK, then. I'll call and book tickets for us."

Of course, I knew nothing about Handel or the *Messiah*, so I set off for the local bookstore in the village and was soon browsing the music section for Handel. And there it was, the piano score for Handel's Messiah. It was a large paperback edition. I could just afford the five shillings it cost. Back in my room, I worked my way through the entire score, amazed that one phrase of a chorus could occupy so many pages of music.

The evening of the concert, Johnny Heweston drove us into Liverpool and parked near the Philharmonic Hall on Hope Street. Crowds were already pouring through the doors of the massive building. We made our way up the carpeted stairs to our seats in the front row of the first balcony. The orchestra was beginning to assemble and behind them a huge choir was ranged in a great sweeping curve, row upon row, gleaming in elegant tuxedos and gowns. And above them, the mighty columns of the pipe organ rose to the ceiling. The audience began to clap as the soloists entered. The conductor strode to the podium. With a bow to the audience, he raised his arms and the audience hushed.

With the very first note I was lost in that amazing music. I was overwhelmed by the power of the monumental choruses. The aria, *I know that my Redeemer liveth,* brought me to tears. I tried to hide them from Johnny Heweston, but I felt his hand squeezing my shoulder. Then the mighty choruses swelled and soared again. As the audience rose to its feet for the Hallelujah chorus, the great organ thundered and the whole building reverberated to the incredible music. I was stunned. I had never experienced anything like it.

Afterwards, as we drove back to the seminary, we were both strangely quiet. For some reason that I did not understand, it seemed that Johnny Heweston had been as moved by the experience as I had. I suppose the music somehow evoked the warmth of a love that we both missed; the warmth that we both needed to feel, in hearts frozen by the cold, hard self-denial of priesthood.

After that Christmas I felt a special bond with Johnny Heweston. I had to be careful not to let the other boys sense it, as that would have left me wide open to their ridicule. But in many ways, I felt more fondly towards him than I had ever felt towards my own father. It was not that he showed me any special favours. It was more a feeling of warmth and security that he conveyed.

The long winter term of 1951 finally gave way to spring and I turned fourteen. There was no birthday card from my parents. The scraps of newspapers we used for toilet paper were full of stories about the Cold War and the Korean War. America was exploding nuclear bombs in the Pacific. Senator McCarthy was raging against the Reds. Britain, still struggling to recover from the Second World War, decided to hold a National Festival to raise morale.

Then suddenly I got a postcard from my father. Michael, Elizabeth, and I were to fly out to Uganda for the summer.

"You will see Mill Hill missionaries at work," he wrote.

CHAPTER 21

"All right you lot, what are you up to?"

The doorman of the Grosvenor Hotel was an imposing figure, resplendent in his gold-braided top coat and embossed peaked hat. He gazed down suspiciously at the three excited teenagers who had just been deposited by a cabbie on his front steps.

"What do you think you're doing?" he growled, bending slightly to inspect our grubby suitcases.

"We're here to spend the night," Michael said evenly, in his best English public school accent. "We have a reservation. And tomorrow, we're flying to Africa."

"You're what?" The doorman fixed Michael with a cold stare from beneath bushy eyebrows. "You expect me to believe that?"

He straightened up, touching the peak of his hat to an elegant woman wrapped in a fox fur who swept down the steps to a waiting limousine. Then, with white-gloved hands behind his back, he stood barring our way to the front door.

The Grosvenor Hotel is situated in Mayfair, London, opposite Hyde Park. An imposing Victorian building, it had survived the bombs of the blitz. That day, in the early summer of 1951, it stood like a stolid monument to the fast fading glories of the British Empire.

My father had sent us detailed instructions on how to meet each other. We were to take a cab to the hotel where he had booked two rooms for us. We were to have supper there and breakfast the following morning. Then we would be driven to Heathrow airport to board the plane that was to take us to Africa.

The three of us were bubbling with excitement. It was more than a year since we had seen each other. Michael was about to turn sixteen and was now almost six feet tall. He looked handsome and very fit from all his rugby training at school. But it was Elizabeth who surprised me the most. I had not seen her since the Christmas at Annie's a year and a half ago. Somehow she had been transformed from a rough and tumble tomboy into a sparkling young woman, with gorgeous red hair and lively blue eyes.

Michael was not the least bit intimidated by the hotel doorman. "I don't care if you believe us or not," he said. "We're going in to register." He picked up his suitcase and marched right up the steps to the front door. Elizabeth and I followed, full of admiration at his supreme self-confidence.

We crossed an acre of plush red carpet to the marble and mahogany reception counter. Here the roar of the London traffic outside was reduced to a dull murmur. Uniformed valets moved around the hushed foyer like the ushers in a church, ready to deal with any inappropriate behaviour from unruly teenagers.

Unlike the grumpy doorman, the clerk at the reception desk was smoothly courteous.

"We have been expecting you, Sir," he said to Michael. "Your rooms are ready."

Elizabeth and I grinned at each other, impressed by the 'Sir.'

"The porter will take your luggage up," the receptionist continued, handing Michael our room keys. "Your supper will be served in the banquet hall. I have arranged for you to be called in the morning so that you can be in time to catch your plane."

The three of us were escorted across the lobby into a massive dining room. Row upon row of tables, covered in white linen, sparkled with silver place settings and crystal glasses. Each table had its own little lamp glowing faintly in the late evening sunlight streaming through the enormous windows that overlooked Hyde Park.

The room was empty except for a group of waiters and some musicians setting up at the far end. It was clearly too early for adult diners. We were ushered to a table where three waiters stood behind three high-backed chairs to seat us. As we sat down, they unfolded stiff linen napkins and handed us elegant, leather-bound menus.

Elizabeth and I looked at each other and immediately got the giggles. Neither of us had ever experienced this kind of luxury before. The waiters stood by impassively, seemingly unperturbed, while

Michael ignored us and focused on his menu. We struggled to control ourselves, finally succeeding only by using the tried-and-true method of examining our fingernails.

The menus were incomprehensible. Most of the dishes had French names. Michael handed his back to the head waiter.

"Why don't you decide for me?" he said.

"Very good, Sir," said the head waiter with a slight bow.

"That goes for me too," I said, handing back my menu, and Elizabeth nodded her head in agreement.

It felt strange to be the only ones in that enormous dining room. We began speaking in whispers as if all the empty tables around us were listening. But the sound of a saxophone suddenly filled the room. The musicians were starting their warm-up, so we were able to talk a little more naturally.

"This place is incredible," said Elizabeth, looking up at the rows of chandeliers dripping with crystal.

"Mother told me she and Dad used to come here often," Michael said. "That was before they got married. They had pots of money then. They must be doing OK now, though, to pay for all this."

"I'm not so sure," Elizabeth said. "I think he tends to throw money around even when he can't afford it. Maybe he wants to impress us. Or maybe he's trying to make up for leaving us the way he did."

"Could be," Michael said, "but Mother says he wastes his money hanging out in bars. She says he's always buying drinks for strangers and talking about far-fetched money-making schemes."

Michael seemed to know much more about my father than I did.

"I feel I hardly know him," I said. "It seems so long ago since we've seen him. It doesn't seem like we're a real family."

We were interrupted by the waiters bringing our dinner.

It was an amazing meal. There was oxtail soup, followed by a salad and salmon, and then a main course of roast rack of lamb. Best of all, there was a huge choice of desserts: cakes, custards, pastries, fruit, and different kinds of ice cream, everything our young hearts could desire.

"I'm completely stuffed," Michael said afterwards as we rode up to our rooms in the elevator. "I probably won't want any breakfast in the morning."

Michael and I said good night to Elizabeth and then went to unlock our door. For a moment we stood there in awe. It was the grandest bedroom either of us had ever seen.

The ceiling was impossibly high, with an ornate, gilt-framed fresco above the beds. It depicted a young shepherdess clad in a diaphanous robe that revealed more of her anatomy than it concealed. She was apparently swooning in the arms of a peasant in an impossibly idyllic landscape.

The walls of the bedroom were covered by rich, tapestry-like wallpaper that was furry to the touch. There were two enormous beds with elaborately quilted duvets already folded back. Our suitcases had been opened and our pajamas laid out for us. Our toothbrushes were neatly arranged on the marble countertop in the bathroom. All this luxury seemed sinfully extravagant after the spartan environment of the seminary. But it was definitely fun.

"This is going to be quite the holiday," I said to Michael as I climbed into bed and snuggled down between cool, soft sheets. "I hope it isn't just a dream!"

CHAPTER 22

At exactly six o'clock in the morning, the telephone rang. It was the wake-up call from the front desk. We dressed quickly and Michael knocked on Elizabeth's door. We went down for breakfast together, almost too excited to eat. Half an hour later we were at the front entrance with our luggage. The now deferential doorman touched his cap with a "Good morning, Sir. Good morning, Ma'am." A shiny, black limousine purred patiently at the front steps. Our luggage was stowed in the trunk and we were off to Heathrow Airport.

"I wonder what kind of plane we'll be on," Michael said, as the limousine threaded its way through London's early morning rush hour.

"Mine was a flying boat," Elizabeth said.

"What did you say?" Michael was looking at her in disbelief.

"Oops! I wasn't supposed to tell you," Elizabeth said, covering her mouth.

"What do you mean, not supposed to tell us?" Michael demanded.

"Well, Daddy flew me out last summer. I wasn't supposed to tell you. They were afraid you'd be jealous."

Michael was instantly furious. "That's so unfair. How could they? And we had to spend those awful summers with Granny. I don't get it."

"How come you got to go and we didn't?" I asked.

"I don't know," Elizabeth said desperately, "but we're *all* going now. Don't let's spoil it. We were having such a good time."

"I just think it's so unfair," Michael said bitterly.

"You're right," I said. "But perhaps they didn't have enough money for us all to go last year. Let's forget it."

"I'm so sorry," Elizabeth whispered, and she started to cry softly.

This had a magical effect on Michael. He immediately put his arm around her.

"It's OK, it's OK," he said. "It's not your fault. I'm not angry at *you*. I'm angry at *them*. And you're right. We're all going together now, and that makes up for it."

Elizabeth's sobs began to subside.

"It was a beautiful plane," she said quietly, "that flying boat."

The sky was overcast when we arrived at the airport, seeming to reflect our change of mood. We were given seats facing each other with a table in between at the very front of the plane. The fourth seat at the table was occupied by a rather distinguished looking gentleman in a pin-stripe suit and a bowler hat. He was still wearing the hat when we arrived, but he quickly got up and carefully set it into an overhead bin as we sat down. He took a sheaf of papers from a briefcase and began working at them even before the plane left the gate. At first we thought he was going to ignore us, but after a while he put them away and leaned back in his seat.

"So," he said with a little smile, "where are you all off to?"

"We're going to visit our parents in Uganda," Michael said.

"Well, that's exciting. What are they doing in Uganda?"

"Our dad's a Queen's Counsel with the circuit court in Kampala," Michael explained.

"Kampala? That's where I'm going. My name is John Selwyn-Lloyd."

Just as Michael was introducing us, the plane began to move. We leaned towards the windows, watching the airport buildings slide past. Then the engines roared and we were rushing down the runway. Suddenly, the ground dropped away. Below us roads stretched into the distance, cars and trucks becoming tiny toys. Thin wisps of cloud streamed past the windows and, moments later, the plane burst through into sunshine. The sky was an incredible blue and our spirits perked up. We were on our way to Africa. Our adventure had truly begun.

It turned out that Selwyn-Lloyd was a person of importance, a real VIP. He was the Minister of State for Foreign Affairs and was on his way to Uganda for a meeting to discuss the possibility of the country becoming independent.

"At the moment, Uganda is a British protectorate," Selwyn-Lloyd explained. "That means that other countries have to deal with the

British government if they want to get involved in Uganda. But soon, hopefully, it can become a completely independent country with its own government to manage things."

"I suppose when that happens my father will be out of a job," Michael said thoughtfully.

"Not necessarily," Selwyn-Lloyd said. "Often, a newly independent country will want to keep people like your father in their jobs until they have enough of their own lawyers and judges to take over. And that can take quite a while. But eventually, yes, he would have to leave."

"Well, I hope it happens soon, then." said Michael, an edge of resentment in his voice. "I don't like the way he left us by ourselves in England. It makes me feel he doesn't want to have us around."

"I can imagine it does," Selwyn-Lloyd said. "Anyway, would you mind if I used the table to finish up some paper work? Then, afterwards we can have a game of cards or something. It's going to be a long trip."

"OK," Michael said. He fished out a bundle of comics that he had brought with him and we all settled down to read for a while.

About an hour or so into the flight, the captain came out of the cockpit and introduced himself.

"We'll be flying over Switzerland quite soon, Sir," he said to Selwyn-Lloyd. "Would you like to come forward and take a look? The Alps are quite spectacular."

"Of course I would! Can the children come too?"

"Well, there's not much room up there," said the captain looking at us cautiously, "but they can come if they take turns and don't touch anything."

So, amazingly, we were each given a turn standing behind the pilot's seat while the captain explained where we were. We could see craggy, white-capped Alps far below us and, among them, the steep-sided slopes of the Matterhorn. In the far distance the sun was glinting off the glassy surface of the Mediterranean.

It was a long flight, broken by short stopovers in Rome, Cairo, and Khartoum. We were allowed to leave the plane at each stop to stretch our legs.

When the stewardess opened the door at Khartoum, the desert heat hit us like the blast of a furnace. We had to climb down a set of steel steps from the plane, the railing almost too hot to touch. Inside the airport lounge huge ceiling fans stirred the air without seeming to moderate the temperature in the slightest. We sat in wicker chairs and were served ice-cold drinks by Sudanese waiters dressed in long white robes and red fezzes. It could have been a scene from one of my favourite Henty novels.

Uganda turned out to be very different. As we were coming in to land, the countryside below looked lush and green, not at all like the dry, yellow sands of Khartoum.

"Uganda is approximately 3,700 feet above sea level," Selwyn-Lloyd told us, "so the average daily temperature is quite comfortable."

The plane sank lower, curving over the edge of Lake Victoria. It was already late in the day. The slanting sun highlighted the rich colours of the tropical vegetation along the shore. Then, with a bump, we were on the ground and rolling towards a long, low, yellow building that had ENTEBBE AIRPORT spelled out along its roof.

Chapter 23

Tumbling down the steps from the plane, I saw a small group of people waving. One figure detached itself from the group and came running towards us. It was my mother. Laughing and crying, she rushed up to hug us over and over again.

"You all look so different," she said as we walked across the tarmac to the terminal. "You've grown so tall! And Elizabeth, you cut your hair!"

Michael, embarrassed at the fuss she was making, asked, "Where's Dad?"

My father had hung back. As we got closer, I could see a pleased smile on his face. He didn't look as tall as I remembered, and his hair had turned grey at the sides. He had developed a beer belly, but still looked handsome in his light, tropical suit.

Selwyn-Lloyd introduced himself. "They were very well-behaved," he said, looking sideways at us with a grin. "No trouble at all." It was only then I realized my father must have asked him to keep an eye on us.

"Well, goodbye, you lot," Selwyn-Lloyd said. "Enjoy your stay in Uganda." He walked over to a small delegation of officials waiting to greet him.

"Where's Dominic?" Elizabeth asked eagerly as we walked into the terminal.

"Over there," my mother said.

An elderly African man wearing a long white robe was standing just inside the exit. He was holding a little red-haired baby in his arms.

"This is Dominic and this is Simonie, our head boy. He takes care of Dominic for us when we're away."

Dominic was looking curiously at us. The two middle fingers of his right hand were stuck in his mouth. He was barely nine months old but not the least bit shy. He bounced excitedly in Simonies' arms, trying to reach out to us, almost falling.

I wondered why mother had called Simonie a head boy. He looked older than my father, with his wrinkled black skin and work-worn hands. He stood there with such quiet dignity that calling him a boy sounded absurd. I looked up at him and his eyes had a blankness to them that spoke of the huge distance separating us. I felt uncomfortable and looked away.

"Come on, you rats," my father said. "Get yourselves into the car." 'Rats' was his favourite way of referring to us as a collective. "It's about a twenty-minute drive to our house in Kampala and Simonie has to get supper organized."

As we drove out of the airport parking lot, I had my face glued to the window, taking in the exotic palms and mango trees that confirmed I was now in Africa. At first I was disappointed that the road was paved and we were passing cars and trucks that looked the same as those in England. But then my father started telling stories, just as he had done when we drove across Ireland.

"Did you see that big school we just passed?" he asked. "Two boys were attacked by crocodiles behind there just a week ago. Lake Victoria is on the other side of the school, and they went for a swim in an unprotected area."

Crocodiles! Now that was more like the Africa I had imagined.

"The lake is huge," my father said, "as big as Scotland."

Soon we were passing a whole plantation of young trees with small, light green leaves.

"Those are eucalyptus trees. They've been planted in a ring around the town to keep mosquitoes away. The roots absorb stagnant water and stop mosquitoes from breeding. They also produce a kind of gum that mosquitoes don't like. It helps to keep the place free of malaria."

I knew all about malaria. We had each been given quinine tablets before leaving England and were supposed to take them every day.

"Malaria's not too bad," my father went on, "but sometimes it can develop into blackwater fever. That's very dangerous. So at night tuck yourselves under your mosquito nets really well."

Soon we were driving down the main street of Kampala. It was lined with shops and office buildings that looked different from the ones in England. These were mostly built of concrete, stained red where rain had splashed mud up against the walls. The rooms above had open balconies with intricate trelliswork.

We turned off the main road onto a street that wound up the side of a hill. There were little bungalows on each side, set in lovely open gardens with green lawns and luxurious shrubs and trees.

"This is where we live," my father said as we drove into a driveway near the top of the hill.

In front of us was a white bungalow, a replica of the ones we had passed. It was a simple enough house, with a corrugated tin roof and glass-louvered windows. To one side was a large garage.

"That's where you boys will be sleeping. There are only two bedrooms in the house, so we've done up the garage for you. Come and take a look."

Doing up the garage meant having two camp beds set up on the concrete floor with mosquito nets hanging from the roof. There was a small bamboo table with a kerosene lamp in between the beds. It looked very much like a set from *The African Queen*.

"Where's the bathroom?" I asked.

"You'll have to come over to the house," my mother said. "But this is kind of cozy, don't you think?"

She looked anxiously at Michael, who obviously was not as willing to forgo comfort as much as I, with my austere seminary background.

"It's OK, I guess," Michael said somewhat reluctantly.

While Simonie was preparing supper, Michael and I explored the garden. The sun was just disappearing behind the surrounding hills. They were wreathed in hazy blue smoke from countless cooking fires. Dozens of fireflies winked in the African dusk that was creeping up around us. At the side of the house, red earth had been scraped level to make a badminton court. Behind it, we saw the long, low silhouette of a building, dark against the flaming yellow and orange sky. It was the house where Simonie lived with his wife and his young son.

A small figure detached itself from the shadows.

"Jambo," he said. "I'm Yusuf. Welcome to Kampala. My father says you have never been here before."

"Supper's ready!" It was my mother calling from the house. There was something sharp about the way she called to us, as if she had seen us talking to Yusuf and disapproved.

"See you later," Yusuf said with a smile, and we ran back to the house.

My father was already sitting at the dining-room table. We quickly joined him and for a moment there was an embarrassing silence. This was the first time we had all sat down as a family since that long-ago summer in Ireland. It was one of those silences that is broken by everyone beginning to talk at once.

"Hold on, hold on," my father said, "Let's say grace."

We shut our eyes and started to say the formal prayer together: *Bless us, O Lord, and these thy gifts . . .*

I took a quick peek at Michael through my fingers. He was sitting with his eyes wide open, his mouth shut tight, his face flushed with resentment. He had clearly not forgiven my father for abandoning us. He was in no mood to thank God for anything. As the prayer ended, there was another uncomfortable silence.

Simonie came in to serve supper. He wore his white gloves and quietly ladled out a light, brown soup.

"Goody, my favourite," Elizabeth cried out, "peanut soup!"

"How *do* you make it, Simonie?" my mother asked in a slightly condescending tone. Without waiting for an answer, she said to us, "Of course, we don't go near the kitchen. That's Simonie's kingdom."

Simonie ignored her and silently left the room with calm dignity. He brought in a large plate of curried goat's meat and a bowl of mashed unripe bananas called *mutoki,* a staple dish in Uganda.

"That looks scrumptious," Elizabeth said to him. "Thanks, Simonie."

Simonie gave her a little smile. "You're welcome, *kisichana,*" he said.

After supper, we were all sent off to bed for an early night.

"So what do you think?" Michael asked as we lay under our mosquito nets, the kerosene lamp hissing on the table between our beds. Outside a shrill chorus of crickets filled the night.

"It's not quite what I'd expected," I said. "I imagined we'd be living in a mud hut in the middle of a jungle. This place feels very civilized."

"Call this civilized? We're sleeping on camp beds with only a hurricane lamp to see by. It seems pretty primitive to me!"

"I know, but at least there are roads and cars and things. And we're probably the only people sleeping in a garage."

"I suppose so," Michael said, "and it *is* a treat having servants to wait on us hand and foot."

We were quiet for a moment as I thought about that.

"I'm not so sure," I said. "Did you see how Mother sort of put Simonie down? That wasn't nice. He's an old man and they call him a head boy. What do we need servants for, anyway? It makes me feel like we're supposed to be superior or something."

Michael's bed creaked as he shifted onto his side.

"Now you're talking like a missionary, Peter. Go to sleep."

He reached out and turned down the lamp. The shadows that had lurked in the corners of the garage gradually closed in around us as the flame slowly dimmed. With a little flicker it finally went out and we were lying in total darkness.

The stuffy cotton smell of the mosquito net filled my nostrils.

Michael's breathing settled into an even rhythm.

As I stared up into the darkness, my mind was alive with excited thoughts. We were a family again. And I was in Africa. And I was going to see Mill Hill missionaries in action.

It was a while before I fell asleep.

CHAPTER 24

" So, what would you rats like to do on your first day in Africa?" my father asked as we sat down to breakfast the next morning.

"Why don't you take a drive over to the Nsambya?" my mother suggested. "Peter can see what a real Mill Hill mission is like."

"I don't want to go," Michael said sulkily. "I'd rather stay here with Elizabeth."

It was obvious Michael was still angry at my father but didn't want to talk about it.

"I was there last year," Elizabeth chimed in. "I don't mind staying here. Michael and I can set up the badminton net and have a game while you're gone."

"Whatever you like. There's no point in going if you don't want to become a missionary. How about you, Peter? Would you like to go?"

"Absolutely," I said.

Kampala, like Rome, was built on seven hills. Catholic and Protestant missionaries had been there ever since the late 1800s. Perched on top of each of four hills were two separate Catholic cathedrals, plus a Protestant cathedral and a mosque. Of the remaining three hills, one was occupied by the Kabaka's (king's) palace and the High Court; another was the site of the ancient tombs of previous Kabakas. The third was the site of the ruins of a British fort.

The Mill Hill compound was called Nsambya and included a hospital run by Franciscan nuns. Rubaga Hill was where the other Catholic cathedral was located. It was the headquarters of a Catholic missionary organization popularly known as The White Fathers because they wore white robes, like the Arabs.

As we drove up the hill, my father filled me in on some of the history.

"The first Catholic missionaries to work here were the White Fathers, who were French," he said. "They were followed by Protestant missionaries who were British. A huge rivalry developed between the two missions and, in the 1890s, their followers actually started a civil war!"

"That's crazy!" I said. "Missionaries aren't supposed to fight."

"Well, both sides behaved more like the representatives of a colonial government rather than a Christian religion. In the end, when Uganda became a British protectorate, the Pope asked the Mill Hill priests to come, just because they were British."

The car strained as it climbed the steep dirt road. We passed groups of women, some with enormous bundles balanced precariously on their heads, and others with tiny babies tied to their backs with colourful cotton shawls. Sometimes two or three children would run, laughing and waving, in the red dust thrown up behind the car.

Near the top of the hill we parked under a huge mango tree. On the other side of the road was a long, low, wooden building with peeling white paint and green trim. It had a veranda running along its length, crowded with people. They were sitting against the walls and on the steps. Others sat in the shade of another mango tree at the side of the building. A plank of wood nailed against the rusty tin roof had the word HOSPITAL painted in crude red letters.

An African nun in a white habit sat at a folding table by the entrance. She was listening to a young, barefoot African man dressed in khaki shorts and a grimy, grey T-shirt. He was supporting a withered old lady so bent it was a wonder she could stand at all. The nun glanced up at us as we walked across the road towards them, but only for a moment. She continued listening to the young man. Then she got up and, speaking gently, put an arm around the old lady as the three of them disappeared inside.

And then, I saw a tall, white priest standing in the doorway. To my amazement, I recognized him. It was Father McKee, the priest who had met me in Walsingham and got me into the seminary at Freshfield.

"Hello, Peter," he said with a slight smile. "Fancy meeting you here; your father told me you might be coming."

"Hi," I said shyly. "I didn't know you had been sent here."

He seemed to have lost a lot of weight. He was quite skinny. He had an anxious, almost haunted look.

As soon as the people around us saw him, pandemonium broke out. They leapt up, elbowing me out of the way, pushing and shoving to get close to him. I stepped back and he gave me a helpless, apologetic look. "We'll talk later," he said.

"Come on, Peter," my father said. "We're in the way here. Let's go up to the cathedral."

As we went on up the hill I looked back, but Father McKee was hidden by the crowd.

We were walking toward a very simple building that hardly deserved to be called a cathedral; it was just a tin roof supported by open brick arches. Rows of rough, grey, wooden benches were ranged on each side of a centre aisle. A small choir of women stood on a raised platform near the altar, practising for Sunday Mass.

We sat on one of the benches and listened for a while. The choir seemed to be enjoying themselves. There was much giggling and chatter between songs. When they sang it was like a dance; they moved their whole bodies, clapping and swaying to the rhythm of the music. A cool breeze swept through the open sides of the building. Brightly coloured birds flew in and out, from one side to the other.

"It's too bad," I said. "I wish Father McKee could have stopped to talk with us. I suppose he feels that he has to spend all his time with the Africans. Perhaps we could invite him over to the house when he can take a break."

"You know," my father said thoughtfully, "Father McKee's been having a rough time since he came here. Many Africans treat missionaries like witch doctors. They still believe in evil spirits. They want the priests to ward off bad magic by blessing their houses and children and fields."

"It was scary," I said, "the way they swamped Father McKee as soon as he appeared."

"That's what happens if you believe priests have a special 'in' with God. Even back home a lot of Catholics still believe that priests have a unique power. Believing in magic and superstition is a convenient way for people to avoid taking responsibility for their lives."

I looked at him, surprised at the angry tone that had crept into his voice. He stood up abruptly and we began walking back down the hill to the car.

"The hospital was started by an Irish nun at the request of the Mill Hill Mission," my father said. "She had to overcome a lot of prejudice and superstition. The site was occupied by a big tree. The Baganda sacrificed chickens in front of it to appease the evil spirits. She chopped it down and almost caused a riot."

He chuckled, and then went on more seriously.

"She also had to fight the Pope. In those days, the Church didn't allow nuns to become doctors. She won in the end. But it shows how reactionary the Church can be."

As we got into the car, I saw the crowd had settled back down along the hospital veranda. Father McKee wasn't there anymore and I felt a little sad. He had seemed so completely overwhelmed by the demands of those people. He looked scared, like an animal terrified of being torn apart by predators.

My golden dream of heroic missionary adventure was somewhat tarnished by that day's dose of reality.

CHAPTER 25

When we got back to the house, Michael and Elizabeth were sitting in the shade of the front porch with a cold drink. They were hot and sweaty from their badminton game.

"Who won?" my father asked as we got out of the car.

"Michael did, of course," Elizabeth said, pretending to pout. "He's just too tall for me. And he showed no mercy. You should play him, Daddy; he'd have a much tougher time beating you."

"Alright, Michael, how about it? Think you can beat me?"

Michael avoided looking at him, carefully examining his racquet instead. He shrugged his shoulders. "OK, I guess."

"Give me a second, then," my father said. "I'll get changed."

A few minutes later he came out, dressed in snazzy white shorts and a yellow sports shirt.

"Come on, Michael. Let's see who's the better man."

Michael flushed. He tightened his grip on his racquet.

"Let's go, then," he said between clenched teeth.

My father was a skillful but relaxed player. He would reach effortlessly for each shot, his height giving him a big advantage. Michael, on the other hand, was like a coiled spring. He leapt at every return. Time and again, he pounded the shuttlecock into the net as he tried to go for the kill. Gradually the score built up in my father's favour. Michael kept trying to power every shot into the ground while my father calmly placed his shots just inside the edges of the court.

When my father won the first game, Michael challenged him to another.

"I can beat you," he yelled in frustration. "I know I can."

But he was tiring. He struggled for every point, while my father played with calm efficiency.

"That was in!" Michael shouted when one of his shots fell just outside the line. He stormed around the net and pointed to where he thought it had landed. "You just want me to lose. It's not fair."

Suddenly, he broke. He flung his racquet on the ground. His anger came bubbling up.

"I hate you. You don't care about us. You never cared about us. You shouldn't have brought us here. You only care about what other people think. We're just trophies for you to show off to your friends. You don't really want us here at all."

He was almost incoherent with rage.

"That's not true, Michael," my father said. "That's not true. I really missed you all, especially when Dominic was born. I wanted us to be a family again, even just for a little while."

He tried to put an arm around Michael's shoulder, but Michael angrily pushed him away.

"I don't believe you," he shouted. "You're just saying that. You could have got a job in England and stayed with us. Why didn't you? Why didn't you?"

Elizabeth was standing next to me, horrified. I reached for her hand. Together we walked around to the front of the house. My mother was just coming outside.

"What's going on?" she asked, looking at us anxiously.

"It's Michael," I said. "He's really angry."

My mother ran past us and disappeared around the side of the house next to the badminton court.

Elizabeth and I sat down on the flagstones against the wall of the front porch. We clasped our knees to our chests, not looking at each other. I knew exactly what Michael was feeling. But I couldn't let myself feel that kind of anger. I was afraid my father would never want to see me again.

It seemed as if we sat there for a long time. Then, my mother came walking back, her arm around Michael's shoulders. My father walked behind them with the two badminton rackets. They went into the house and, after a little while, came out without Michael.

"He's having a little sleep," my mother said. She looked as if she had been crying. My father avoided looking at us.

"I'm just going out for a bit. I'll see you at supper." He climbed into the car, accelerated backwards out of the driveway, and shot off down the hill towards the town.

That evening my father didn't show up for supper, confirming my worst fears.

Michael woke up and joined us, but was very subdued. My mother hardly said a word. Simonie served the food silently. I wondered how much he understood about what was going on.

"How are you doing?" I asked Michael that night as we lay under our mosquito nets.

"I still feel angry at him," he muttered. "And I don't trust what he said. How could he take Mother and leave us if he really cared?"

"I don't know," I said, "but I think we should give him a chance. After all, we've only been here a day. Let's just see how things work out. At least he knows how you feel about him. Maybe it will make him want to change."

"How was your trip to Nsambya?" Michael asked.

"All right, I guess. I'm not sure Dad likes missionaries. He seems to think the hospital is a good thing. But he thinks priests just encourage superstition."

"Well, I kind of agree with him there," Michael said.

He yawned and I heard him turning over on his side.

"Do you want me to turn off the lamp?" I asked.

"Sure," he said.

CHAPTER 26

Slowly, over the next few weeks, Michael's anger seemed to subside. Sometimes, he was allowed to spend the day at the Court House, watching my father handle a big trial. I was considered too young to go.

One day Michael arrived back just bursting to tell me something.

"Come into the garage, Peter," he called, eyes gleaming with excitement. "You have to hear this!"

He strode across the yard and slammed the door behind us. He sat down on the edge of his camp bed, dragging me down next to him.

"You should have been there," he said. "Dad was furious. He threw all the money into a heap in the middle of the floor and set fire to it!"

"What money? What do you mean? What are you talking about?" I asked.

"It was this Sikh bloke. He left a suitcase full of money on Dad's desk. He wanted Dad to stop the trial. His brother had murdered an African girl. He'd cut her throat with a machete. The Sikh wanted Dad to let him go."

"Dad set fire to it?"

"Yes. You know the huge marble foyer where people wait for their cases to be heard? Well, Dad chased the Sikh man out of his office and threw the suitcase after him. It landed in the middle of the foyer and burst open. All the money fell out. The Sikh just stood there, with Dad yelling at him. Then Dad bent down and set the money on fire with his cigarette lighter. You should have seen the look on their faces!"

Michael was obviously impressed by this dramatic display of righteous indignation. It clearly went a long way toward restoring his respect for our father.

As the weeks went by I discovered our family was part of a small, exclusive circle of British expatriates who socialized together on a regular basis. It included the Chief Justice, the Chief of Police, doctors from the big, government hospital and professors from Makerere University.

Their wives would host dinner parties and more informal tennis or badminton get-togethers. No Africans were ever invited.

The children of the European expatriates were mostly sent to boarding schools in Nairobi or England. They returned to Kampala for the summer holidays. Michael, Elizabeth, and I were quickly absorbed into the teen social scene.

There was one family in particular that we got to know well. They lived just a few houses from us. Dr. Boase was an ophthalmologist at the government hospital. Two of his daughters, Gillian and Josie, were about the same age as Michael and I.

Gillian reminded me a lot of Annie. She had the same raven-black hair and creamy complexion. And there was a similar devil-may-care attitude with which she flung herself into things. My mother, of course, made it very clear to her that I was a seminarian and therefore off limits, but that did not seem to concern her.

We kids often drove over to Silver Springs, a whites-only club, with a large, outdoor swimming pool. We spent long, lazy afternoons there, cavorting in and out of the water.

The pool had a bar that opened onto the patio, with rows of tables shaded by thatched umbrellas. In the evenings white government officials and business men would gather there for drinks. But at other times the only adult in the place was the owner, Antonio, a portly gentleman with a bushy, greasy moustache.

"What on earth possessed you to go to a seminary?" Gillian asked me one day. We were lying together on our stomachs by the pool. She was wearing a particularly miniscule bikini that had already prompted me to ask myself the same question.

"Probably just to avoid thinking about what else I could do with my life," I said, playing it cool.

"Don't be so flippant. I'm serious."

"OK, OK," I said. "It's just that most people don't really care enough to ask."

Gillian raised herself on one elbow and looked at me. "Well, I care," she said emphatically. "I don't understand why anyone would want to be a priest."

I looked around. No one else was listening. Elizabeth and Josie were busy blowing soap bubbles. Michael was floating on his back in the pool with his eyes shut.

"It's kind of complicated," I said, watching the clouds of shiny soap bubbles blowing across the pool. "Being born is such a random thing. Why am I me? And why are you, you? We could have been anybody, or we could have been nobody. I mean, there must be a *reason* for us to be born."

Her question had caught me unawares, and I was struggling.

"What's all that got to do with being a priest?" Gillian looked at me, her clear, blue-green eyes demanding an answer.

I tried to focus my thoughts. Elizabeth had blown a splendidly large, translucent bubble that landed on Gillian's arm before bursting in a spray of soap.

"You know, it seems to me that most of us live in a kind of bubble," I said. "We don't often think about what goes on outside it. All those kids in Korea, killed and crippled by the war; why should that be happening to them and not to us?"

Well, I don't think I live in a bubble," Gillian said thoughtfully. "I can certainly see all kinds of crazy things going on in the world."

"Yes, you *see* what's going on around you, just as you would if you were living in a soap bubble. But our bubbles are not like soap bubbles. They're more like unbreakable glass. They're like a protection. So we don't get to *feel* what's going on outside."

Gillian sat up and wrapped her towel around her shoulders. "Well, what can I possibly do about the kids in Korea?"

"It's not just about kids in Korea," I said. It's about those kids over there."

A small group of African children were clinging to the iron railing surrounding the pool, watching us white kids splash around.

"How do you think those kids feel? They see us having fun and they know that they're not allowed in here. Why do we get to swim here and they don't?"

Gillian looked over at them and then down at her toes. She had very pretty toes, I thought.

"It does make me feel uncomfortable," she said finally. "But you still haven't told me why you want to be a priest."

Michael yelled from the pool: "It's because he thinks he's better than we are!" He had been listening all the time.

I leaped up and did a cannonball jump right next to him.

"You're just a bloody heathen," I shouted as I swam to the side and levered myself out of the pool.

I was grateful for the distraction. Gillian's question disturbed me. My fantasy of heroic missionary adventures was fading fast. She presented me with the conflict I felt; the conflict between sexual attraction and the celibacy demanded of Catholic priests. Perhaps Michael was right. Maybe I did feel I was better than other kids. Maybe that was easier than being challenged by Gillian's sexuality.

Cooled by the water, I stood at the edge of the pool in the full glare of the African sun. I felt the sudden, sharp heat of the concrete patio under my feet. Drops of water ran down my legs, forming little dark patches that instantly evaporated.

As I bent down to pick up my towel, I saw that Gillian had walked over to the fence. She was crouching down, her hands covering the hands of a kid holding onto the railing. She was talking fluently to him in Swahili. Then she stood up and walked along the fence to the entrance gate, the kids following along on the other side. She opened the gate and tried to get them to come in. But they stood bunched together outside, eyes wide with wonder and curiosity. They were like a herd of young deer, ready to spring away at the slightest sign of danger.

"Hey, you there!"

It was Antonio yelling. He waddled round the corner of the bar, flicking a tea towel towards the African children as if he were shooing away flies. He fixed Gillian with beady eyes.

"You can't let them in here. This is for whites only. Didn't you read the sign?" and he pointed angrily to a big board wired to the fence.

The children turned and fled. Gillian looked after them helplessly.

"Antonio! Why did you do that? You scared them away."

"They have no right to be here," Antonio huffed. "This is a private club. Only members are allowed. Those kids' parents could never afford the fees. Besides, they probably have all kinds of diseases. No white person would swim here if I let them in."

"That's nonsense," Gillian insisted. "They can take a shower just like us. I wouldn't mind swimming with them. And where else can they go? They'll get bilhartia if they swim in the lake. Everyone knows that. You make enough money from our parents. Why can't you let them swim here?"

Antonio was not prepared to argue the point. "This is my place and I run it my way, and that's that," he declared loudly. He shut the gate with a bang. "Now, just you go off and play with your friends, or I'll tell your dad you're not welcome here." He turned and shuffled his way back to the bar, wiping sweat from the back of his beefy neck with his towel.

"I bet he uses that dirty towel to wipe the glasses," Gillian said, loud enough for Antonio to hear. She walked back to where we had been lying by the pool.

"What's bilhartia?" I asked as we sat back down.

"It's a kind of microbe that gets into the pores of your skin and eats away at you. It lives in the lake water," Gillian explained, her eyes still flashing with indignation.

"Well, you certainly broke through your bubble," I said.

She gave me a small smile, slightly mollified by the obvious admiration in my voice.

"There, you see. You don't need to be a priest to break a bubble."

CHAPTER 27

That summer was one round of parties after another.

My mother shone at these gatherings. Her infectious Irish laughter always seemed to catch other men's attention. Not to be outdone, my father flirted outrageously with their wives. It was as if the two of them were competing, trying to prove that they were still attractive to other people. Those warm African evenings were thick with suppressed sexual tension.

It gradually dawned on me that my longing for a close, loving family was never going to be realized. We were simply not the focus of our parents' lives. They were totally absorbed by the artificial society they had created for themselves. We hung around on the outskirts of the colonial enclave, fending for ourselves. We might just as well have never left England.

Then, at supper one evening in late July, my father announced that he couldn't afford to send us back to England.

"Elizabeth will go to a school in Nairobi with the Boase girls. You boys will have to stay with us until we can save enough money."

I was appalled. It had never entered my head that I might not go back to the seminary. Suddenly, the whole context of my life seemed to have dropped away, leaving a yawning void. My mother saw the panic in my eyes.

"It's alright, Peter; this doesn't mean you will *never* go back. It's just that we can't send you back right away."

I was surprised at my own reaction. I had so looked forward to being with my parents. But now, I was thoroughly disillusioned. They were completely involved in their own lives, their own battles, their own concerns. They weren't really interested in me at all.

For the first time I began to appreciate the camaraderie of the seminary. I had enjoyed the good-natured joshing and the feeling of being accepted. I felt more at home there than with my real family. It was God who really knew who I was and cared about me.

Michael's reaction to my father's news was quite different. He couldn't have been more pleased. He had always hated school. For him, the chance of staying in Africa came as an unexpected relief.

"I don't need to finish school," he said that night. "I can easily get a job out here. No one's going to ask if I passed my A-level exams. I can get a job at the Public Works Department here, no problem. Dad was saying they need mechanics." He sounded quite excited.

"Well, I don't know what I'm going to do," I said morosely. "The missionaries don't want a teenager getting in their way. And, with everyone away at school, there'll be no one around to be with."

"You're such a softie," Michael scoffed. "You'll be OK. Mother said it would only be for a while. Once they get some money saved, they'll send you back. And if I'm working too, it shouldn't be too long."

I didn't want to listen.

"If they weren't spending all their money on booze and parties," I said bitterly, "I could be at school in time for the start of the new term."

Over the next four months, I babysat Dominic and ran house-keeping errands for my mother. Twice a week I trudged down to the train station with an empty milk churn to exchange for a full one shipped from some farm in Kenya.

Michael went off happily every morning to the public works yard. There he learned how to fix mechanical diggers and broken water pumps. But for me, Africa was now the furthest thing from being an adventure.

Once my father took me upcountry to a place called Gulu where the circuit court was to hold trials. While the court was in session, I sat alone in the government rest house, endlessly twiddling the knobs of a shortwave radio. Eventually, I drained all the power from the old car battery that ran it. When we got back I decided to harass my mother until she came up with a date for me to go back to England.

"Well, if it's that important to him, he can go back after Christmas," my father said when my mother lost patience with me. "But Michael will have to go with him. Michael needs to finish school and get his A-levels if he's ever to have a decent job."

When Michael heard this, he was furious.

"Why did you have to go and do that?" he yelled at me. "Things were going fine. I don't need to go back to school."

"I didn't think he'd send you back as well," I said dejectedly. "I only asked for myself."

But I knew Michael hated me for spoiling his chance to avoid school.

Our mood on the return flight from Africa was very different from six months earlier. Michael refused to speak the whole way. We landed in a London blanketed by gloomy rain clouds. A cold wind rippled the puddles, cutting keenly through our thin tropical clothes.

Instead of the luxury of the Grosvenor Hotel, we stayed at a cheap rooming house in the east end. We shared a drafty room with only the illusion of heat from a solitary gas stove. We draped ourselves in thin cotton blankets, pulled from the beds, and huddled in front of the fireplace. But soon the cold blue flame went out with a faint pop; we had no shillings to put in the gas meter.

The next day we left for our separate train stations without saying goodbye.

CHAPTER 28

"Welcome back to civilization!" Rinty grinned. "Bet you couldn't wait to get back."

Low clouds drifted above the bare trees by the soccer field, threatening snow. We sat on the warm sewer pipe that ran along the edge of the building, waiting for the bell to ring for class, trying to soak up a little heat.

It was my first day back at St. Peter's.

"We all thought you had quit," Rinty said, cupping his fingers around his mouth to warm them with his breath. "You've missed a whole term of work, and you've got O-level exams at the end of next year."

"I know, I know," I answered, not really wanting to talk. "My father just couldn't get us a flight back from Africa until after Christmas. I can catch up, no problem."

Rinty looked at me, sensing that I was holding out on him. "So how was Africa?" he asked.

"Different," I said. "Warm. Not like here."

"OK, you don't have to tell me if you don't want to," he said, getting up as the bell rang for first-period class. We headed for the door with the other boys, pushing and shoving to get out of the cold.

Before I left for Africa I had imagined my return very differently. I had pictured myself as the centre of attention, full of exciting stories about African adventures. But there had been no African adventures. There had been no exciting safaris. No jungles teeming with wild animals. And I wasn't about to tell anyone about being sidelined by my parents.

Now I just wanted to hide. I wanted to plunge into the daily routine of school, to be swept along in the flow of things. I was numbed by the need to forget.

I sat through the morning math class struggling with algebraic equations and a dark, black cloud of depression. But the second class of the day was history. As Vince McCann walked into the room, he looked over at me with a quizzical smile.

"Welcome back, Bruno. We missed you. How was Uganda? We're going to be looking at British colonial history this term, so maybe you can give us some local colour."

"Sure," I said, surprised that he even noticed. "No problem, I'll be the resident expert."

I immediately felt better. There was something very understanding and genuine about Vince McCann.

That evening, as I was going upstairs to bed, I passed his room. His door was slightly ajar and a warm shaft of light fell across the darkened landing. The radio was playing. I hesitated for a moment and then tapped on the door.

"Come in, Bruno, come in," he said, looking up from his desk. He was smoking his pipe while marking some papers. "Sit yourself down. This is a great song, isn't it?"

We sat there for a few moments listening. I looked around the room, remembering how much I had enjoyed staying in it for Christmas the year before. When the song was over, Vince got up and turned off the radio.

"So, what can I do for you, young man?" he asked.

"I don't know," I said hesitantly. "I'm feeling kind of homeless, like I don't have any place where I really belong. I thought going to Africa would be going home, but it wasn't. My mother and father were so preoccupied with their own lives, it was almost as if I didn't really exist for them. And I don't know if I belong here, either."

Vince leaned back in his chair, re-stuffing his pipe from a packet of Amphora tobacco on his desk. Then he looked up at me.

"You know," he said thoughtfully, "when I was a kid, I always wondered about that story in the Bible, the one where Jesus' parents lost him as a young boy. When they found him, all he said was, 'What were you so worried about? Didn't you know I had to start working at my Father's business?' Well, that always seemed a bit callous to me. Then I realized, from his point of view, it was God who was his real father. He must have really missed him and it hurt. I mean, if he was human, he had to have human feelings too."

Vince paused for a minute. The bowl of his pipe glowed orange. A cloud of blue smoke escaped from the corner of his mouth and drifted towards the ceiling.

"We Catholics are always talking about God as our Father," he went on. "If He really is, if we really felt Him as a father, we would miss Him too, all the time. We would never really feel at home anywhere if we didn't feel He was close to us and cared about us."

"That makes sense," I said. "I never thought about that."

"When you feel loved, it frees you up," Vince went on. "Children who truly feel their parents love have no worries about leaving home and exploring the world. They carry their parents love with them wherever they go. You may not be able to do much about your human parents, Bruno, but you could try to think about how much you believe in a loving God. And don't forget, you meet up with God every time you bump into someone who cares about you."

He gave me one of his wry smiles.

"Now off to bed with you, and think about it. Stop by any time you need to talk."

That night I tried to make sense of what he had said. I had felt better after listening to him. It was not so much *what* he had said, as the way he said it, the kindness in his voice. I felt that he, at least, cared about me, and according to him, that meant God did too.

Every year we were required to put on a play as part of our English course. This year it was to be a performance of Shakespeare's *A Midsummer Night's Dream*. Because of the drawings and paintings I had done for his history project, Vince McCann insisted I design the sets for the play. I was relieved of cleaning duties and afternoon sports so as to spend as much time as possible painting.

"Take as long as you need," he said to me. "Just make it look good!"

The backdrops consisted of a number of huge canvases. They were attached to rollers and could be raised or lowered by a set of ropes and pulleys. I learned how to prepare the canvas and sketch out the scenes from smaller drawings. I loved the smell and feel of the paint and the sweeping scale of the brush strokes.

But mostly I enjoyed it because I felt needed.

For weeks I spent the afternoons alone on the stage, creating Duke Theseus' palace and a fantastic fairyland forest for Oberon and Titania. Sometimes, Vince McCann would stop by and stand at the back of the hall to watch my progress. He was clearly delighted with what I was doing and would often drag in one of the other priests to take a look.

When the play was over, it was hard returning to the school routine of classes, sports, and exams.

Then one day I received another of my father's rare postcards. My mother was pregnant again. They would be flying back to England to have the baby. Elizabeth and Dominic would stay behind with the Boase family. Dominic's birth in Africa had been difficult. They felt a London hospital would be safer for the new baby.

"We have rented rooms for the summer at a guest house in Haslemere," he wrote. "It's close to your Aunt Doreen. You will have a chance to see your cousins. We'll all stay there until the baby's born. It's due towards the end of August."

I felt the beginnings of excitement and hope again. Perhaps they had changed. Perhaps this time they really wanted to be with us.

But I was wrong.

When Michael and I arrived at the guest house, we found that our parents were not there. They had decided to rent a flat in London for themselves. "We need to be close to the hospital," my mother said, "just in case anything goes wrong. Doreen will help you if you have any problems."

Once again they had shuffled their responsibilities onto someone else. But this time I decided I would ignore my disappointment. I would stop moping around wishing things could be different. Instead, I would enjoy my independence.

CHAPTER 29

My mother's sister, Doreen, was the aunt whom I had so painfully mistaken for my mother during the war. She now lived with her husband, Ray, in a fifteenth-century cottage in Haslemere, a pretty little market town in Surrey, bordering Hampshire and West Sussex.

Five hundred years earlier their tiny house had been built from ship timbers, likely stolen on the way to the shipyards in Portsmouth. It had an immense fireplace, big enough for people to actually sit in to keep warm. The original wattle-and-daub walls did little to keep out the damp chill of an English winter.

The Elizabethan guest house, where Michael and I had a room, was about two miles outside the town. As a seminarian I was expected to get up early every morning and walk those two miles to church in Haslemere.

When I struggled awake on the first morning, I envied Michael, curled up and warm in his secular bed. But as soon as I set off, I began to feel better. The sun was climbing up into a clear blue sky. Cool, clean country air filled my lungs. The long grass at the side of the road was soaked in dew. Spider webs glistened in the hazelnut hedges. Blackbirds and linnets sang from their hiding places. It was going to be a beautiful day.

As I reached Haslemere, the houses were shuttered and silent. No one was stirring yet. A clinking sound carried down the empty High Street. It was a milkman jumping from his cart with fresh bottles for someone's doorstep. I passed Doreen's sleeping house, on Lower Street, then the railway station, and then continued up a steep hill to the church.

In the vestry, a round-faced priest in his mid-forties held out a chubby hand, as cold and limp as a floppy fish.

"You must be Peter," he said. "I'm Father Borelli. I believe you are to be my altar boy for the summer. This is my mother." He gestured towards a shrunken old lady in a long, black dress.

"Hello," I said, but the old lady was already shuffling through the door into the church.

"She is also our church organist," Father Borelli said. "Every Mass here is sung. The stipend for a sung Mass is twice that of a regular Mass. So please help her by joining in." He slipped on the last of his vestments. "Let's go."

I walked with him into the church. It was a pleasant enough building with solid, stone pillars marching up the nave. Tall, clear windows flooded it with sunlight. But there was no congregation. There was not a single soul in that church other than the three of us.

Father Borelli set the chalice on the altar and began the familiar Latin Mass, with me giving the rote responses:

Introibo ad altare Dei. 'I will go up to the altar of God.'

Ad Deum qui laetificat juventutem meam. 'To the God who gives joy to my youth.'

I could not possibly count the number of times I had repeated these words at Mass over the years. I could say them in my sleep. My mind wandered almost immediately. Kneeling on the altar steps so early in the morning, I did not feel my youth was getting much joy from God in that church. There was more joy in my early morning walk. I was looking forward to when the Mass would be over and I could go back down the hill to visit my cousins.

My daydream was suddenly interrupted by a high-pitched wailing. It came from Father Borelli's mother at the organ. She was racing through the *Kyrie* responses at breakneck speed. Father Borelli continued reciting the prayers of the Mass, his mother periodically interjecting bursts of plainsong recitatives, rattling them off like a machine gun. It was all very bizarre.

I could not join in; I was shaking with suppressed laughter. "Join in!" Father Borelli commanded. But I couldn't.

As soon as we got back to the vestry, Father Borelli turned on me. "Young man, how dare you mock God," he snapped. "You were laughing in His church. I will inform your superiors at the seminary."

Later, I tried to explain how I felt to Doreen. She had invited me to stop by for a cup of tea on my way back from the church.

"It was all so ridiculous," I said. "Mass is supposed to be for people. And there we were, alone in the church, galloping through the service, his mother squealing at the organ, just to get extra money. Whoever paid for the Mass wasn't even there. Martin Luther would have been shocked all over again."

"I know," Doreen said, warming her hands around her cup of tea. "I do the flowers for the church every Sunday. I know what Father Borelli's like. It's too bad we don't have a say about who we get as a parish priest. But you don't have to worry, Peter. He won't take the time and trouble to complain about you. He'll have forgotten all about it by tomorrow."

"But it makes me wonder what on earth I'm doing," I said. "I don't want to be a priest if I'm going to end up like him."

"Well, you don't have to. Not all priests are like that. Your priests at St. Peter's don't sound a bit like him."

She put down her cup and looked at me thoughtfully.

"You mustn't think of giving up, Peter. The Church badly needs *good* priests; priests who can help people with their lives. Not priests who just want to feel important and powerful."

I heard a rush of footsteps coming down the stairs. My sixteen-year-old cousin Clare burst into the room. She twirled around, a bright, new summer dress flaring out in a flash of yellow and white.

"What do you think?" she asked me. "Mummy just finished making it."

"Wow," I said. "You look gorgeous!"

Doreen got up, adjusted the waist band, and then stepped back, eyeing the dress critically.

"It does look good on you, if I do say so myself," she said.

"What were you two talking about when I came in?" Clare asked. "You looked so serious."

"Peter's had a run-in with Father Borelli," Doreen explained.

"He's a creep," Clare said. "Whenever he looks at me I get the willies. Don't pay any attention to him, Peter. Nobody likes him. Mummy hates him!"

"Now then, dear, don't go saying things like that," Doreen said with a rueful smile.

"But you do!" Clare insisted. "You hate him."

"Here, Peter," Doreen said hastily, changing the subject. She picked up her bag and took out a change purse.

"Your mother told me to give you this for pocket money." She held out two pound notes. "There's one for you and one for Michael."

I was thrilled. I decided at once that I would use my money to buy a set of oil paints. I had never used oil paints before. Doreen encouraged me. She was quite the talented artist herself and insisted on accompanying me to a local art shop. I discovered a wonderful set of paints, complete with linseed oil, turpentine, and brushes, all neatly packed into a little wooden carrying case. The lid folded out into a small easel, and Doreen insisted on buying me my first canvas board.

That summer I spent most of my days roaming the surrounding hills, painting bucolic country scenes. I sat in fields and hedgerows, imagining myself to be another Turner or Constable.

But all this time I was aware that my parents were only a short train ride away, up in London. In the end I decided I would go and see them. Doreen gave me their address and I spent my last few precious shillings buying a train ticket. In London I asked a friendly policeman for directions and, after a long walk, I arrived at their flat. It was on the second floor of an apartment building. I checked the number and knocked on the door.

"Who's there?" I heard my father yell.

"It's me, Peter," I yelled back.

After a few minutes my mother appeared at the door. She was looking very pregnant.

"Your dad's still in bed," she said. It was about eleven o'clock in the morning.

"We can't see you now," my father shouted from the bedroom. "Why don't you go off and have a fun day at the British Museum? We'll get together some other time."

"Yes. Why don't you, Peter?" my mother said with a funny, twisted smile. "Goodbye." She shut the door.

I turned away and ran down the stairs, brushing away hot, angry tears. I caught the next train to Haslemere, kicking myself all the way for even trying.

"What did you expect?" Michael said. "You shouldn't have bothered. Dad's not interested in us. And Mother's afraid if she doesn't have sex with him, he'll chase after someone else. She won't use contraceptives, so she'll just go on having babies until she can't stand it anymore."

Their baby boy was born in late August. They called him Barnabas. A week or so later they flew back to Uganda. A whole year would go by before I got to see my new brother. At the end of that year I received another postcard.

"Your mother is pregnant again," it said.

FRESHFIELD

On a walk at Freshfield. I am sitting on the gatepost

Father Turnbull with soccer team at Freshfield (I am the second boy standing at his left)

AFRICA

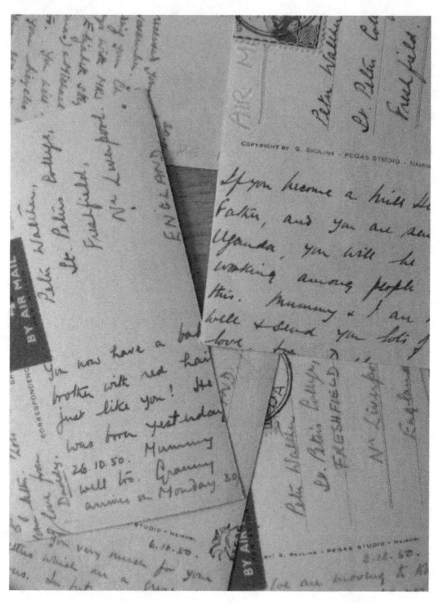

Postcards from my father in Africa

My father with Dominic in Kampala, Uganda

Simonie with Dominic

PART THREE

FARMING AND D.H. LAWRENCE

1953-1955

CHAPTER 30

The school year of 1952-53 was my last at Freshfield. By the time it was over, I had celebrated my sixteenth birthday and successfully passed my O-level exams. Cramming for the exams made it easier to bury the hurt caused by my heedless parents. In that regard, my subconscious skills were already well-developed. The postcard from my father stirred no excitement.

"Your mother will be flying back to England with Elizabeth and the two little ones on the first day of the summer holidays," he wrote. "They will meet your train in London so that you can travel together. I have rented a house in a village called Lane End, near High Wycombe, in Buckinghamshire. Your mother will stay there until the baby's born. It's due in November. Now that Michael has finished school, he will join me here in Uganda and get a job to help support us all."

I read his instructions over. There would have been more feeling in a memo from his secretary.

As my train pulled into Waterloo Station, I hung out the carriage window, scanning the crowds on the platform.

There was no happy family waiting to greet me.

I jumped down and followed the other passengers to the exit barrier.

My mother was not there either.

I hung around until the platform was empty. Then I made my way over to the huge station clock, where people often arranged to meet. For an hour and a half, I sat on my suitcase, waiting. Finally, I decided to buy a train ticket to High Wycombe. There, at least, I would be closer to Lane End.

It was five o'clock in the evening when the train arrived at High Wycombe. I stood outside the station, wondering what I should do. The late afternoon sun was already casting dark shadows across the street. People were hurrying home, glad that work was done for the day. Shopkeepers were pulling shutters across windows and locking doors. Then I remembered what had been drilled into me as a child: 'If you ever get lost, find a policeman'.

A helpful stranger directed me to the local police station.

"Well, the first thing to do is to find out whether your family has actually arrived at Lane End," the burly police sergeant said, peering down at me from his perch behind a tall desk. He had a black walrus moustache and intimidating bushy eyebrows. He seemed skeptical of my story. "We'll radio the local constable in Lane End. He can check at the address your father gave you and see if your mother is there. It might take an hour or so. He has to do his rounds on a bike. You can wait on the bench over there. I'll give you a shout as soon as I hear back from him."

For what seemed like an eternity I sat clutching my suitcase to my chest, trying to look inconspicuous. I tucked my feet tight under the bench to make room for the occasional miscreant being escorted to the holding cells. With agonizing sluggishness the minute hand of the station clock crawled around the dial. I must have dozed off.

"They're there."

I was startled awake by the burly sergeant giving my shoulder a shake.

"Your mother says she forgot she was supposed to meet you."

"Forgot?" I said.

"The bus to Lane End leaves from just down the street, in about five minutes."

It was already dark when the bus arrived at the village. "The house you want is over there, across the green," the driver said.

I walked through the damp grass of the village green towards a long, low cottage. Light from its windows cast a comforting glow through the night mist that was beginning to settle. I unlatched a small wooden gate and walked up the gravel path to the front door. Lifting the horseshoe knocker, I tapped tentatively. Nothing. I tried again, a little more forcefully. Suddenly the door flew open and there was my mother.

"Why did you tell the police where we lived?" she demanded.

"Hello," I said, not knowing quite how else to respond.

"Peter!" Elizabeth brushed past her and gave me a big hug. "It's so good to see you," she grinned. "It's been such a long, lousy day.

Mummy's in a tizzy with all the unpacking. But it's good to have you here." She took my hand and dragged me into the house. "This place is quite lovely. Mummy and I have our own rooms and the two boys will be sleeping with you. They've only just gone to bed so they're probably still awake. Come on upstairs. They'll want to see you."

Barnabas was already fast asleep, curled up in his cot clutching a worn, blue blanket. He was almost a year old and this was the first time I had seen him. But Dominic was awake. He was three now and had been promoted to a real bed. He had heard all the commotion downstairs and was sitting up, wide-eyed, waiting for us.

"Hello, Dominic," I said.

"Hello," he answered with a shy smile, "are you staying with us?"

"Absolutely," I said. "I'm going to be here for the whole summer."

"Good." He snuggled down under his blanket and shut his eyes.

I turned off the light and Elizabeth and I crept down the stairs together. It felt good to be with her and my new brothers. But I was still furious at my mother for forgetting to meet me and then blaming me for going to the police. She was totally oblivious to all the anxiety and panic she had put me through.

It was only later, when I heard her sobs from behind the bedroom door, that it dawned on me what she herself had been through that day. Four months pregnant, she had been pushed onto a plane in Africa, with three children to look after, flown to England to find a place she had never seen before and set up home in a strange, empty house. She had clearly been nursing bitterness and resentment all the way.

That summer money was tight. My father barely sent enough to cover the rent and food. One day, while shopping at the village grocery store, my mother overheard a local farmer complaining about a shortage of workers. She immediately volunteered me and I was hired for the princely sum of five shillings a week. The next morning I tramped over to the farm with a lunch box to start my first paying job.

The farm was owned by two brothers. They had several hundred acres of wheat and barley ready for harvesting. Every day, we would stook the sheaves of grain in the fields and afterwards throw them onto a wagon to be taken to the barn for threshing.

It was strenuous work. At first I had difficulty keeping up with the two older men. I would pray for rain just to have a break. Unfortunately, rainy days were few and far between that summer. Each evening I fell into bed exhausted. But the muscles in my arms and shoulders soon grew stronger, and before long I was more than holding my own.

I began to enjoy the long hours in the open fields. Sometimes I worked so fast that I caught up with the binding machine as it flailed along behind the tractor. I would stop for a moment and stand up straight to stretch my back, stiff from all the stooping. I would look back at the long rows of wheat sheaves behind me, following the contours of the field. Crows wheeled above in the deep blue sky, just like a Van Gogh painting.

I felt comfortable working for the two brothers. They accepted me cheerfully and treated me kindly. They showed me how to stook the sheaves without the skin on my arms becoming raw from the sharp spikes of wheat. Sometimes they let me drive the tractor that pulled the binder. By the end of the summer I was tanned and fit and almost reluctant to go back to the seminary. I would be going to Burn Hall, a college near Durham City, in the north east of England, to study for my A-level exams.

The night before I left, Elizabeth and I sat with my mother at the kitchen table playing cards. The two little boys had been packed off to bed. My mother was looking very pregnant. Her eyes were unusually bright as we laughed and joked.

"It will be too early in the morning for me to wake up and see you off," she said after the game. "I'll say goodbye to you now. Make sure you don't make too much noise when you leave." She gave me a hug, and went off quickly upstairs.

"I don't think she likes goodbyes," Elizabeth said, as she gave me a hug too.

It felt strange to be leaving the house alone in the cold pre-dawn; strange tiptoeing down the gravel pathway with the rest of the family still asleep. It was if I had been shut out of their lives before I had even left.

Burn Hall is a magnificent, Victorian mansion set in a sixty-nine acre estate. The house and grounds are so impressive that Queen Victoria is said to have described it as 'the finest looking estate between the Humber and the Tweed'. Mill Hill purchased it in 1926 to use as a sixth form college for the students who graduated from St. Peter's and their two other junior seminaries in Ireland and Scotland.

My first sight of the building was from the train as it curved along a spectacular viaduct that crosses the river Weir into Durham City. From the train there is a wonderful view of the house and grounds in the valley.

Tall, wrought-iron gates guard the main entrance. A half-mile-long carriageway leads to an imposing pillared portico. It continues on down the side of the valley to a small stream, or burn, which accounts for the name Burn Hall. Next to the stream there is a wide lawn, once used as a tennis court. It is overlooked by a large Victorian conservatory, adjacent to a walled vegetable garden.

It was September 1953, and I was sixteen when I first walked up that long driveway. I was in awe of the building. It seemed too grand to be a boarding school. Off to the right was a row of sandstone farm outhouses designed to complement the architecture of the mansion. Cows were grazing contentedly in the surrounding fields. Somehow I already sensed that the splendour of the building and its pastoral setting was going to be significant for me in the months ahead.

The prospect of meeting new classmates made the long walk with a heavy suitcase seem quite short. Those of us from St. Peter's would now be mixed with students from the Mill Hill seminaries in Scotland and Ireland. But what I looked forward to most was meeting Rinty Monaghan again. I had missed him during my last year at Freshfield. It turned out that he was part of a group designated to welcome new students at the front door.

"So, Bruno," he grinned, relieving me of my suitcase, "you survived. I assume you passed your O-level exams OK." Of the forty boys from my class at Freshfield, more than half had failed.

"You bet," I said. "So what's this place like, anyway? It seems a bit posh for the likes of us."

"It's pretty good, actually," Rinty said as we climbed the stairs to the dormitory. "We have more freedom to roam around on days off, and most of the teachers are good sports. I hear Vince McCann has been sent up here too. He must have wanted to keep an eye on you."

I stopped, surprised and pleased. Vince was still going to be one of my teachers. I hadn't expected that. Perhaps it was Mill Hill's way of ensuring continuity; there would always be one teacher who knew us really well.

Before very long, I was caught up in the routine of seminary life and began to get to know my new classmates. I particularly liked Paddy Cahill, a cheerful Irish boy with the gift of the blarney. He played a small concertina that he would bring out for a singalong at the slightest excuse. He was a fun person to have around.

I was pleased to be connecting with Rinty again. We soon began to ignore the restrictive rules about personal friendships. One day the two of us were walking down by the river. "Bruno," he said seriously, "you've got to make sure you pass your A-levels. They're the passport to university. A lot of the lads here don't think about that."

I was surprised at his earnestness. I had always thought of Rinty as a carefree, happy-go-lucky boy.

"Mill Hill doesn't really care if we pass our A-levels," he explained. "They would lose too many of us if it was a requirement for philosophy and theology. So a lot of the boys don't even bother trying. But, if we ever decided to quit being priests, we'd be sunk. What could we do? We wouldn't have any job skills worth talking about. Nobody's going to hire somebody just because they spent a long time trying to be holy."

I hadn't really thought about that.

"Do you ever think of quitting?" I asked him.

"Sure," he said as the smile came back to his eyes, "every time I see a pretty girl!" He punched me on the shoulder. "No, just kidding. But if I want to be a priest today, who knows about tomorrow? God is the only one who never changes His mind, and I'm not God."

CHAPTER 31

At Christmastime, I returned to Lane End to find that I had a new baby sister. My mother had given birth to her just six weeks earlier. I had never seen a newborn baby before. She was amazing, tiny and perfect. I was completely in awe of her. I loved to hold her in my arms and feel her little fingers exploring my face. Her name was Gemma.

On Christmas Eve we took the three little ones across the village green to Midnight Mass. They all slept soundly through the service, including Dominic, who had insisted he would stay awake.

Afterwards we tucked the sleeping kids into their beds and stuffed their stockings with a few tiny toys. Then my mother, Elizabeth, and I sat around the kitchen table, its white top bare from countless scrubbings. My mother had prepared some hot apple cider. The air was thick with the scent of cloves and cinnamon.

"I wonder what Michael and Daddy are doing for Christmas in Africa," Elizabeth said as she rubbed her glass between the palms of her hands.

"Probably out partying," my mother said with a bitter laugh. "They won't be thinking of us, that's for sure."

"I can't believe he did it," Elizabeth said, staring into her glass.

"Did what?" I asked.

"Tell him," Elizabeth said.

"Well, Peter dear," my mother said, "your father isn't such a model Christian as he would have us all believe. Last year he borrowed some money from his legal budget for a wild business venture. It was an idea suggested by one of his drinking buddies. The whole thing collapsed. The Chief Justice discovered the money was missing. He agreed to take no further action if your father resigned and left the country. So now he and Michael are living in Kenya."

She brushed away a strand of hair that had fallen in front of her eyes.

I was shocked.

"How could he do a thing like that? He was always so strict about honesty. Remember how he treated that man who tried to bribe him? And how he yelled at me when I took some money from your purse?"

My mother looked at me with tired eyes.

"I know, I know. It doesn't make sense. But your father has always spent more money than he could afford. He was forever obsessing about winning the Irish Sweepstakes; always looking for a pot of gold at the end of a rainbow."

"I'm more worried about Michael," Elizabeth said to me. "When he and Daddy arrived in Kenya, Michael joined the special forces to fight the Mau-Mau rebellion."

"What's that?" I asked. "What's the Mau-Mau? I've never heard of it."

"It's a secret group of Africans who want to drive the white people out of Kenya," my mother said. "They hide in the jungle and sneak into Nairobi at night and murder people."

"Michael is part of a team that tries to track them down," Elizabeth said. "He's out in the jungle for weeks at a time."

For a moment we sat there in silence.

"Why didn't you write and tell me?" I asked.

"What good would it have done?" my mother said. "There was nothing you could do. And you have to focus on your studies."

"But at least I would have felt for you all," I said, exasperated. "At least I would have felt that I was part of the family."

Elizabeth reached out and took my hand.

"Let's just be glad that we're together for Christmas," she said.

It was hard leaving my mother and the little kids to return to Burn Hall. My mother was quite depressed. She had heard nothing from my father. What little money appeared in their joint account fluctuated alarmingly. But she was adamant that I should go. "You have been called by God to be a priest," she said. "He will provide." So off I went again, trying my best to forget about my family.

One of the features of life at Burn Hall was a spring retreat. It meant that, for two or three days, we were not allowed to talk to each other. A guest priest would be invited to give a series of spiritual lectures. In between these talks we would roam the grounds, supposedly reflecting on the state of our souls.

I loved those solitary days. I used them to explore the magnificent woods and gardens that surrounded Burn Hall. There were huge, hundred-year-old beech trees arching their branches over meandering paths. Bluebells carpeted the clearings between, filling the still air with their subtle scent.

I often imagined how, years ago, the children of the big house would have played and laughed in this paradise of nature. At the edge of the river I discovered the hull of an old wooden punt half submerged under overhanging bushes. I pictured the children pushing it out, as I would have done, poling it up and down the river, pretending to be pirates. In these silent woods it wasn't hard to see and hear the ghosts of the past.

Once, as I sat by the river, I saw one of my classmates walking along the opposite bank. He was swinging a stick heedlessly back and forth, decapitating daffodils and bluebells left and right, sending their blossoms flying. I was horrified. How could anyone be so insensitive and still think they could be a priest? For the first time I began to wonder about the emotional barrenness of our training.

But perhaps it was not by chance that Mill Hill chose Burn Hall for its senior seminary. Hopefully, whoever made that decision was aware of the impact it would have on someone like me. I soaked up the beauty of the place as if by osmosis.

Durham, with its spectacular cathedral, was only a short distance away. On our so-called free days I would wander through the echoing aisles of the cathedral, marveling at the stolid stone pillars of the nave and the delicate Gothic tracery of the windows. I had just discovered D.H. Lawrence. I felt exactly as he did when he described the horizontal lines of Norman arches marching down the centre of the building. For him they represented *the dogged leaping forward of the persistent human soul.* They contradicted the perpendicular lines of the Gothic arch, which *leapt up at heaven and touched the ecstasy and lost itself in the divine.*

I was aware of this kind of contradiction in my own life. I wanted to explore the urgency of my sixteen-year-old sexuality, to understand its strong connection to the immediate beauty of nature all around me.

135

It contrasted so sharply with the sterility of priestly asceticism we were being urged to pursue for a remote mystical reward. Like Lawrence, I felt the earth teeming around me. I felt *the rush of the sap in spring . . . the intercourse between heaven and earth, the sunshine drawn into the breast and bowels, the rain sucked up in the daytime, the nakedness that comes under the wind in autumn, showing the birds' nests no longer worth hiding.*

Lawrence's words articulated for me the power and mystery of sexuality. It seemed to me, as it did to him, to be a natural and even spiritual force of life. It felt much more significant than the arid celibacy we were being prepared for as priests. But, at that time, I could not see my way out of the trap of Catholic culture that enclosed me.

CHAPTER 32

While Elizabeth and I were back at school for that spring term of 1954, my mother's situation at Lane End became precarious. Money from my father arrived sporadically and was not enough to cover the rent and living expenses. Somehow she managed to find a cheap, two-bedroom apartment on the beach front of St. Leonards-on-Sea, Sussex. This was where we ended up for the next summer holidays.

The apartment was in a rundown, Victorian rooming house. Paint was peeling from the ceiling; carpets were stained and worn; plumbing creaked and groaned as if inhabited by a group of ghosts. Elizabeth and the three small children occupied the only bedroom. My mother slept on a couch in the living room. I slept in the bathroom, on a board laid across the bath tub. Over my head the pilot light of a large, copper, gas-fired water heater flared in the night. I was terrified that I might die in my sleep if the pilot light went out.

For the children, though, the apartment was a wonderful place. The beach was just across the road. They spent the entire summer playing there. My mother would take a deck chair and sandwiches and lie in the sun reading while Elizabeth and I played with the little ones. But she was getting more and more depressed. She insisted that Elizabeth leave school after completing her O-level exams and stay at home to help with the three young ones.

Then, suddenly, while I was away completing my last year at Burn Hall, my father returned to England. He had abandoned Michael, leaving him to fend for himself in Kenya. His attempt at starting his own business had failed. He had gotten himself deeply in debt and was now being pursued relentlessly by his creditors. In England, he turned to his mother for help.

With his slick, professional eloquence, my father persuaded my grandmother to sell her house in Walsingham. He got her to agree to support my mother financially while he took the proceeds and left for

Canada to start a new life. He had been offered a job as a public trustee in Toronto. Once settled, he promised to have the rest of the family join him there.

My mother was bitterly resentful. This had all been arranged without consulting her. Nevertheless, she was relieved to be financially secure for the time being. She found a house to rent in a village called Fernhurst, near her sister, Doreen, in Haslemere. It was a fortunate arrangement. The two of them had always been close.

Elizabeth continued to live at home and help my mother. She took a job as a secretary to augment the family finances. Michael remained by himself in Kenya, fighting the Mau-Mau, and completely out of touch with his family.

Meanwhile, at Burn Hall, I was working hard to prepare for my A-level exams. I found the last few months of studying particularly difficult. The weather in May and June of that year was unusually warm and sunny. I hated being cooped up indoors for the extra study time that I knew I needed. I could hear the carefree shouts of the other boys playing in the woods. The newly minted leaves of the beech trees beckoned and the rhododendrons bloomed in glorious profusion all the way down to the river. Nevertheless, remembering Rinty's advice, I stoically plugged away at my studies. Nick Morgan and I, and one other boy, were the only ones who passed our A-level exams that year.

All this time I had known nothing of my father's arrangements with my grandmother. It was only when my mother wrote to me at Burn Hall to tell me where to go for the summer that I found out. When I arrived at Fernhurst, I got the whole story.

"It's entirely your grandmother's fault that Daddy left us," my mother complained in tears. "She's destroyed our marriage. I don't even know where he is. He hasn't written since he went to Canada."

Now, every night before going to bed, the children were summoned to kneel down to pray the rosary. "We have to pray that Daddy will bring us all together again," my mother insisted.

The children hated kneeling through the long rosary prayers. I watched them playing a game, shuffling backwards on their knees, to see how far away they could get before my mother noticed. They did not know who their 'Daddy' was.

Whenever my mother felt particularly depressed, I was sent to the local pub to get a bottle of cider. After a few glasses she would forget her misery and reminisce about her childhood. She told me stories of her school days at the convent in Sherbourne.

"We all had to wear little straw hats," she said. "It was part of the school uniform. In Lent, I gathered brambles and stuck them inside my hat. I would cram it onto my head so that it would feel like a crown of thorns." She collapsed into hysterical laughter at the memory.

"When I finished school I wanted to join the convent. They wouldn't let me. 'Betty,' they said, 'you are too rambunctious. You wouldn't be able to keep the rules.' They were right." And off she went into hoots of laughter again.

"I wanted too much fun. I liked boys too much. I got a job with a Catholic publisher in London. I met a lot of literary people like G. K. Chesterton and Hilaire Belloc. I would go with them to a pub on Fleet Street where they would discuss writing, religion, and politics and get drunk. That's when Kenelm Foster asked me to marry him." She paused with a wistful look on her face. "Perhaps I *should* have married him. He wouldn't have run off like your father!"

It was disconcerting to hear her talk about herself like that. She was talking to me as if I were already an adult.

I did not feel like an adult. I had just turned eighteen.

BURN HALL

Burn Hall, Durham

Conservatory and Tennis Court, Burn Hall

PART FOUR

PHILOSOPHY IN HOLLAND

1955-1957

CHAPTER 33

"In September you will be going to St. Joseph's, Roosendaal, to study philosophy."

Vince McCann had called us together to explain the next step in our progress towards the priesthood.

"Roosendaal is a small town in the south of Holland. It's close to the Belgian border. You will be living with students from all over Europe. The common language is English, but you will have the opportunity to learn Dutch."

I was excited. At eighteen it seemed like a coming-of-age kind of thing. I would have my own private room at the college. I would be allowed to smoke if I wanted to and visit local pubs on free days.

Vince McCann gave us a checklist of the practical things we would need to bring with us. The list was comprehensive. We would be away from home for a full school year without Christmas and Easter holidays. I noticed that one of the items we were required to bring was a black, trilby hat.

"How can we afford that?" my mother asked in horror. "A trilby costs a fortune!"

A trilby hat was a kind of fedora with a narrower brim. In those days a hat was an essential part of the male dress code. My mother took my travel list with her on her next visit to Doreen in Haslemere.

"I don't suppose Ray has a spare trilby he could loan Peter?" she asked hopefully.

Doreen shook her head. "No. He's only got one and he wears it to work every day. And, besides, it would never fit Peter."

"So what am I going to do?"

"Why don't you go to the church and talk to Father Borelli? Perhaps he'd help. He's got lots of money. He could afford it."

So off we went the following Sunday to beg from Father Borelli. As my mother pleaded her case, it occurred to me that generosity was not one of his strong points. He was too obsessed with raising money for himself. But then I noticed him looking at me appraisingly. Was I, perhaps, an investment opportunity that might offer future returns? Once I became a priest, I could be useful if he wanted to take a holiday away from the parish.

"How about if Peter earns it?" he said finally. "I need help with the garden. What if he comes and works for me?"

Thus it was that I became the parish gardener for the summer, in order to equip myself with a trilby hat. I weeded flower beds, trimmed hedges, and mowed lawns all around the church property. At the end of August, on my last day, Father Borelli's mother came out of the rectory and handed me an envelope.

"Now don't you go spending that on anything foolish," she said, glaring at me. "This money comes from the pennies of the poor. It's not to be used frivolously!"

On the bus back to Fernhurst, I opened the envelope. It contained five rather-tired-looking pound notes, more than enough for a trilby hat.

My mother's knowledge of hat shops was restricted to Dunn & Co. on Regent Street in London. "They are hatters to Her Majesty the Queen," she said grandly. "You can stop there on your way to catch the boat train to Holland."

I found the shop without difficulty. It was a splendid emporium, all French-polished paneling and carved teak display cases. I was greeted by a stiffly elegant gentleman in formal tailcoat and bow tie. He had the mannerisms of a retired butler.

"And what can I do for the young gentleman?" he murmured.

"I need a hat, a trilby hat."

"Of course," he said. A bright yellow tape measure magically appeared in his white-gloved hand. Standing behind me, he looped the tape around my head.

"Aha!" he said as he checked the result.

The tape disappeared into his waistcoat pocket. He stepped over to a glass showcase where rows of hats were displayed on plaster heads. Gently lifting one down, he smoothed away an imaginary speck of dust with a light brush of his hand.

"Try this one, Sir," he said, inserting a ribbon of tissue inside the headband to protect it from my fashionably greased hair.

I lifted the hat with two hands and settled it on top of my head.

"No, no, Sir, that's not the way," he said, horrified. "You start at your forehead and gently push it back."

I tried again and he offered me a mirror in which to view my new sartorial self. I was impressed. Suddenly I had been transformed into a gentleman of 'the City.'

"I'll take it," I said, handing over one of Father Borelli's grubby pound notes. He accepted it, disdainfully, between his gloved finger and thumb. With hat firmly in place, I boarded a London Transport bus for Liverpool Street Station where I was to meet my classmates.

I found them clustered on the platform, waiting to board the boat train. We were all very self-conscious in our black trilby hats and clerical coats. A gaggle of teenage school girls, equally uncomfortable in prim blue uniforms, giggled at us from under yellow straw hats. For a moment we shared a common bond of discomfort, branded by our clothes. Then I saw Rinty Monaghan walking up the platform towards me, and the discomfort was forgotten.

"Good to see you, Bruno," he said with his characteristic grin. "What have you been up to?" Being in the class ahead of me, he had already experienced a year in Holland while I was still at Burn Hall.

We clambered aboard the train and spent the short trip to Harwich catching up on our year's experiences. We were chattering so much that we hardly noticed when the train pulled into the ferry terminal. I lost Rinty in the crush of passengers lugging their suitcases through customs but felt confident we would meet again on the boat.

Once on board, I walked through the various saloons looking for him. I climbed the narrow steel stairs to the upper deck. As I scanned the passengers lining the rails, the rhythm of the throbbing engines increased. A long, loud blast from the ship's horn bounced off warehouse walls, setting seagulls squawking into the sky. Slowly, the huge ferry moved away from the dock, out into the grey waters of the English Channel.

I made my way to the stern rail to watch our departure. The long, roiling wake, churned by the growling engines, stretched out behind us. The docks and houses of Harwich slowly shrank together into a blurred blue line. It would be a whole year before I would see England again. The wind picked up, sending long slivers of dark grey cloud racing across the sky. Seagulls hovered and swooped and the boat began to rock in the North Sea swells. I grabbed onto my trilby, afraid the wind might take it.

"Where are you going?"

I turned to see one of the girls from the platform at Liverpool Street Station standing next to me at the rail. Her head was tilted towards me, the wind blowing her long brown hair into the corners of her smile. She clutched at her hat with one hand and clung to the rail with the other, bracing herself as the ferry heaved through the water.

"Holland," I said.

"Why?"

"To study philosophy," I said, hoping the implication of latent wisdom would impress.

"Wow."

Her shoulder bumped mine as the boat lurched sideways.

"Sorry," she said, grasping my arm to steady herself.

"That's OK," I said. "And where are you going?"

"Switzerland. My parents think I need refining. They're sending me to a finishing school."

She laughed up at me as the boat rolled again.

"My name's Brenda," she said. "What's yours?"

"Peter," I said. "And I'm studying to be a priest."

Her face went blank. She looked at me, dumbfounded.

"A priest?"

She grabbed the rail with both hands.

Instantly, the wind whipped off her hat. It went whirling down the deck and caught on a stanchion. Then, it tore loose and sailed out over the water, becoming a little, yellow dot swallowed by the waves.

"Oh God! My hat! My hat!" Brenda shrieked.

The boat rolled again. It threw her against me. Instinctively, both my arms went around her. Suddenly free, my splendid trilby hat took flight also. It was like a gull in a storm. For a moment, it hovered over the waves. And then it, too, was gone.

The wind blew wildly, mocking the irretrievable nature of our loss as we clung to each other.

"My mother's going to kill me," Brenda wailed into my coat.

"Hey there, Bruno, what's up?" It was Rinty, lurching across the deck towards us, grinning, his trilby hat firmly secure in his hand.

"I thought your name was Peter," Brenda said, looking up at me suspiciously.

"Bruno's my nickname," I said. "This is my friend, Rinty."

"He made me lose my hat," Brenda said.

Rinty looked at Brenda and then back at me. "Well, let's go and console ourselves with a beer," he suggested sensibly. "My treat."

We made our way down to the comparative calm of the saloon. Some of Brenda's friends joined us at a large table, and I got to order my first-ever beer. The girls were intensely curious about why we wanted to be priests. They laughed when Rinty talked about being an only boy with five sisters and wanting to escape from a house full of females.

In the warmth of the saloon, time passed quickly. The gale outside blew long beads of spray against the salt-grimed windows. The boat heaved its way through the surging sea towards Holland. For most of us, this was our first time drinking in a public bar. By the time the boat docked, neither Brenda nor I were concerned about the loss of our hats.

"This was fun," she said, giving me a quick hug. "When do you finish in Holland?"

"Not for two years," I said, somewhat ruefully.

"Well, let me know how things go. You never know, you might change your mind about being a priest." She bent down and tore the label from one of her suitcases. "Here, this is my home address, just in case." She looked up at me, her eyes teasing.

I felt myself blush. Confusion was back full blown, just when I thought I was all set to push on with answering God's call.

I took the little brown label and stuffed it into my pocket.

"Brenda, if I do change my mind, you'll be the first to know," I said, hiding my face in her hair as I returned her hug.

On the train, speeding from the Hook-of-Holland to Roosendaal, I caught a glimpse of a new and delightful country. Flat fields, edged with dikes, stretched for miles between clusters of farming villages. Each had a mediaeval church spire that rose above the rooftops. Groups of children straddled their bicycles at rail crossings, waving, as the sleek, modern train whisked by. Innumerable canals, glinting in the late afternoon sun, were bordered by ancient, wooden windmills. There seemed to be no sign of the devastation so recently wrought by the German occupation.

St. Joseph Missiehuis in Roosendaal was a massive building, with yellow brickwork still dark and smudged from the smoke of war. We were met by Dutch and Austrian students who had arrived earlier. They quickly gathered around us, eager to practise their English. I was amazed at how fluent they were. Before very long we were trading swear words in our different languages and laughing at pronunciation mistakes.

It seemed to me that the Dutch education system was much broader than our English one. The Dutch students were interested in art and classical music, subjects ignored in our single-minded pursuit of A-level exams. This, plus the fact that they had begun using tobacco at an early age, made them seem very sophisticated. They manipulated cigarettes, cigars, and pipes in an impressively relaxed and confident manner.

I was tired from all the day's travel and excitement. It was a welcome relief to be able to retire that night to the privacy of my own room, one of many forming a long row on the fourth floor. It was small and simply furnished but felt cozy. There was a wooden desk and chair, a washstand with a large porcelain water jug sitting in a bowl, and a black metal-frame bed.

I walked over to the single dormer window that looked out over the town. It was dark now, with only the occasional glow from curtained windows in the street below. It felt comforting to see that there were regular families living close by. We were not to be as isolated from ordinary people as we had been at Burn Hall and Freshfield.

CHAPTER 34

An English cardinal, Herbert Vaughan, had founded The Mill Hill Missionaries, officially known as *St. Joseph's Society for Foreign Missions*, in 1866. As a young man, he had become convinced that English Catholics needed to take some responsibility for what was happening in the colonies. He had been educated in Belgium and had travelled widely throughout Europe and America. In an era of rampant nationalism, he recognized that his organization needed to have an international character. His missionaries would be recruited from various countries, not just England.

He also realized that missionaries would be trained more effectively if they lived and studied together in an unfamiliar culture. Their national prejudices could be more easily identified and resolved in a foreign environment. So he set up a college in Holland, where international students could complete their philosophy studies before going to Mill Hill in England for theology.

At Roosendaal, I plunged with enthusiasm into the eccentricities of philosophical thought. Happily, we were not restricted to the works of Thomas Aquinas who had been, for centuries, the official philosopher of the Catholic Church. A broader perspective of ideas was provided by a course in the history of philosophy.

My professor, Father Jaap Nielen, was a young and enthusiastic priest who had recently graduated from his studies in Rome. There, he had come to know Father Camilo Torres Restrepo, a Colombian priest whose writings tried to reconcile revolutionary Marxism with Catholicism, and who later would die fighting as a guerilla in Columbia.

Thanks to Father Nielen, I started exploring the world of ideas, but not just from a detached academic point of view. I needed to find a rationale for my own desire to be a priest. I found myself attracted to the writings of Father Restrepo. It made sense to me that what really

149

validated Christianity was its mission to bring justice to the poor and the oppressed. I understood the desperation that leads Marxists to see class war as the only effective way to change society. For centuries, it seemed, the Catholic Church had been a party to oppression and injustice. It had, more often than not, ignored the plight of the poor by trying to focus attention on the rewards of an afterlife.

Early Christian communities, on the other hand, had formed a kind of proletarian revolution against privileged Roman oppressors. They banded together to share goods in common. Perhaps what the Church needed was a return to those original ideas. In any event, with all the idealism of a nineteen-year-old, I set out to feel my way towards my own *apologia pro vita sua*.

It was an enormous advantage to have a friend like Rinty a year ahead of me. His humour was always there to counterbalance my earnestness. He refused to let me take myself too seriously.

"Bruno, you have to get yourself a pipe," he said to me one day as he puffed away at his polished briar. "You can't be a real philosopher unless you smoke a pipe. It gives you the necessary air of wisdom."

"Maybe," I said, a little apprehensively, "but I haven't got the budget to take up smoking in a big way."

"Don't worry. You don't have to actually smoke the pipe. It's just something to hold in your mouth. It gives you time to think of clever things to say!"

Confronted with such unassailable logic, I visited the local tobacco shop. Two of my new Dutch friends came along to assist with translation. Piet Van Breemen and Jan Swagemaker were both pipe smokers, so I felt I was in good hands. After examining pipes of all shapes and sizes, I finally chose one that I thought had an elegant, rakish look.

"You need a good tobacco to go with it," Jan said. "How about Amphora? That's what I smoke." He fished out a packet from a side pocket and opened it up for my approval.

"Sure," I said, "If it tastes as good as it smells, I'm hooked."

Piet was a tall, blond-haired boy who, like Rinty, had a delightful sense of humour. He came from Breda, a small town not far from Roosendaal. "You must come and meet my mother on our next travel day," Piet said.

Sure enough, a few weeks later Piet took me to his home and introduced me to his mother. She was a plump, cheerful lady with round, rosy cheeks and a welcoming smile. Her strong hands were red and rough, the result, Piet said, of constantly scrubbing the spotless flagstone floor.

We sat at a round table covered with a lovely tapestry-like cloth that Piet told me was common in Dutch homes. His mother served us *uit-smijter*, a huge plate of thick buttered bread, topped with ham and fried eggs. It was a treat compared to the sparse seminary food.

Afterwards, we took a walk over to the *Grote Kerk*, a large Gothic church in the marketplace at the centre of Breda. We sat at a table outside a coffee bar, leaning back in our chairs, soaking up the warmth of the late afternoon sun.

Suddenly a bell clanged. Hundreds of school children poured onto the street, laughing, running, coats and scarves flying. It was a scene from a child's picture book. The stolid Dutch buildings around the square were transformed, walls echoing the children's shouts, windows reflecting the riot of coloured clothing. I was amazed. I had never seen anything like it. There were so many children, happy, carefree children quite unlike the scruffy, depressed urchins of England.

It seemed that Holland was bursting with young children. They were everywhere. The streets were crowded with bicycles. When the canals froze over after Christmas, they skated to school. They used wooden skates strapped to the bottom of their shoes.

One day that winter the weather got so cold all the schools had to close. The children flocked down to the canal to skate, and we went also. Jan gave me an old pair of his skates and showed me how to tie them securely under my shoes.

I had never skated before. After a few wobbles and falls, I managed to launch myself onto the ice. My friends got impatient with my slow, stumbling pace and soon disappeared into the distance. I was left to skate along the canal on my own.

Gradually I was able to relax and establish a rhythm of long, smooth strokes. I kept my hands clasped behind my back, leaning slightly forward, pretending to be a pro. Only an occasional awkward wobble kept me humble.

Before I realized it, I had left the shouts of the children behind. I was alone, skating silently through the frozen countryside. I kept my head down, watching my feet glide over the ice, seeing the trapped air bubbles and strands of weed in the dark depths below. At first, I followed the lines cut into the ice by the skaters ahead of me, but then I grew more venturesome and made for the untouched, glassy surface at the side of the canal.

The more comfortable I became, the more I was able to lift my head. I saw weirdly shaped icicles cascading from shrubs and trees along the verge, glinting in the sunlight. I passed a tall wooden windmill, its ladder-like sails motionless against the cold blue sky. It loomed high above me like a giant sentinel, guarding the canal bank. The sole sound in all that stillness was the hiss of my skates and the occasional crack of expanding ice. I was the only thing moving in that silent, frozen world.

My head seemed suddenly clear. Gone were all the tangled philosophical arguments and conflicting ideas that had been clogging my brain for the past few months. I felt alive and free. I drew the freezing air down into my lungs, feeling its keen cutting edge as I glided over the ice.

Suddenly I realized that it was not the cold air that was liberating; it was the children that had freed my mind. I was feeling the same freedom that they felt at being released from school. They were boisterous and loud and carefree. They felt no pressure to appear older and wiser than they really were. Spontaneous, exuberant joy spilled out of them. I quickly turned and skated back towards the town, wanting to see them again as they chased each other all over the ice-covered canal.

Later that afternoon, Jan asked me, "So how was your first skating day?"

"Amazing," I answered. "I discovered how much I wished I were a child again."

As winter slowly released its grip on the frozen fields, and the warm spring sunlight coaxed the famous Dutch tulips from the soil, I looked for other outlets for my energy. In the smoking room, where we all gathered between classes, there was an old, upright piano. Ben Beemster, a musically gifted Dutch student, often sat there playing tunes from classical opera. I would stand at his shoulder totally entranced.

"We should write our own opera," I said to him one day. "We could choose melodies that we both know, and I'll write the lyrics. What do you think?"

Ben stopped playing and turned to look up at me. He was a short, stocky boy, with a domed forehead and horn-rimmed, Buddy Holly glasses.

"Of course," he said with a grin. "We could jazz up the tunes a bit and make them sound like rock and roll!"

He turned back to the piano and started to pound out a rock version of the soldiers' chorus from *Il Trovatore*. "How's this?" he asked.

"Perfect. If you can find the tunes, I can write the words."

Ben proceeded to play through a number of well-known tunes. Almost immediately, words and phrases started to form in my head.

"This is going to work," I said to Ben as we left for our next class. "Give me a few days and I'll have a complete libretto ready. Then, we can hold auditions and perform at the next smoking concert." These concerts were often organized as entertainment on weekends. They were an opportunity to lampoon any of the professors who dared to attend.

Writing the libretto wasn't quite as easy as I had thought. I needed a suitable storyline that could be carried by an all-male cast. I finally settled on *Ali Baba and the Forty Thieves*. It did not require a heroine and had enough potential for grand operatic bravado to be entertaining.

For weeks Ben and I spent all our free time, and even class time, developing scenarios and devising *leitmotifs* to fit the characters. Ali Baba was transformed into an earnest student in search of philosophical jewels and the thieves became boastful philosophers hoarding treasures of truth in a magical cave.

It was relatively easy to recruit singers for our opera. We knew who the good tenors, baritones, and basses were from the regular Sunday liturgies. As our stage was miniscule, we cut the forty thieves to twelve. I had a crew of amateur carpenters and painters create a makeshift cave and props. It took a while to coordinate the movement of the blanket that we used to open and close Ali Baba's cave, but somehow the stagehands managed it.

We performed the show as an end-of-year concert. The cast sang with enthusiasm. Philosopher brigands died spectacular deaths. Ali Baba poured scalding 'logical' oil over their heads. As a grand finale, they arose from their jars to sing an adapted version of Verdi's *Chorus of the Hebrew Slaves*. It was a splendid way to end a year of intensely abstract thought. The audience, including some of the professors whom I had pilloried in verse, applauded with enthusiasm.

CHAPTER 35

"I have something very important to discuss with you," my mother said. I had just arrived back from Holland for the summer holidays "We'll talk about it once Elizabeth has gone to work."

Elizabeth still had her job at the nearby agricultural research facility. It was a short walk from the village. She had just turned eighteen and clearly enjoyed the admiring glances of the boys at the bus stop as she set off to work every morning. She was the epitome of fifty's fashion with her carefully starched petticoats and matching bobby socks, her ponytail bouncing jauntily behind her.

"She has a boyfriend," my mother announced, once Elizabeth had left the house. "He's an older man. I don't know what to do about it."

"Why do you have to do something about it?"

"Well, he's a lot older than she is. He's thirty-three. He has his own business. He's a hop factor, a middleman between farmers and brewers."

"So, don't you like him?"

"Oh, of course I do," she said hastily. "It's just that I was afraid you wouldn't approve. He's so much older than she is."

"I don't think they need my approval," I said. "When do I get to meet him?"

"This weekend. He's coming to take Elizabeth to dinner."

"What's his name?"

"Kenneth Hook. Quite the name for a sea captain, don't you think?" She giggled, "He probably got teased a lot as Captain Hook!"

In spite of all her talk about his age, I suspected she was excited at the prospect of acquiring a wealthy son-in-law.

The following Saturday we were sitting around the kitchen table at lunch when we heard the crunch of tires on the gravel driveway.

"It's Kenneth," Elizabeth said. She jumped up and flew to the front door. A few seconds later, Kenneth strode into the kitchen with a wide smile. He was a broad-shouldered, stocky man, dressed in stylish

English country gear, a tweed jacket with leather elbow patches, tan slacks, and shiny, brown brogues.

"Hello, Peter," he said, giving me a firm handshake.

My mother was fussing around getting an extra place setting, her face pink with excitement.

"Come and sit down, Kenneth. You must be tired after that long drive. How was it? Were the roads busy? They must be crammed with holidaymakers at this time of year."

Elizabeth looked embarrassed. Kenneth ignored our mother's chatter and turned to me.

"I hear you're studying in Holland, Peter. How do you like it? I had a couple of Dutch boys on my boat during the war. They were gunners. Steady as a rock, even when the boat was bouncing all over the place."

"I've made some very good friends," I told him.

Kenneth's shoulders began to relax as we talked. I was surprised at how shy he was for a man with all his experience. He could hardly keep his eyes off Elizabeth. She positively glowed in his presence. Very soon he suggested that they leave. He was going to take her to dinner in Lewis, quite a long drive from Fernhurst.

"Well, Peter, I think we'll be seeing a lot of each other," he said, before climbing into his car. "We'll have to go for a sail in my boat sometime."

That summer was memorable, not so much for meeting Elizabeth's boyfriend as for the fun of getting to know my young brothers and sister.

The house at Fernhurst was surrounded by farmers' fields. It was built on the side of a hill and the back garden sloped down to a little stream. The children and I spent long summer days roaming the countryside together just as Michael, Elizabeth, and I had done on the Isle of Wight. We waded into thickets of blackberry bushes that grew wild at the edges of the fields, trying to avoid the stinging nettles that lay in wait for unwary legs.

I learned to use a scythe to cut the tall weeds and grass that choked the garden, making more space for the children to play. I would stack all the grass into a bonfire and we would watch the thick, white smoke drift across the valley, startling the cows in the nearby fields.

One day the children came screaming into the house in terror. The cows had found a hole in our hedge. They pushed their way through, one behind the other, plodding up the garden to the house.

While I was on the phone to the neighbouring farmer, the lead cow ambled ponderously through the kitchen door and started to climb the stairs. The unfortunate animal got stuck, wedged between the banister and the wall. Pandemonium reigned supreme. The cow bellowed, the children screamed, and I tugged ineffectually at the cow's tail. Fortunately, the farmer soon appeared with two of his men. He successfully extricated the beast before any harm was done.

Watching the children play, my heart went out to them. They so obviously needed a father. Already, a lot of affection that should have been going to him was coming to me. I hated leaving them when it was time to go back to Holland again. I tried telling them I would only be away for one short year, but for them a year was a lifetime. I could only say I would be back soon.

Their sad, confused faces reflected my own pain.

CHAPTER 36

I n the fall I returned to Holland for my last year of philosophy. Rinty was no longer there. He was now at Mill Hill in London for his first year of theology.

Life in Roosendaal seemed dull without Rinty. I missed his cheerful companionship. I had come to rely on him for help with my studies. He had an acute mind that could cut through bad logic with ease. He was infinitely patient explaining concepts that I found difficult to understand.

At the end of September my mother wrote, telling me that Elizabeth and Kenneth had decided to get married. In November I received a wedding picture showing a beaming Kenneth, standing at attention, gripping Elizabeth's hand firmly in his. He looked as if he was afraid she might slip away. I spent hours pouring over the picture, struggling to comprehend that my eighteen-year-old sister was now a married woman. How was it that I, at nineteen, still felt more like a child than an adult?

That year the prospect of celebrating Christmas so far away from home seemed particularly sad. The Dutch students did not celebrate Christmas the same way we did. Their gift-giving time was the 5th of December, St. Nicholas' Eve. So I was surprised and pleased when a parcel was delivered to my room a few days before Christmas. It was from Elizabeth and Kenneth.

They had sent me a traditional English Christmas pudding. It was all ready to cook, wrapped in tin foil. A small bottle of brandy and a large bottle of sherry were packed with it.

"Party time," I thought. I immediately got hold of Piet and Jan to invite them to my room for Christmas Eve.

Entertaining visitors in our rooms was strictly against the rules of the college. The rules were enforced by a humourless old priest who was the dean of discipline. It was his task to see that all college regulations were followed to the letter. Nevertheless, Jan and Piet accepted my invitation with enthusiasm.

Elizabeth had thoughtfully included instructions on how to prepare the pudding. It had to be deposited in boiling water for three hours prior to serving. How I might do that was a problem. The solution came to me in a rare moment of inspiration.

Deep in the basement of the building was a student-run bookbinding shop. In the shop was a small electric stove used to heat glue for binding books. The glue pot would be perfect for cooking a Christmas pudding.

By ten o'clock on Christmas Eve the whole building was asleep. I hid the pudding in a plastic wastepaper basket and crept downstairs to the glue shop. Three hours? I could not afford three hours. Two would have to suffice. While the Christmas pudding bubbled in the glue pot, I sat on a stool and read one of the unbound books.

Close to midnight, I realized I had another problem. How to fish a boiling pudding out of a glue pot? I looked around the shop and found two wooden rulers. After a couple of tries I managed it. I lifted the pudding, poised precariously between the rulers, and deposited it into the wastebasket. Success!

I clutched the basket to my chest and sped softly up the darkened stairs. Only a faint light glimmered from the windows at each landing. As I passed one floor after another, I breathed more easily. But at the very top, my luck ran out. A Scrooge-like figure was glowering down at me. It was the dean of discipline.

"So, Bruno, what have you got there?" he growled.

"Just my wastepaper basket," I offered.

"And what are you doing carrying a wastepaper basket upstairs at midnight?"

Before I could answer, disaster struck. There was a soft thump. The hot Christmas pudding had melted through the bottom of the basket. It landed on the step between us.

The dean looked at the pudding and then at me.

Then I noticed an unusual wrinkle at the corner of his mouth.

"Better pick it up," he said, and swept on down the stairs.

I gaped after his shadowy form as it disappeared into the darkness. I picked up the pudding and ran for my room. I could not believe my luck. For one night, at least, Scrooge had turned into Santa Claus.

Jan, Piet, and I, had a great party.

After the brief Christmas break it was back to the last semester of philosophy. That year happened to be the thirtieth anniversary of the publication of Martin Heidegger's *Being and Time*. It is probably one of the most influential philosophical books of the twentieth century. Jaap Nielen tied our minds in knots trying to explain Heidegger's abstruse terminology. Many of my fellow students just gave up. A few were angry at the very idea of studying a man who, in 1933, had joined Hitler's National Socialist Party. But Nielen pleaded with us not to be prejudiced. Heidegger's politics, he argued, might have been adopted more for cover than from conviction.

In any event, I chose to work on some of Heidegger's ideas for my final paper. He intrigued me because of his refusal to accept the authority of philosophical tradition. He insisted on the need to examine personal experience to understand the meaning of existence. He demanded that we be authentic and resolute in taking responsibility for our own lives.

How Heidegger managed to reconcile his ideas with becoming a member of the Nazi party thirty years later, I could not imagine. I simply recognized in myself an affinity for refusing to accept, unquestioningly, truths which were claimed to be self-evident. I was becoming increasingly aware of glaring anomalies in the teaching of the Catholic Church, relying, as it did, so slavishly on Thomistic metaphysics.

I was encouraged by the writings of Karl Rahner, who had been a student of Heidegger's at the University of Freiberg. Rahner was beginning to question the absolutist claim of the Catholic Church to be the 'sole way of honouring God.' For the first time, I felt the chains of Catholic culture, tethering me since childhood, had begun to work loose.

At the end of the school year, as I sat on the deck of the ferryboat watching the coastline of Holland recede, I felt an enormous gratitude that I had been given the opportunity to learn with Mill Hill priests.

Most of my teachers were truly authentic men who were not afraid of new ideas. They had encouraged me to think for myself and make sense of my life.

The bow of the boat rose and fell as it ploughed through cresting waves, sending plumes of salt spray over the deck.

I found myself wishing that Brenda was with me.

HOLLAND

At a pub in Roosendaal, Holland: Jan Swagermaker (left), me (right)

Outside a tobacco store, Roosendaal: Piet Van Breemen (left front), me (right front)

PART FIVE

Calling
the Question

1957-1961

CHAPTER 37

Fighter pilots, coming in to land at Henley Airport during the Battle of Britain, used the tall statue of St. Joseph atop Mill Hill's college tower as a marker.

"There's Holy Joe. We're home," they would yell over the roar of their engines.

Shining in gilded splendour below them, the statue was a distinctive landmark, visible for miles around. It was the first thing I saw as I came out of the tube station at Mill Hill in September 1957. The founder of St. Joseph's College for Foreign Missions clearly had no intention of hiding its light under a bushel.

Hefting my suitcase, I looked for a momentary lull in the rush hour traffic streaming up the Great North Road. I finally managed to cross and began walking up a steep hill towards the college. I had to stop several times to put my suitcase down and catch my breath. Each time I would look up and absorb the details of the huge, red-brick Victorian building where I was to spend the next four years studying theology.

I finally turned into a long driveway that circled around an island of late summer flowers to the front entrance. A wide flight of stone steps led up to the main doors. Terraced lawns flowed down the hillside. A family of ducks gently ruffled the placid surface of a lily pond. It all seemed so peaceful after the roar of the London traffic far below.

I set my suitcase down at the top of the steps and pressed a bell in the wall beside a pair of massive oak doors. After what seemed a long wait, one of the doors swung open. A cheerful young man dressed in a black cassock with a bright-red sash ushered me in.

"Welcome to Mill Hill," he said with a smile. "My name is Martin. I've been assigned to show you around. What's your name?"

"Bruno," I said. "At least that's what they've called me since Freshfield. My real name is Peter."

Martin laughed. "I've heard all about you, Bruno. Rinty told me. You're the great opera man!"

We were standing in the centre of a long hallway that formed one side of a large, open quadrangle. The thick yellow and blue stone tiles of the floor were worn from years of use. All down the hallway, glass museum cases displayed exotic artifacts from the different mission countries where Mill Hill priests worked. There were ebony carvings from Africa, Dyak masks and mats from Borneo, Maori bone carvings from New Zealand, and multi-armed bronze statuettes from India.

"You can look at all this later," Martin said. I'll take you to your room first and get you settled. Then, I'll show you around."

After dumping my suitcase, Martin took me to the college chapel. Built in nineteenth century French Gothic style, every square inch of its wall was decorated. Elaborate geometric patterns surrounded pictures of missionary saints preaching to primitive-looking inhabitants of foreign lands. They seemed like illustrations from a Victorian child's picture book. Circled behind the main altar, in the walls of the apse, were tall, white, marble slabs engraved with all the names of Mill Hill missionaries who had died since 1866. Along the north wall, were small side chapels where Mass could be said by the many resident priests.

Back in the quadrangle, Martin took me past the refectory and then out through a breezeway to the ground floor of what he called the D-Wing. A pair of swing doors opened onto a landing that overlooked a large hall. The room was crowded, the air thick with tobacco smoke. Students in long, black cassocks were reading newspapers, playing cards, or just sitting around in groups, chatting away to one another.

"This is the smoking room," Martin said, "our home away from home."

"Hey there, Bruno!" Rinty's round, cheerful face looked up from a table near the door. He pushed his chair back and came up the steps to where we were surveying the scene.

"I see you've met Martin. He's a deacon already. You'll suffer through one of his practice sermons before very long."

Piet Van Breemen and Jan Swagemaker were threading their way towards us between crowded tables.

"How come you're so late getting here?" Jan asked with mock sarcasm. "We've been here for hours."

"Welcome to England," I said.

It felt good to be back in their company again. Even though the building was strange, seeing them made me feel immediately at home.

The Mill Hill Missionaries are an order of secular priests. Although they do not take vows like monks, they are still bound by Canon Law with its obligation of celibacy. To become a member of the order, I would be required to take an oath of obedience. Once ordained, I would have to work wherever I was told to go.

Rules for the education of priests had been established by the Catholic Church hundreds of years earlier at the Council of Trent. There had been no significant changes since then. As a result, our lives at the College were minutely regulated, with little room for personal decision or initiative. Classes slavishly followed Latin texts of dogmatic and moral theology. They were delivered from an antique wooden pulpit in a large lecture hall.

The only course that I found interesting was Scripture studies. It was taught with enthusiasm by a priest who had worked with Father Roland de Vaux, at the *École Biblique* in Arab East Jerusalem. De Vaux had led the Catholic team that initially worked on the Dead Sea Scrolls. I was intrigued at the new light they might throw on the Jewish religion as practised in the century before Christ.

However, it was not the academic courses that were my main concern. What was bothering me most at this time was the question of celibacy. Would I be able to live the celibate life required of a priest? Like every other student, I had been assigned a personal spiritual director. I began to realize that I needed to talk to him.

My director was a priest from the Italian Tyrol, Father Maserai, who taught moral theology. With his thin, gold-wire spectacles and round, semi-bald head, he was very much the intellectual theologian. It was not until well after the New Year that I finally summoned up courage to see him. One night I made my way to his study and tapped nervously at his open door. He was working at his desk, his face lit by the reflected glow of his reading lamp.

"Bruno," he said, glancing over towards me. "What can I do for you?"

"I need to talk," I said, my heart beginning to pound uncomfortably in my chest. "Do you have time right now?"

He hesitated for a moment and then leaned back in his chair, pushing the papers he was working on to the back of his desk.

"Of course," he said. "Come in and sit down."

He gathered up some books from a straight-backed, wooden chair next to his desk.

"Sit here," he said. "What is it you want to see me about?"

I sat down and tried to gather my thoughts.

"I don't know if I should be here at Mill Hill," I said finally. "I don't know if I can be a priest."

Suddenly, I felt in danger of crying.

"I've always wanted to be a priest, as long as I can remember." I struggled to keep my voice steady. "But I don't know if I can be celibate. I'm twenty years old and still swamped by sexual thoughts. I thought I would grow out of it. But I haven't." I covered my face with my hands, wishing I could hide.

"Look at me," Father Maserei said quietly, reaching out to pull my hands away. "You mustn't think you're the only one. You're young. All young men have sexual urges like this. They are powerful. But they are natural. God gives them to you as an integral part of being a man. Men are designed to marry and have children. It's not a sin to be a human being."

"I know that," I said. "But what if I can't handle being celibate when I'm a priest? Right now, whenever I meet an attractive girl, I always want her to like me. I say and do things that I hope will make her like me."

Father Maserei looked at me, an amused smile on his thin face.

"Perhaps you need to get to know girls a little better," he said, "long enough to get to see them as real people."

"That's never going to happen," I said. "We live in a seminary restricted to males."

"Then, you have to do the next best thing," Father Maserei said. "You have two months holiday every summer. Use them as an opportunity to meet girls. Meet as many as possible. Get to know them. You have three more years of study in front of you. That's plenty of time to find out if you truly want to be a priest."

I was amazed. It was the last thing I had expected to hear from him.

Later that evening I stayed behind in the chapel. Everyone else had gone to bed. I looked up at the altar. A little red sanctuary lamp glowed in the shadows.

"Help me, God," I prayed. "Help me to know what to do. I think I still do want to be your priest. But you make it so difficult. I'm afraid of being lonely. I'm afraid that all I'm looking for is some kind of recognition; that all I want is to be admired. If I quit, I'll feel lost. What would I do? Where would I go? My mother, my grandmother, they would be horribly disappointed. They think I'm wonderful for wanting to be a priest."

I looked above the altar to where God was supposed to be. He seemed so remote. I didn't know what I expected.

"Very well," I thought to myself. "I'll just have to keep on going until things seem clearer."

CHAPTER 38

On May 13, 1958, I turned twenty-one. I had not told Rinty or anyone else, so there were no celebrations. I didn't want anyone to know. I felt that I was no way near attaining the maturity that a twenty-one-year-old was supposed to have.

At the end of June I traveled to Fernhurst for the summer holidays. My mother greeted me with the news that my sister had just given birth to twin girls. Now that Elizabeth was safely established with her own family, my status as a seminarian was increasingly the focus of my mother's attention.

Traditionally, it was the dream of every Irish Catholic mother to have a son become a priest. At any possible threat to that divine purpose, my mother, like some wild swan, would spread her fearsome feathers to protect my vocation. Thus, when a very attractive young girl drove up in a Land Rover one morning and knocked on our front door, my mother bristled.

"And what is it you want?" she demanded, eyeing her from head to toe.

"My name's Pamela," she said. "I've come to see Peter."

I had first met Pamela earlier in the year at a conference organized by the Jesuits. It was to encourage young people to get involved in social issues by forming so-called Catholic Action groups. As delegates introduced themselves on the first day, I discovered that Pamela was from Guildford, the nearest big town to both Fernhurst and Haslemere. She and a dozen of her friends had formed a group there. At the end of the conference, they asked me to join their meetings over the summer holidays.

I looked forward to those weekly meetings. I particularly liked Pamela. She was very bright. She was the first one of the group to focus on the neediness of the teenagers who inhabited the downtown espresso bars. She was a natural leader and was able to win over the other members of our group to support her projects. Often she and I would get together over coffee before the meetings to exchange ideas.

My mother made it very clear that she disapproved.

"Guildford is a sordid city. It's nothing but a hangout for loose women. Any girl that comes from Guildford is up to no good."

Now one of those loose women was standing at our front door. And she was asking for me. It didn't help that Pamela was looking particularly attractive that morning. She was dressed, casually enough, in light blue overalls, a plaid shirt, and farming boots. But her cheerful brown eyes mirrored her wide smile. Her gold-blonde hair gleamed in the sunlight. She had tied it back with a knotted blue scarf, but random ringlets still curled around her ears. I pushed past my mother who was trying to block the doorway.

"Hello, Pamela. It's good to see you. What brings you here?"

"I've just started a new job here in Fernhurst," she said, "down the road at Tudor Farm. I only started on Monday. I have to drive one of their horses to Tichborne tomorrow. It's not something I can do by myself, so I wondered if you could give me a hand."

"Of course, no problem. What time do you want to go?"

"I could pick you up at eight."

"That's fine," I said.

"Good. Then, I'll see you tomorrow."

She drove off with a cheerful wave, her blue scarf flapping jauntily over her shoulder.

"I can't see the likes of her needing much help," my mother said, throwing a baleful look in the direction of the disappearing truck. "She's just after your body, Peter, that's all."

"Don't be so ridiculous," I said, laughing. "She's a nice girl and I like her. You're just being a grouch."

Pamela showed up early the next morning in the Land Rover. The cloudless, blue sky gave promise of a warm, sunny day.

"Hi there," she said with a smile as I climbed aboard. "We have to go over to the farm and hitch up the horse-box."

It was parked next to a row of stalls in a yard behind the Tudor farmhouse. Pamela backed up the Land Rover and together we lifted the trailer tongue and hitched it onto the drawbar at the back. We slid a ramp from under the trailer and secured it at the rear door. Pamela led a big, brown mare out of a stall, talking softly, stroking its neck to keep it calm. Carefully, she guided the mare up the ramp and into the trailer. Then we stowed the ramp and drove out of the yard towards the road.

"You certainly know how to handle horses," I said. "I'm impressed. You didn't really need me at all."

Pamela looked over at me and laughed. "It's always better to have two people, just to be safe. Besides, it's a long drive to Tichbourne. It's good to have the company."

"So, what's your job like?" I asked as she turned onto the main road. "Is it hard work?"

"No, not really. It's not a real farm. I get to work in the house most of the time. The man who owns it is up in London all week. For him it's just a hobby farm. He's one of those swinging bachelor types. He has huge house parties on weekends with lots of people doing drugs and getting drunk. It's quite scary sometimes."

"Sounds like you should be careful about working in a place like that."

"I know," Pamela said. "They're a strange bunch. But I need the money."

Pamela was clearly a competent driver. She handled the Land Rover with its heavy trailer skillfully, making me realize that, unlike most boys of my age, I still did not know how to drive.

Shortly before noon we pulled off the road and parked at the entrance to a hay field.

"I brought us some lunch," Pamela said, switching off the engine. We climbed down from the Land Rover and she pulled out a satchel from the back seat. After checking the horse, we sat in the shade of the hedge next to the road.

"Hope you like ham and cheese; it's the best I could do. Here, hold this." She handed me a tin mug and poured some tea from a thermos.

We munched away quietly for a while, soaking up the sun and the silence of the surrounding fields. It was a welcome relief from the constant roar of the Land Rover. Gradually, as my ears attuned to the stillness, I realized that it wasn't that silent after all. There was the buzz of insects in the tall summer grass and the rustle of a breeze in the hedgerow. After finishing our sandwiches, we lay back in the grass. Above us the sky was a deep, deep blue with only the occasional wisp of white cloud. A perfect summer day, just warm enough to make us feel comfortably drowsy.

I turned my head and looked at Pamela beside me. She was lying with her arms under her head, her stomach gently rising and falling.

"What are you looking at?" Pamela asked quietly.

I felt a hot blush rising to my face.

"You," I said. "You're very beautiful."

"Thank you," she said. "Not many boys seem to think so."

"What makes you say that?" I asked.

She hesitated.

"At school all the other girls seemed to get boyfriends, but I never did. I kept thinking that there was something wrong with me. That's partly why I joined the group in Guildford. I thought it would be a chance to meet someone. And then I started noticing you. But you're going to be a priest."

She sat up quickly. "Drat," she said, "now I'm sounding sorry for myself. C'mon, let's go."

She started to pick up the remains of our picnic, stuffing them into her satchel.

"I'm sure there are lots of boys who would love to go out with you," I said, helping her clean up. "I don't think I'm that unique."

"Then how come I haven't I met any?" she said.

"You have to give yourself a chance. There's no way that I'd be the only one who finds you so attractive."

"Really?" She stopped and looked at me curiously.

"Of course," I said, "and you know it."

She turned suddenly and gave me a quick, hard kiss.

"Thanks," she said.

She bent down to pick up the satchel she had dropped and we walked over to the Land Rover. We climbed in and she slipped it into gear, pulling back onto the road.

I was surprised and pleased that she had kissed me. But I did not know how to respond. At first, we both just sat there while she drove, with neither of us saying anything.

"So, tell me about your family," I said finally.

Pamela looked over at me and laughed.

"There's just me and my mother," she said. "My dad left us when I was six. I don't know why. One day he just wasn't there anymore. My mum had to sell our house. We've lived in a small one-room flat ever since. She works as a cleaning lady at a bank."

Pamela seemed quite content to talk about herself and her mother as we drove along. I told her about my mother and how she was clinging to the idea that one day she would join my dad in Canada with the three little ones.

"My sister's already married, with twin girls," I said. "It seems really odd. She's younger than me. But I feel she's all grown up and I'm not."

We drove through Tichborne to a small farm on the far side of the village. Pamela backed the trailer into the farmyard. Together we coaxed the mare out of her box and safely down the ramp. The farmer was very appreciative and handed Pamela a large manila envelope to give to her boss.

The drive back passed quickly. Pamela was curious about the time I had spent in Africa and Holland. She had never in her life travelled much further than London and was full of questions. As we got closer to Haslemere she said, "I know a pub where we can stop for a pint and a bite to eat. What do you think? It's not far to Fernhurst from there and we're making good time."

"Sure," I said. "That's a great idea."

We pulled up in front of the Swan on Haslemere High Street. Even with the trailer, we had plenty of room to park, as it was quite early.

"My Aunt Doreen lives just around the corner," I said, as we settled at a quiet table in the back. "She often comes here with my uncle. I hope she won't be shocked if she walks in to find me drinking with a pretty girl."

"Would that really make you feel uncomfortable?" Pamela asked, wide-eyed. "We could always go somewhere else."

"Not at all, my aunt is a very open-minded person. Not like my mother. My mother would scratch your eyes out if she thought you might entice me away from the priesthood." We were well into our second pint.

"So what about you, Peter?" she said with a smile. "How do you feel about sitting here having a beer with me?"

"Great," I said. "It's great to be here with the prettiest girl in the room. I'm really glad you asked me to come with you today. I'm already jealous of the lucky guy who's going to end up being the love of your life."

"It could be you," she said lightly. She reached across the table and touched my hand. "I've enjoyed getting to know you. Why don't you give this priesthood thing some second thoughts?"

"I *have* been giving it second thoughts," I said. "In fact I've been having second thoughts for a long time. My advisor at Mill Hill said I should get to know as many girls as possible, though I don't think he actually meant it the way that sounds."

Pamela laughed, and I took a long swig of beer to hide my confusion.

"Actually, I like you very much," I said, "and I'd love to spend more days with you like this. But you have to understand, I've always wanted to be a priest, ever since I was a child. I can't remember ever *not* wanting to be a priest."

I paused, frustrated at my own ambivalence.

"Go on," Pamela said. "Tell me. Why would it be so hard for you to quit?"

"I don't know," I said, suddenly feeling quite miserable. "I don't know. It's like I'd be betraying something in myself. I just think I need to follow through right now. I mean, I can always quit later if I really find I've done the wrong thing."

I buried my face in my beer to avoid looking into Pamela's eyes.

"Well if that's the way it is, that's the way it is," Pamela sighed. "Let's order some food before we get too depressed."

By the time we finished our supper and had another beer, we both felt more cheerful. The bar had filled with regular customers coming in for their pints after work. The noise level had increased exponentially, and it was becoming difficult to talk. We decided to pay our bill and make our way out to the street. After the loud and smoky atmosphere of the pub, it was good to be in the calm, cool freshness of the summer evening.

"Let's just go for a short walk," Pamela said, putting her arm through mine. "There's a park at the bottom of the high street. We can sit there for a bit. I don't want to go back to the farm just yet."

We found a bench next to a little stream that meandered through the town. We sat there, watching the water reflect the changing colours of the evening sky. After a while, as the light faded, a mist began to form along the edge of the stream and slowly drift across the surface. I felt Pamela shiver. I put my arm around her and she huddled closer.

"I hate evenings," she said. "They're so lonely." She looked up at me. "Oh drat! There I go again, feeling sorry for myself." Then she reached up and kissed me. But this time it was a warm, soft, lingering kiss. And I kissed her back.

Suddenly she pulled away.

"We should go," she said. "I shouldn't have done that." She stood and pulled me up off the bench. "Come on. I'll race you back to the car." She turned and ran ahead of me, across the grass and up the high street. I took off after her, but she was too fast for me. When she reached the Land Rover, I barely had time to scramble in before she let in the clutch and roared off in the gathering dusk towards Fernhurst.

After a few minutes she started to ease up on the accelerator.

"I'm sorry, Peter," she said. "That wasn't fair. I promise I won't bother you anymore. You have to do what you have to do. You don't need me around to confuse you."

It was dark when she dropped me off at the house. She refused to look at me as I got out.

"Goodbye, Peter," she said, looking straight ahead. "Thanks for your help."

A small tear in the corner of her eye glistened in the dashboard light. She threw the clutch into reverse, spun the Land Rover around, and roared off. I stood there watching as she paused at the corner, the amber signal light flashing. Then she turned onto the road to the farm.

I felt awful. I hated myself.

The following week Pamela didn't show up at our group meeting in Guildford. When I got back I walked over to the farmhouse where she worked. I really wanted to talk to her, to tell her how torn I felt.

I saw a long chain hanging next to the front door. I yanked at it and was surprised to hear the tones of an electronic chime instead of a real bell. The door was opened by a skinny, waxen-faced man dressed in fashionable Carnaby Street clothing.

"How can I help you?" he asked with an extravagantly arched eyebrow.

"I'm looking for Pamela," I said. "I understand she works here."
"Used to work here," he replied. "Apparently she left us."
"Well, can you tell me how I can get in touch with her?"
"Fraid not. Left without telling anybody. Good day."
The door was shut firmly in my face.

CHAPTER 39

I was shaken by the intensity of my feelings for Pamela.
When I returned to Mill Hill in September, I knew I had to confront my ambivalence. I could not ignore the power of the sexual attraction I had felt. There was also a gnawing feeling of guilt. Had I been stringing everyone along all these years? Was this drive to be a priest all a pretense? Perhaps it was nothing more than the continuation of my childhood desperation to win approval.

However, dramatic events in Rome that autumn revived my flagging, religious idealism. Four weeks after the start of the new semester, Pope Pius XII died. Nineteen days later, Pope John XXIII was elected to succeed him. The cardinals had chosen him as a kind of harmless, caretaker pope. He was seventy-seven years old, and they did not expect him to live very long. Their plan was to use the time to search for a more permanent successor. But the old man surprised them. He immediately set in motion a process of radical Church reform.

What first impressed me about Pope John was his evident concern for people. He did things that no pope had done for years. Previous popes never left the Vatican except to holiday in their mountain villa. In December Pope John went to visit the children's hospital in Rome. He talked to the kids there who were suffering from polio. He visited the Regina Coeli prison and told the inmates, "You could not come to me, so I came to you."

Then, in January 1959, scarcely three months after his election, he announced his decision to summon all the bishops of the world for a general meeting. He realized that the Church desperately needed to be more relevant in the modern world. He used the Italian word *aggiornamento* to describe what he wanted. I liked the story of how, when asked what *aggiornamento* meant, he simply walked over to a window and threw it wide open.

At Mill Hill, we were well aware the Church needed to change. For so long it had isolated itself behind its fixation with morality. Far from paying attention to people's needs, it busied itself with preserving its own power and authority.

At church services priests stood with their backs to the people, shielded by stiff gold-brocade vestments, reciting prayers in a language that few understood. Its prohibition of birth control and sex before marriage made a lot of Catholics cynical. Many left the Church altogether. The failure of Pope Pius XII to condemn Hitler's Jewish genocide during the war seemed symptomatic of the Church's disengagement from real human concerns. But here was a new pope promising change. That encouraged me to set aside the doubts I had been feeling about becoming a priest.

"Life here is getting far too serious," Rinty declared to me one day. "We all need to laugh more."

"You're right," I agreed. "What can we do about it?"

"I think we should put on a play," he said, "a comedy." He reached into his pocket and pulled out a book. "I found this in the library. It's called *Arsenic and Old Lace*. Read this tonight, and let me know what you think."

That night I ignored the notes I was supposed to be reviewing for next day's lecture and read the play voraciously. The story revolved around a young man, Mortimer Brewster, who discovers that his two spinster aunts are murdering their lonely lodgers with homemade elderberry wine. They bury the bodies in the basement, where their crazy brother, who believes he is Teddy Roosevelt, is digging locks for the Panama Canal.

"I think it's great," I told Rinty the next day. "It's so ridiculous. I think everyone will like it. And it all takes place in one room, so there are no complicated scene changes. We could put it on at the next Christmas concert."

"Exactly!" Rinty said. "You could play Mortimer Brewster, the serious, responsible one. I'll be the brother who thinks he's Teddy Roosevelt. Who do you think should play the aunts?"

We decided to make a list of people who we thought might be good for the other roles and, after some friendly arm twisting, we had a full cast. Once we had done a read-through, everyone was super keen. For the next eight weeks we rehearsed every day, and by Christmas we were all ready.

On the whole, our play ran quite smoothly. The two students who played maiden aunts had managed to smuggle a bottle of real wine onto the set. They served it whenever the script called for the poisoned elderberry wine. They claimed afterwards that it steadied their nerves and cured them of stage fright.

At one point Rinty almost caused me to lose my lines. The script required him to show me a family photograph of the two of us at a holiday camp. "That's me," he said, pointing, "and that's you." But instead of the blank piece of paper, it was a picture of two monkeys sitting on a rock. I managed to choke back a laugh and carried on.

Afterwards, the rector of the college, Father Anthony Galvin, called us to his office to thank us. He was a stocky man, about forty years old, with greying hair and a round chubby face. He came from Durham and had the same relaxed, comfortable attitude that I admired so much in Rinty. He was liked and respected by all the students. Everyone called him 'the boss,' though he certainly didn't behave like a bossy person.

Father Galvin was a gifted administrator. Besides ensuring the smooth running of the day-to-day events of college life, he fearlessly undertook major projects to maintain and upgrade the physical fabric of the building. The huge statue of St. Joseph perched on top of the college tower had been deteriorating for a number of years. The cost of refurbishing it seemed prohibitive. Undaunted, he managed to persuade a local contractor to donate a helicopter crane. It carefully lifted the statue from the top of the tower and carried it off to a nearby sculpture studio to be restored.

It was this kind of creative enterprise that Father Galvin sought to encourage in us students. He believed that we should learn how to tackle practical, physical problems, not just abstract theological ones.

Mill Hill owned and ran a small farm that had been part of the original property since 1886. There were chickens, pigs and a few cows, and enough land for potatoes and other vegetables to help feed us all. One day Father Galvin mustered a dozen of us in the yard by the henhouse, issued us with shovels and spades, and marched us out to one of the pastures.

"I'm going to teach you lads how to dig a latrine," he said. "You could easily find yourselves at a mission station in the middle of a jungle village with no toilets. There's no knowing where you might end up. So, grab a spade and start digging."

He explained the importance of making sure the latrine was hygienic and environmentally friendly. He showed us how to keep it from contaminating a water supply and how to keep away flies and odour.

It was by far the most practical class I had ever attended.

Chapter 40

In June, at the end of each scholastic year, voting took place to elect a new student president. These elections were a big deal in our little world. I was delighted when it was announced that Rinty had been elected as president for his final year.

To celebrate I took him downtown for a beer at the St. George, an old Elizabethan coaching inn. It was in the heart of London's hop district where, for centuries, hops were marketed to the brewing industry. Kenneth, Elizabeth's husband, was in the hop business and had recommended the pub.

We were lucky to find a table outside in the cobbled yard. The place was crowded with noontime office workers. Many were in shirt sleeves, their business jackets draped over chair backs, enjoying the warmth of a late June sun. Jugs of beer with bangers and mash seemed a popular lunch. The courtyard hummed with cheerful chatter. Waitresses carried heavy trays high above people's heads, skillfully negotiating the narrow spaces between tables.

"Dickens must have loved this place," Rinty said, looking around appreciatively. "I read somewhere that he used to come here quite regularly."

"That's right." A waitress was standing next to us, pencil poised to take our order. "Except in those days it was a coaching inn and he came here for coffee. What can I get you?"

"I'll have a Watney's," I said, "and a pub pie."

"And I'll have a Red, with bangers and mash," said Rinty.

"I'll be right back with the drinks," she said.

She disappeared into the bar and returned with two foaming pints and, a few minutes later, a tray with the food.

"Here's to your last year at Mill Hill, Rinty," I said, raising my glass. "I wish it were mine. Two years seems a long time, right now."

"It will go fast," Rinty said. "And after that . . . I wonder where we'll be." He sat contemplating his beer for a minute. "I hate how we just disappear once we get ordained. We've been together for so many years. Then, all of a sudden, we're gone. You and I have been a great team, Bruno. They should consider sending the two of us somewhere together."

"Well, let's make the most of next year," I said. "We should do one last spectacular play."

"What do you have in mind?" Rinty asked.

"I've always liked Eliot's *Murder in the Cathedral*," I said, "especially the part where the archbishop recalls all the good times he's had with the king. *Fires devouring the winter season, eating up the darkness, with wit and wine and wisdom.* Wit, wine, and wisdom! What more could anyone want?"

I took a quick gulp of beer. Rinty was looking at me shrewdly.

"Is that a real question?" he asked.

I gave a rueful laugh. "I think you've got me," I said.

I was, in fact, in the middle of a major anxiety attack. In two weeks I would be ordained a sub-deacon with the rest of my class. It was a decisive step because it meant taking a vow of celibacy. I would be given a tonsure, the top of my head shaved like a monk. It would be a visible sign that I was now a cleric.

"I remember feeling panicky last year too," Rinty said. "This year I'll be ordained a deacon. You'd think I'd be even more anxious. But I'm not. Being ordained sub-deacon last year was pivotal. In the end, it just seemed logical after all these years of preparation. But what's making you so scared now?"

"I've been confused ever since last summer," I told him. "I was very attracted to a girl I met. It knocked me for six. Made me question if I really wanted to be a priest. I don't know how I'd handle it if it happened again." And I told Rinty the whole story about Pamela.

"And another thing," I said, feeling that I needed to get everything off my chest. "I find it hard to pray these days. Prayer just feels like I'm talking to myself. And there's all the emphasis the Church puts on God being physically present in a piece of bread at Mass. That just doesn't seem relevant. And then there's the political machinations going on in Rome right now: a bunch of old men clinging to power, afraid of sex, afraid of women. I don't want to be like that."

I stopped and looked at Rinty. He didn't say anything right away. Then he leaned his elbows on the table and looked back at me with a bit of a grin.

"I don't think you really have to worry about becoming an old, misogynist priest," he said. "Remember what you've always thought about the Church needing to tackle real problems, like injustice and poverty. You obviously feel deeply about those things. Just because you're suddenly attracted to a girl doesn't mean you have to give up everything else you've felt so strongly about all these years."

We sat quietly for a little longer, thinking our own thoughts amid the laughter and chatter all around us. Rinty took a last, long swig of beer, put his glass on the table and stood up.

"Time to go, Bruno," he said. "I can't make up your mind for you. You have to decide for yourself. Just make sure you look at the whole picture. It's easy to get bogged down with one little part and find you've missed the whole thing."

"OK," I said. "I'll try. Thanks." I finished my beer and paid the bill.

"Sorry for dumping on you," I said as we made our way through the crowds to the tube station. "Today was supposed to be a celebration, and I made it more like a wake."

Rinty stopped abruptly and turned to face me. We became a little island in the stream of office workers parting around us as they hurried back to work.

"For goodness sake, don't apologize, Bruno. We all need to talk. There are too many priests who end up lonely and isolated because they can't talk to each other."

Two weeks later we were ordained, Rinty as a deacon and I as a sub-deacon. Afterwards, as I rode the train home for the summer holidays, I experienced a strange feeling of relief. I had made the decision. Now I could go on preparing to be a priest with more peace of mind.

CHAPTER 41

Gemma gave a shriek when I walked in the door at Fernhurst. She
ran across the room and jumped into my arms. "You're home!
You're home!" she said, hugging my neck.

I was surprised that Gemma even remembered me. She was only
two when she had seen me last summer. Dominic and Barnabas rushed
over and clutched my legs until we all collapsed in a heap on the
floor.

"They've been looking forward to having you home," my mother
said, pulling me up. "And so have I."

I played with the children until it was their bedtime. After they
were settled, I sat in the hall outside their open bedroom doors and
read to them from the *Narnia Chronicles*. When they finally fell asleep,
I went down to join my mother in the kitchen.

She was sitting at the table with a cup of tea. She looked up as I
came in, her face still surprisingly youthful, her eyes bright. She was in
her mid-forties now. Her hair was shot through with threads of grey,
the backs of her hands ridged with veins.

I sat down next to her, and she reached over to rub my newly
tonsured head. "I'm so proud of you," she said. "You're almost a priest
already. Now I'll have to address my letters 'To the Reverend Peter
Walther'." And she grinned at me impishly, like a small child.

"As if you'd ever send me a letter," I said sharply. "You hardly ever
write to me, even for my birthday."

Her face crumpled. "It's just that I forget," she said. "I'm so sorry.
The children are such a handful. I never have time to think. Look
at the mess they make, toys everywhere. They never clean up after
themselves." She dissolved into tears.

"Please don't do that," I said. Tears were her biggest defense
whenever she felt I was upset with her. "I don't imagine your parents
ever remembered your birthday either."

185

"You're right," she said, shocked. "I never thought of that before. I just took it for granted. They seemed too far away in India. It took weeks for letters to get there in those days."

"Have you heard anything from Malcolm yet?" I asked. Somehow I had difficulty forming the word 'Dad'.

"Nothing. I don't even know where he is in Canada."

"Well, that's ridiculous. He's been gone almost four years now."

"I know. I'm very worried. I'm afraid something's happened to him."

"We should find out. We could get the Red Cross to look for him."

"Will they do that?"

"Of course they will. They're an international organization. They can find him. And then you can get child support. He's got to be earning some money by now."

I phoned the local Red Cross office the next day. They gave me a number to call in London. A very efficient-sounding woman answered the phone and asked for all the details: my father's name, age, birthplace, date of departure for Canada, and so on. A few days later I got a call back.

"He's alive and well in Toronto," the woman said.

"Hold on while I get a pencil and paper," I said excitedly. I put the phone down and pulled open the kitchen draw where my mother kept her writing things.

"Can you give me his address?" I said, grabbing the phone again.

"I'm sorry, but I can't do that without his permission."

"You mean he doesn't want us to know?" I was stunned.

"It would seem so," the woman said. "But, if he has dependent children, you can hire a lawyer to track him down and get him to provide child support. I can put you in touch with a good lawyer if you want to go that route."

"Thank you," I said. "We'll think about what we can do." I hung up.

I repeated what I had just heard to my mother. Her eyes clouded over. She slumped down in her chair.

"He must be with that woman again. How could I have been such a fool? I should've known. He met a girl in London during the war, a Canadian girl. She was a nurse. He said she'd gone back to Canada."

She buried her head in her hands, her shoulders shaking with sobs.

"I should have known, I should have known," she repeated over and over again.

I stood there feeling helpless. She had never spoken about my father being unfaithful before. I suddenly felt enormously angry. How could he treat her like this, leaving her alone with three little children to manage by herself? I bent down and put my arms around her.

"We have to do something," I said. "We can't just let him abandon us. I'll talk to a lawyer. It's not fair that his mother has to support us. I'll call a lawyer in the morning."

She jumped to her feet. "No, you won't," she shouted at me. "I won't let you. He's still my husband. We're married. I don't care what he's done." She started sobbing again.

"Well, you can't go on living in limbo like this. Why don't you go into Haslemere tomorrow and talk to Doreen? Maybe she'll have some ideas. I'll stay here and look after the children."

"Would you?" She looked up at me through her tears. "I'd like that. Doreen will know what to do. She's always known what to do."

"Of course," I said. "You go up to bed now. I'll bring you a cup of tea."

The next morning she went off to catch the bus into Haslemere, and I took care of the children for the day. We had fun playing in the backyard, and they seemed to enjoy my efforts at cooking.

It was already dark when my mother got back that evening. She was a much happier person; too happy. She and Doreen had ended up in the Swan after a day of window shopping. They had clearly consumed more than a couple of drinks.

"I'm not going to do anything about Malcolm," she confided when the children had gone to bed. "He can go off with his little slut if he wants to. I'm not chasing after him. I'm never going to leave my children ever again. They're happy here and I'm happy, too. So there!"

I was taken aback.

"Is that all that you and Doreen could come up with?"

"Peter, there's nothing else we can do," she insisted. "We can't get hold of him. We could never afford a lawyer. Even if we could, we probably would not get anywhere with him in Canada. We'll just have to pray that he comes to his senses, that he'll start missing us and come back."

"How can you just do nothing?" I was shouting at her. "How can you let him abandon you and the children like this? They need him! You need him! You need him to be responsible and help take care of them. You can't just let him get away with this."

I was seething with anger.

"What's the point of making the children pray that he'll come back? You always say God only helps those who help themselves. You have to see a lawyer. You have to get help."

The house suddenly felt claustrophobic. I needed out. I made for the front door and stumbled up the laneway. Moonlight made dark hollows in the uneven path. I was running, the anger burning inside me. I had to slow down to let the pounding in my chest subside.

I stopped and leaned against a rail fence. Why did I feel so angry? It wasn't just my mother's refusal to take responsibility. It was the fact that the children were going to suffer. Just like me, they would be growing up without a father. They would feel the same hurt that I felt. And I was helpless to prevent it.

CHAPTER 42

The late afternoon sun filled my room with a golden glow. It was September 1959, the first day back at Mill Hill after the summer. From my top floor window I could see the distant highrises and church steeples of London gleaming in a soft blue haze. I thought of Gemma and the two boys playing in that same sunshine in Fernhurst. I felt a lump in my throat. I missed them.

"Don't worry about us," my mother had said as I left that morning. "We'll be fine. Now that the children are all in school I'll have more time for myself. You just make sure you concentrate on your studies. Two more years to go and you'll be a priest."

I unpacked and hurried down to the smoking room. I needed to be with my friends.

A few months later, in December, Rinty and I were walking outside doing our exercise rounds in front of the college. Once again time and the college routine had succeeded in distancing me from those uncomfortable feelings for my family.

We walked briskly. A cold wind whipped at the few remaining leaves still clinging to the trees. When they finally tore loose, they hurtled high, twisting and twirling into the turbulent sky.

"The Catholic Church needs a wind like this," said Rinty. "It needs to be shaken up and blown apart. It's been guarding its ghetto for far too long."

I was surprised at the intensity in his voice.

"What brought this on?" I asked.

"I've been thinking about how the Church controls us," he said. "It behaves like an over-protective parent. Everything has to be Catholic. We must attend Catholic schools, join Catholic youth groups, marry only Catholics. We're surrounded by exclusively Catholic symbols and traditions: Benediction, Forty Hours Devotions, and Stations of the

Cross. Good Catholic girls have to belong to the Legion of Mary and boys to the Altar Society. It's all too much. It's not healthy."

The wind beat against our faces as we rounded the corner by the pond.

"But isn't that what this new Pope hopes to change?" I asked. "He wants a more open Church. One that appreciates today's world, respects other faiths."

"That's going to scare a lot of diehard clerics in Rome," Rinty said with a laugh. "I wonder if they can handle it. The Vatican bureaucrats would have to change their job descriptions. What's going to happen to all those *monsignori* who spend their lives looking for heretical books to burn?"

"It's not just the Roman Curia," I said. "We have to change as well. As missionaries, we can't go on acting as if we have a monopoly on truth. If God reveals himself in other religions, we have to listen to them too."

Rinty stopped for a moment to relight his pipe, sheltered by the broad trunk of a beech tree.

"I agree totally," he said between puffs. "The Church is far too dogmatic and intolerant. It invented the catechism to make sure we have only approved answers to life's questions."

"I hate how it classifies every little thing we do wrong," I said. "Mortal sins. Venial sins. That's when I question if I should be a priest. I can't see myself controlling people like that."

Rinty gave up trying to light his pipe. The wind was too strong.

"So what's keeping you here?" he asked, tucking the pipe into his pocket.

"Hope," I said. "Hope that the Church is about to change. I read this article by Christopher Butler. He's been appointed an advisor to the Vatican Council. He says the Church needs to acknowledge the positive aspects of other religions. *Let us not fear that truth might endanger truth*, he says. Isn't that splendid?"

We walked on in silence for a while. Then Rinty stopped and turned towards me.

"All this presupposes that the Council will actually make changes."

"I don't see how it won't," I said, "if the Pope himself is pushing it."

"Aren't you being a little naïve?" Rinty said. "After all, the old cardinals who ran the Roman Curia under Pius XII are still there. They are the ones who are drafting the agenda for the Council. I'm not sure that Pope John is the kind of person to deal with the Machiavellian politics practised in the Vatican."

"Perhaps I *am* being a little naïve," I said. "But then, maybe you're being a little cynical. We'll just have to wait and see."

While Rinty and I speculated about Church reform, the tired old courses in Thomistic theology still continued at Mill Hill. Christmas provided a brief distraction, but with the New Year it became obvious that we all needed a fresh project to engage our energies.

"Let's do one last show," I suggested to Rinty after breakfast one morning. "How about the play we talked about last summer, *Murder in the Cathedral?*"

"Eliot's poetry is difficult," Rinty said, "but it's worth a try."

We called a meeting and ran off some copies of the script on a Gestetner. A surprising number of students showed up. We gave them a rough synopsis of the plot and then started reading the chorus parts together. Rinty was right. Eliot's poetry took a lot of explaining. But everyone seemed to enjoy the session. By the end, most were willing to join us.

Five intense weeks of rehearsal later, we were ready to go. We decided to present the play on Easter Monday. The actors in the chorus, who were mostly Dutch, were particularly anxious about their ability to tackle the poetry. As it turned out, they need not have worried. They were very effective in conveying the fear and foreboding of the peasants at the impending political violence. The four tempters enjoyed their roles in trying to entice the archbishop to submit to the king. And the audience got a break when they reappeared as the knights and spoke in prose to justify the murder.

The central theme of the play was particularly appropriate for an audience of seminarians. Thomas Becket, Archbishop of Canterbury, knows he is to become a martyr, but he must face the question of whether he is doing the right thing for the right reason. Is he doing it because he wants to serve his God or because he wants the glory of immortality?

The following day we sat around on the log benches in an outside smoking area to rehash the performance. It was the middle of April. The weak spring sunshine was barely warm enough for us to be without winter jackets.

But it was good to be outside. Fresh new leaves had already burst from winter buds. Next to us, behind a wire fence, a few chickens scratched in the dirt. They frantically flapped their foolish feathers whenever one of us made a sudden move. Piet Van Breemen was being unusually quiet. While everyone else was reminiscing about the performance, he was sitting with his head down, picking at the loose bark of an old sycamore twig.

"What's the matter, Piet?" I asked him.

He looked up, surprised that I had noticed.

"There's something that still bothers me about the play," he admitted. "You know the part where the fourth tempter says Thomas is really seeking martyrdom for his own glory? Well, Thomas justifies himself by saying that he's only doing God's will. But how does he *know* it's God's will? How do any of us know what God's will is?"

"People always say there's a still, small voice inside that tells you," I said, laughing.

"That's ridiculous." Piet was annoyed. "That's just like saying that anything you want is God's will."

He stood up and kicked a pebble towards the fence in frustration, setting the chickens squawking. "I don't see how I can know I'm not kidding myself. Perhaps I just want the glory and respect that our parents give to priests."

"You *don't* know," Rinty said quietly. "That's the point. It's like telling someone you love them. It's a leap in the dark. You simply have to trust. *Confident ignorance*, that's what Thomas says in the play."

Piet stood up and looked at him for a moment. Then, he shrugged his shoulders and walked away. We sat there silently, feeling his frustration. We knew we were all asking ourselves the same thing. And the time to call the question was getting closer.

One morning after breakfast, Jan Swagemaker came over to me. "The boss wants to see you," he said.

I made my way up to Father Galvin's room and tapped at his door.

"Come in," I heard him say.

He was standing in the middle of the room, one hand rubbing the back of his neck.

"You wanted to see me?" I asked.

"Oh yes, Bruno. I need to talk to you."

He walked around behind his desk, pulled up his chair and sat down.

"I've just got a letter from Rome," he said. "They've decided to make me a Bishop. They want to send me to Miri, in North Borneo. I'm supposed to be in Rome at the beginning of May for the consecration. That's only two weeks from now. I'm feeling rather overwhelmed. It's not every day I get a letter from the Pope."

"Anyway, I'm supposed to have an official coat-of-arms," he went on. "I think it dates back to the time when bishops were warlords. I have to submit a design to the College of Heralds for approval. Could you make one for me? I heard you had some experience with that kind of thing."

It was true. Way back, when I had spent Christmas at Freshfield, Johnny Heweston had asked me to design a coat-of-arms for his friend, Monsignor Ireland, who had been appointed Bishop of the Falkland Islands.

"I'll be glad to," I said.

With Rinty's ordination coming up in June, an election had to be held for a new student president. No one ever campaigned to be president. Students simply tossed names around amongst themselves in an informal way.

The day before ballots were to be filled out, I started feeling uncomfortable. Groups of students would stop talking when I approached. First year students, whom I didn't know, would come up to me in the hall just to chat. And then that night, it dawned on me; they were considering me for president.

Rinty announced the results at breakfast the following day.

"Your next student president is Bruno Walther," he said, looking at me with a big grin on his face. The place erupted with cheers and the banging of spoons on plates. I was embarrassed, but pleased too. It was good to be so universally liked.

"Congratulations, old chum," Rinty said to me afterwards. "They chose the right person."

Rinty's class was ordained by the newly consecrated Bishop Galvin on the last Sunday in June. After a celebratory breakfast with parents, the new priests were given their appointments. The majority were assigned to different missions around the world. However, a few were sent to universities for further studies. We waited in the smoking room for the new priests to come and tell us where they were going. When Rinty appeared, he was not looking happy.

"They're sending me for further studies," he said with a rueful smile. "It's Durham University. I'll be staying at Burn Hall again."

CHAPTER 43

T *his time next year I will be a priest, too*, I thought. I was on board the train going back to Fernhurst for my last summer as a student.

Watching the towns and villages slide past the window, I thought of all the train journeys I had taken to reach this point in my life. I thought of Mrs. Lily on the way to Freshfield; how she had been so shocked at an eleven-year-old boy going off alone to a seminary. I thought of that first long train journey up to Durham and the sight of the warm yellow sandstone walls of Burn Hall glowing like a jewel in the Weir valley. And then there was the boat train to Harwich and catching the ferry to Holland, and Brenda and I losing our precious hats to the English Channel. It seemed as if the years had gone by faster than the speeding train.

Every morning during the summer holiday, I took the bus to Haslemere for Mass. One day Father Borelli invited me to have breakfast with him. I had never been inside his rectory before. The level of luxury took my breath away. The dining room gleamed with polished teak and crystal ware. A pure white linen tablecloth covered one end of an enormous mahogany dining table. It was laid with a sparkling, solid silver tea service, silver egg cups, a toaster, and napkin rings. I would have felt very uncomfortable living this kind of life had I chosen to be a priest in England.

Before I left Father Borelli went over to a large bookcase and took down a set of St. Thomas Aquinas' *Summa Theologica* in five volumes. They were bound in white leather and embossed in red and gold. They looked expensive.

"These are for you," he said. "I used them when I was in the seminary. I haven't opened them since. They take up too much space. I think you should have them."

They would have been more useful three years ago when I first started theology, I thought. It seemed a little late now that I had only one year

195

left. Father Borelli stuffed them into an old shopping bag and sent me off with a paternal pat on the back.

"Just remember who gave them to you," he said.

It was not only Father Borelli who seemed suddenly aware of how close I was to ordination. My mother and my aunt were already making plans for the big day.

"Doreen and I are saving money to buy you a chalice," my mother said. "That way you can say Mass wherever you happen to be as a missionary and be reminded of us."

"You don't have to do that," I protested. "It would be far too expensive. The inside of a chalice has to be real gold. Mill Hill has a group of rich benefactors who donate chalices for all the newly ordained priests."

"But we want to do it," my mother said, her eyes moist. "We may never see you again. You'll be going off to Africa or some place. This way you'll never forget us."

"Don't be so dramatic," I said, annoyed. "We get a six-month leave every five years, no matter where we're sent."

Her sudden sentimental concern bothered me. I wondered why she had never seemed to miss me much before now.

Doreen was busy making me a fancy new cassock to replace the old, ratty, threadbare one that I had worn for so many years as a student.

"You have to have one with a cape," she insisted. "It's the latest clerical fashion."

I was summoned periodically to her cottage to stand on the coffee table while she draped me in black serge, her mouth full of pins, marking it with tailor's chalk. I kept banging my head on the low beams, much to the glee of my cousins who sat around in awe watching my new robe take shape.

One day my mother and I were sitting at the kitchen table over a cup of tea. Gemma and the two boys were outside in the garden at the back of the house. They were running in and out of the smoke of the small bonfire I had built that morning.

"I hope you're not becoming a priest just to please me," she said, playing with the teaspoon in her saucer, not looking at me. "I worry that I got you into this and that you will blame me if it doesn't work out."

"Of course not," I said, surprised. "If anyone's to blame it's the nuns at St. Dominic's. But who said anything about blame?"

"I don't know. Sometimes I think if I'd been around for you a bit more when you were a little boy you wouldn't have even thought of becoming a priest."

"Well, it's a bit late now," I said. "I've been thinking about being a priest for a long time."

She looked up at me directly, her eyes questioning.

"But is that really what you want to do?"

I hesitated and looked away.

"I think so," I said carefully. "I don't think anyone ever knows for sure about something like this. In the end you just have to decide, one way or the other. I think, all things considered, this is what I want to do."

There was a long pause. I could hear the delighted squeals of the children outside as they ran through the smoke of the bonfire.

"I hope you don't mind," my mother said, "but I've invited Kenelm Foster down for the weekend. I'd like the two of you to have a good talk."

We met Kenelm at the bus stop. As we walked down the street to our house, the neighbours stared in astonishment. He was the quintessential Dominican monk in his black cowl and sandals. He carried a very small backpack, barely big enough for a change of underwear and a couple of books. He had a deliberate way of talking, his eyes searching some distant horizon as he sought to clarify his thoughts.

In the afternoon my mother insisted on taking the children out for a walk.

"I'll just leave you two to talk," she said, giving me a meaningful look.

"So, Peter," Kenelm said after they had left, "your mother obviously wants me to make sure you genuinely want to be a priest."

"Looks like it," I said, feeling a little uncomfortable.

"Don't worry. I'm not going to give you the third degree. You're old enough to have made up your own mind without my help. But tell me, I don't know much about the Mill Hill Fathers. What are they all about?" And he gave me a reassuring grin.

The two of us spent the afternoon discussing the differences between our two organizations, and I told him the story of how the nuns at St. Dominic's had tried to divert me to the Dominicans.

"Well, you're obviously more of a doer than an academic," he said. "I think you chose the right place to be in the end. We Dominicans tend to live in our heads. I don't think you would have liked that very much."

After supper I could hear my mother questioning Kenelm downstairs while I was putting the children to bed. He must have reassured her because she looked distinctly relieved when I joined them later.

Chapter 44

"Our last year together," Jan Swagemaker remarked, sorting his cards carefully.

We were sitting in the smoking room, playing a hand of bridge. It was our first evening back in September 1960. By the end of July 1961, I would be twenty-four and an ordained priest.

"It's hard to imagine," I said. "This time next year, we'll be thousands of miles apart. Who dealt these cards anyway? Pass."

"I pass too." Piet Van Breemen surveyed his hand ruefully. "You're right, Bruno, it does seem strange. We've been together all these years. And soon we'll be scattered all over the globe."

Nick Morgan was sitting across from me.

"One no trump," he said.

Nick and I had long ago repaired the friendship I had fractured as a twelve-year-old at St. Peter's. Not that we were actually close now, but we were able to be casually friendly without any further expectations.

"I pass," Jan said.

"Three hearts," I said, looking at Nick hopefully. I had the ace and the queen and some low hearts in my hand.

"Pass," Piet said.

"Three no trump," Nick said confidently. He had always been good at cards, just as he had been at math. Everybody passed, and Nick proceeded to win comfortably.

"This year's going to be quite a challenge," Piet said, shuffling the cards for another round. "I'm worried about learning how to say Mass; all those tiny details. There are rules for every minute movement."

"It's true," said Nick. No wonder we hated going to church when we were kids. All that standing, sitting, and kneeling. For the longest time I didn't realize we were mocking the Mass when we did the hokey-pokey dance."

Piet began dealing the cards for another round.

"And don't forget all the other sacraments we have to get under our belts," Nick said, sorting his cards. "Baptism, Confession, Marriage. It's going to be a really busy year."

"Nine o'clock. I don't think we have time for another round," Jan said.

Students were already drifting through the double doors towards the chapel for night prayers. He collected the cards as we got up to leave. "See you in the morning. Hopefully tomorrow will be a good start for our last year."

I joined the crowd of students heading down the hallway. I was a little apprehensive. All that talk about workload had me worried. As student president, I would have even more responsibilities than the others.

At the end of the previous year, Rinty had handed me a stack of journals from past presidents. "Reading these should help," he had said. "The seminary system is pretty archaic. It's quite ridiculous. We have to get permission to go into town to buy a toothbrush. You'd think they'd give us more independence now that we're about to be ordained. Just to win minimal changes I had to push unbelievably hard."

I soon found he was right about trying to change things. However, there were more personal challenges that required my attention. One of these was my first sermon.

Father Noel Hanrahan was our moderator for this enterprise. He was a rotund, red-haired Englishman, supposedly possessed of exemplary oratorical skills. At Sunday Mass, we frequently cringed with embarrassment as some unfortunate neophyte lapsed into incoherence. We practised our delivery beforehand from a lectern in the empty refectory. Father Hanrahan would sit at the far end to make sure we projected and articulated. Microphones and associated audio technologies were not yet common in churches.

Eventually, one Sunday morning, it was my turn to climb the curved stone stairway to the pulpit. I was feeling fairly confident. After all, I had performed in front of audiences for many years. Why should I be nervous now? I stepped to the front of the pulpit and gripped the cold marble balustrade with both hands. A sea of upturned faces stretched before me. I took a deep breath.

"Dearly beloved brethren," I began.

Suddenly, horribly, my brain froze. My mind became a complete blank.

"Dearly beloved brethren," I repeated desperately.

Awkward silence.

Several students started to grin in gleeful anticipation.

Then, from out of nowhere, Father Hanrahan's words came to me, *Focus on a person at the back of the church.*

My eyes locked on to our new rector, Father Hennesey, who was sitting in the last pew. Huge relief. The lines I had so laboriously memorized came flooding back.

"Dearly beloved brethren," . . . my voice seemed unnaturally loud . . . "In two months time, on June 29, the Church celebrates the feast of St. Peter and St. Paul. It's strange, isn't it, that these are the only two saints in the Church's calendar that don't have their own individual feast days . . ."

More confidently now, I described how Peter and Paul had quarreled about the organization of the early Church. At one point Peter had insisted only Jews could become Christians. Paul had disagreed. He felt that Gentiles could become Christians without first having to convert to Judaism. Both men were equally rigid.

"It's interesting," I said, "that there was such a fundamental disagreement at the very beginning of the Church. It was only finally resolved by calling a council, the Council of Jerusalem."

"Today we still have disagreements in the Church. So now the Pope is calling another council. He is calling it to decide, among other things, the status of Catholics who disagree with Church rules. Can they still be members of the Church if they are truly following the voice of their own conscience?"

"The story of St. Peter and St. Paul's disagreement is particularly relevant today. If we exclude people with all our self-righteous rules and regulations, we may well find that the Vatican Council disagrees with us."

Suddenly I noticed Father Hennessey looking at me. He had a puzzled expression on his face. He was a fairly conservative Irishman. I hesitated. But I could not stop now.

"In the story of early Christianity, both St. Peter and St. Paul had visions. These visions gave them an insight into what Jesus was all about. They realized that it is not laws and prescriptions that make us children of God; rather it is our connection with Him and with each other. Perhaps this is why it is good to honour St. Peter and St. Paul on the same day. They remind us that the church is primarily about a caring community and only secondarily about following the laws and the prophets."

As the last sounds of my own voice dissipated among the rafters, an oppressive silence seemed to fill the church. Ordinarily, a short period of reflection follows the sermon. But this silence felt different. Father Hennessey was still looking at me, but now I thought I detected a frown on his face. Was my sermon too confrontational? Had I sounded like a modern Martin Luther challenging the Church? I felt acutely self-conscious as I turned and walked down the stone steps of the pulpit.

"Well done, Peter," Father Hanrahan said when I met him in the hallway after the Mass.

"Father Hennessey wasn't looking too pleased," I said.

"Don't worry. He always looks like that if the sermons are too long. And you did go on a bit."

CHAPTER 45

The biggest hurdle we had to overcome, in our final year before ordination, was an oral exam in theology. The Archbishop of Westminster, Cardinal Godfrey, was to officiate at our ordination. Since Mill Hill was within his diocese, it was his responsibility to ensure the doctrinal conformity of those he was about to ordain. So one day early in June a Father Charles Davis was sent to interview each one of us.

Father Davis was a professor of dogmatic theology at the diocesan seminary in Ware, Hertfordshire. As one of England's leading Catholic theologians, he edited a prominent periodical called *The Clergy Review* and had just published a book entitled *Liturgy and Doctrine*. I had carefully read everything he had ever written to bolster my chances in the exam. The location of my name at the end of the alphabet ensured that I was one of the last candidates to be interviewed. It was late in the afternoon when I was summoned.

Father Davis was sitting in one of two wooden chairs in an otherwise empty room. He gestured towards the chair in front of him.

"Take a seat," he said.

He was a slightly built man in his mid-thirties, his dark hair showing the first few strands of grey. There were tired lines around his eyes. He had already interviewed thirty-five of my classmates. It was obvious he was just as keen as I to get the session over with.

"So, Peter," he said, "What do you think about transubstantiation?"

I gulped.

"Transubstantiation?"

He leaned forward in his chair.

"Yes. Transubstantiation."

It was the last thing I had expected him to ask. Here was one of the leading lights of the new theology and he was asking me about *transubstantiation*? Thomas Aquinas, in the Middle Ages, had used this concept to explain the process by which the bread and wine at Mass became transformed into the body and blood of Christ. It was about distinguishing between what Aquinas called the *substance* of a thing as opposed to its *accidents,* or appearance.

"What do I think about it?" I repeated.

"Yes. Go on. Tell me."

He leaned back in his chair, pursing his lips between two fingers.

I took a deep breath.

"Well, as a matter of fact, I don't think much about it at all," I said. "I don't see the point of using Aristotelian metaphysics to explain a religious mystery. After all, that's not really what the Eucharist is all about. Surely it's more important to understand the Eucharist as a communal celebration renewing Christ's life in His people."

I paused. He looked at me impassively.

"So you think Aquinas is old hat?" he asked.

"For people today," I said. "He's simply irrelevant. People today don't worry about arcane rationalizations of mysteries. They have to get on with their lives. What they need from religion is the strength and encouragement they can get from being part of a caring community. And that's what the Eucharist is supposed to offer them, isn't it?"

Father Davis slowly got up out of his chair. He raised his arms high in a long stretch.

"I've been sitting here too long," he said. "You're right, of course. That is what the Eucharist is all about. So go off and make it happen. You'll be a good priest."

He laughed and held out his hand. Surprised, I shook it and made for the door. Then, I turned back to look at him.

"Thank you," I said.

Seven years later, I was to read another of his books, *A Question of Conscience.* He had written it to explain why he had left the Church.

On June 29 1961, I was ordained a priest, along with thirty-five of my classmates. I was twenty-four years old. Because there were so many of us, we were each allowed to invite only two family members to the ceremony. My mother and Doreen arrived early to secure front seats. When the long ceremony was over, they came up to receive my first official blessing as a priest. I was uncomfortable seeing them kneeling there in front of me. I quickly made the sign of the cross over them, and the official photographer snapped a picture for posterity. My mother got up and hugged me. There were tears in her eyes. For her, it was the moment she had prayed about for years.

Afterwards, we all went to the refectory where brunch had been laid out for us. We sat with some of the other families. The big room was unusually loud with excited chatter.

"How did you like the ceremony?" I asked Doreen. "It's a long time to spend in a church."

"I thought it was wonderful," she said, her eyes gleaming. "All those young men with their strong male voices singing that gorgeous Gregorian chant!"

After our families left, we all gathered in the smoking room. From there, we were called individually to the Superior General's office to be given our first appointments as priests. The office was on the second floor of a part of the college known as the Superior's Wing. Piet Van Breemen passed me coming down the stairs. He was looking glum.

"I'm being sent to Dublin University," he said, "for English studies. It's all your fault, Bruno. They must have thought I liked English after doing that Eliot play."

Halfway down a short corridor was a door marked OFFICE. Seated at a large mahogany desk was the Superior General, Father 'Jock' McLaughlin. He was a heavy-set Scotsman with thick, hanging jowls and bushy eyebrows. I had never actually spoken to him before, though I had seen him in the halls and in the chapel.

"Congratulations on your ordination, Peter," he said without looking up. "The Council has decided that you should go to Durham University. Go and see Father Duggan for details. Good luck." That was all. I was clearly dismissed.

"Thank you," I said.

I stood in the hallway outside, feeling slightly dazed. After six years of philosophy and theology, I had just been sentenced to three more years of study. I would be twenty-seven by the time I graduated. I had known this was a possibility. But I was quite unprepared for the reality.

A head popped out of an office further down the hall.

"Bruno, get yourself in here."

It was Father Louis Duggan, the procurator in charge of finances. He was a cheerful, overweight priest who wore spectacles with thick, bottle-glass lenses. Spending all day at a desk, working with enormous ledgers, probably accounted for his weight and short-sightedness.

"Here are your Mass stipends," he said, handing me an envelope. "They should see you through until you get to Durham."

Pious Catholics pay priests to say Mass for their intentions. While Mill Hill priests were housed and fed by the Society, these personal stipends helped pay for our other incidental expenses.

"Thanks," I said, turning to leave.

"Hold on, there," Father Duggan said. "You need to know where you're going in Durham. You will be living at Burn Hall. You'll commute into the university from there. You've been accepted at St. Cuthbert's, a college for non-resident students. Rinty Monaghan will help you get settled."

Rinty! I was surprised and pleased. I had forgotten that Rinty was there.

That night I packed my suitcase so that I would be ready to leave first thing the next morning. As I lay in bed looking at the empty bookshelves and bare walls, it finally sank in. I was now an ordained priest. My life was going to be very different. I was off to become a student at a secular university surrounded by students six years younger than me. And half of them would be girls. What would they think of me? What would they think of this strange, clerical creature in their midst? A man set apart by God.

But I was going to be with Rinty again for another two years. I would not be alone. Encouraged by that happy thought, I quickly fell asleep.

MILL HILL

Arsenic and Old Lace at Mill Hill, London, England

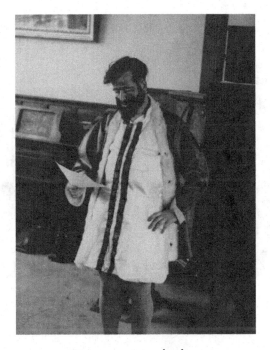

Rinty, practicing his lines

New member of the Mill Hill Order, June 1959

Smoking room at Mill Hill where all the plays were performed

My ordination at Mill Hill. June 29, 1961

PART SIX

DURHAM UNIVERSITY AND THE USA

1961-1964

CHAPTER 46

"I don't want to go to church!" Six-year-old Barnabas was standing in the front hall at Fernhurst, sulking.

"You have to," my mother said. She was holding his shoe, loosening the lace.

"Why? Just because Peter's doing the Mass?"

"No. Because it's Sunday."

"I don't want to go!"

"You have to. I can't leave you here by yourself."

"I'm not going!"

It was the summer break before school started. Barnabas was not the least bit impressed that his elder brother was now a priest. I was upstairs going over my sermon. I had been asked to do the noon Mass in Midhurst, a small town a short distance from Fernhurst.

"Come on, Barnabas, put your shoe on," my mother said. "We'll miss the bus if you don't hurry."

I ran down the stairs, stuffing my notes into my pocket. I snatched Barnabas up from behind and swung him around in the air. He started to giggle in spite of himself.

"So you don't want to come to my Mass, then? Well, we'll see about that. Do you want to be tickled to death instead? Do you? Do you?"

By the time I had finished with him, Barnabas had quite forgotten that he didn't want to go to church.

Midhurst was a busy little country parish and the pastor, Father O'Rourke, had asked me to help him over the summer. Before long I was assisting at baptisms and weddings and the occasional funeral. The parishioners were mostly middle-class civil servants, shopkeepers, and farmers, but there were also a few semi-aristocratic families who had lived in the area for many years. These people typically owned large country estates, sent their children to elite Catholic boarding schools, and bred ponies to compete in the polo matches at nearby Cowdray Park.

On Sundays I usually heard confessions for half an hour before Mass. I had quickly learned that most people confessed by rote. It was as if there was no connection between the sins confessed and their real lives. They almost always confessed in generalities and were happy to be sent away with three *Hail Marys* or an *Our Father* as a penance. But one day, a woman came into the confessional who did not follow the usual pattern.

"Bless me, Father, for I have sinned," she said, and added in a dramatic whisper, "my husband forces me to practise birth control."

She paused, as if expecting me to make a comment, and then continued.

"We have two children and I really don't want to have any more. But he just won't leave me alone. He wants sex two or three times a week. There's no way I can stop him."

"So why do you think you're committing a sin?" I asked. "Contraception is not something evil in itself."

For a moment there was silence, followed by a more intense whisper.

"That's not what Father O'Rourke says. Father O'Rourke says using a condom for sex is always a sin. He says the only way it's not a sin is if I lie there and make sure I don't enjoy it. Well, I've tried that but it doesn't work. My husband just gets horribly angry."

"I'm not surprised," I said. "In any event, at the moment, the Church is quite divided about contraception. It will certainly be debated at the Vatican Council. For now, all you have to do is decide what is right for you. It only becomes a sin if you act against your own conscience."

"What do you mean?" She sounded indignant. "You think you know better than Father O'Rourke? He's been a priest much longer than you. You're just a beginner. If Father O'Rourke says it's a sin, it must be a sin."

I tried to explain the Church's teaching on the primacy of conscience but she refused to listen. Clearly she did not want to give up on the idea that she was a sinner. In the end, I told her to say one *Our Father* as a penance and recited the traditional rite of absolution. As she left, I heard her muttering something about 'young priests these days'.

When Mass was over, a distinguished looking gentleman came up to me and introduced himself. He was dressed in fashionable country tweed and sported a trim, military moustache.

"Brigadier Henry Caruthers," he said in a loud, parade-ground voice. He shook my hand vigorously. "Great sermon. Don't often get intelligent ones these days."

"Thank you," I said. "I hope it was helpful."

"You free for dinner?" he boomed. "Be glad to have you. Great cook. Send the car to pick you up. Six o'clock tonight. Sound alright?"

"Well, thank you," I said. "That's very kind of you."

That evening, promptly at six o'clock, our doorbell rang. A chauffer was standing there, resplendent in a dark blue uniform, his cap under his arm.

"Here to pick up the Reverend," he said to my mother as she answered the door.

"Peter, your ride's here," my mother called.

Outside, a sleek, black Bentley purred in the driveway.

"My name's Robert," said the chauffer, holding the rear door open for me. I sank into a soft, brown, leather seat that smelled of cigar smoke. I noticed a built-in silver tray with a crystal decanter and matching glasses. "The Brigadier says for you to help yourself to the scotch," Robert said, over his shoulder, as we pulled out onto the road.

Fifteen minutes later the Bentley slid past two massive gilded gates that opened smoothly in front of us. A long, gravel driveway led up to an imposing Georgian mansion, its tall mullioned windows aglow. Robert ushered me into the front hall.

"There you are," boomed the Brigadier, advancing on me from an open doorway to the left. "Come and meet the Grangers. Arrived just before you."

He took my elbow and led me into a large, richly carpeted drawing room. The red brocade walls were almost hidden by a huge collection of gilt-framed oil paintings. A cheerful log fire burned beneath a white marble mantle. A young couple stood by the fireplace holding martini glasses, and an older woman came towards me with outstretched hand.

"My wife, Annabelle," the Brigadier roared. "Call her Belle."

"Father Peter, so glad you could come," Belle said with a warm smile. Her dark eyes glowed against pale, almost translucent skin. She wore a simple, black cocktail dress with a light silk scarf gathered at one shoulder. "Come and meet Frances and Tony Granger. They live next door."

Frances Granger was an attractive girl in her late twenties. Her blond hair was cut short and tucked behind her ears, revealing two tiny diamond earrings. Her husband was wearing a dark blue business suit and a monogrammed silk tie. He gave me a keen, appraising look as he shook hands.

"Good to meet you, Father Peter," he said. "My wife and I are relative newcomers to the parish. I hear you belong to a missionary order."

"Mill Hill Society," the Brigadier boomed as he mixed a martini for me. "Capital chaps. Met some in Pakistan. Ran schools. Not allowed to convert Muslims, y'know."

A butler appeared in the doorway. "Mr. and Mrs. Galsworthy," he announced. A tall woman, wearing a long pink gown with a white fur stole swept into the room. Behind her a short bald man in a yellow plaid jacket was handing the butler his hat and gloves.

"So good to see you, Belle," said the woman in an exaggerated upper class drawl. "It's been absolutely ages since Basil and I've been here. We simply *must* see you more awften, don't you think?"

By 'awften' I imagined she meant 'often' in ordinary speech. I recognized the voice immediately. It was the woman who had come to confession that morning.

"Irene, m'dear, this is Father Peter," the Brigadier declaimed, introducing me. "Basil, meet Father Peter."

"Oh, I know you," Irene said, dismissing me. "You're one of those new priests in training at the parish. I don't know where Father O'Rourke drags them up." She turned to the Brigadier. "I'll have one of those divine martinis you make, Henry dear."

Tony Granger came over to me, giving Irene a look of distaste. "Ignore her," he said quietly. "She's just too full of herself to have any regard for other people. I don't know how Basil puts up with her."

I was already beginning to regret accepting the Brigadier's invitation.

"Dinner is served," the butler announced from the doorway. Belle came over and gave me her arm, leading me through the hall to the dining room. "Would you mind saying grace for us, Father Peter?"

she asked when everyone was seated. I obliged and began to feel more comfortable as the food was served. Frances was curious to know more about the Mill Hill Fathers. She was surprised to hear that I was going off to university. Then, inevitably, the conversation turned to the topic of the upcoming Vatican Council.

"What did your professors have to say about birth control?" Tony Granger asked. "I'm kind of hoping the Council will come up with a more enlightened view of marriage and sex."

Before I had a chance to reply, Irene turned on me.

"Some young priests don't follow the Church's teaching," she said, her eyes full of spite. "They say contraception is not sinful. How can they be priests if they say that?"

It was like a slap in the face. There was an awkward silence.

I felt trapped. She was challenging me to break the confidentiality of her confession. I had to struggle to refocus on the conversation.

"The Catholic Church has always preached the primacy of conscience," I said, choosing my words carefully. "The Church's position on birth control is still being discussed by theologians. It's obviously going to be discussed at the Vatican Council. Right now, we just have to decide for ourselves, which is perhaps a good thing. Ultimately we have to take responsibility for our own lives, no matter what the Church tells us. We have to be adult about our religion, just as we have to be about everything else."

Irene refused to let up.

"You trivialize what the Church says is a mortal sin," she said. "How can you give an *Our Father* as penance for using a condom?" She glared at me.

Everyone froze. Then her husband stirred uncomfortably.

"This is an excellent wine, Henry," he said, turning to the Brigadier.

The Brigadier was still gaping at Irene.

"Yes, it is," Frances added hastily. "Where did you get it, Henry?"

The Brigadier shifted his attention to Frances, relieved.

"Paris," he roared. "The only place for wine. Chose it myself. Little shop in Montmartre."

For once, I appreciated his stentorian voice. It broke the chill that had descended on the dinner table. Individual little conversations started up. Tony began to talk to me about an article he was writing for *The Tablet*, a rather esoteric magazine for Catholic intellectuals. Frances and Belle were discussing French cooking, while the Brigadier and Basil were into vintage wines. Irene sat isolated for a while before breaking into Frances and Belle's conversation with her own dogmatic views on French cooking.

Irene and Basil were the first to leave. As Belle returned from seeing them off, she came over to me with an anxious look on her face.

"Father Peter, I have to apologize for Irene. She's terribly conservative about the Church. It's strange, because she doesn't seem to be an insecure person. But she wants the Catholic Church to give her certainty. She doesn't want to have to question anything about religion. I hope she didn't make you feel too uncomfortable."

"I must admit, it was a bit hard to take," I said. "I never thought anyone would use the seal of confession against me. I suppose a sharp learning curve is to be expected for a new priest."

"Should never have invited the woman," the Brigadier muttered through his moustache.

"Don't feel you have to apologize," I said. "Dinner was delicious and I enjoyed meeting you all. Thank you."

It was a relief to sink into the leather comfort of the Bentley as Robert drove me home. The tension in my shoulders began to ease and I realized how unprepared I was to meet the challenge of other people's problems. For too many years, I had focused exclusively on my own.

CHAPTER 47

September came, and with it the long train journey up to Durham. Rinty greeted me at Burn Hall with a smile as wide as a bus.

"Looks like we're going to be together for another two years," he said. "Guess who else is here? Nick Morgan. It's going to be like old times. Come and meet Ray Klapper. He's the boss here now."

Father Raymond Klapper was a genial, older priest who had never been to a university himself, so he was happy to leave us students to our own devices.

We were allocated rooms on the top floor. They would have been the servants' quarters when it was still a stately home. My room had a low ceiling that sloped towards a single dormer window. Outside, blocking the view over the valley, was a sandstone balustrade that ran all the way around the top of the building.

The room was quite large. It had probably accommodated four servants at one time. The faded, flowered wallpaper looked as if it had not been replaced since those days. There was a large table with a gooseneck desk lamp, a small bookshelf, a washstand, and an iron bed that looked as if it, too, was a relic from the previous century.

"What do you think?" Rinty asked, standing behind me as I surveyed the room.

"It's grand," I said. "Much bigger than we were used to at Mill Hill."

"All the better for partying. Last year we had quite a bash up here with some of the Catholic students from the Newman Centre." Rinty walked over to the window. "We put a case of beer outside on the balcony to chill. We must have had fifteen or sixteen people in here."

"Sounds promising," I said.

The following day, Rinty took me on a tour of Durham University. The older colleges were clustered around the cathedral. One, University College, was housed in the old Norman castle. Our college,

St. Cuthbert's, was located on a narrow street called the South Bailey. Rinty introduced me to the principal, Professor Grant, and helped me register for my courses.

"You have to wear a gown to all your lectures," Rinty told me. "There's an extra one at Burn Hall you can use. It's a bit ratty but it'll save you having to buy one. You might want to get yourself a Cuthbert's scarf, though. You can tell which college students come from by the colour of their scarves. St. Cuthbert's is white and green."

In those days the requirements for the first year of the General Arts degree were four subject areas, one of which had to be a language. The language requirement was not a problem as I was reasonably proficient in Latin. The other two subjects that I had taken for my A-levels were history and English. But I needed a fourth. Rinty suggested I take geography.

"There's a first year geography course in climatology that's a breeze," he said to me. "The professor is an old guy who's been here for years. He teaches out of St. Cuthbert's and is an easy marker. You should sign up with him."

"But I've never taken a geography course since Freshfield," I protested. "Are you sure I can manage it?"

"No problem," Rinty stated cheerfully. "I took the course last year and it was a breeze."

"OK," I said doubtfully. "I'll give it a try."

It was a big mistake. With no background in the subject, I struggled from the outset. It did not help that the old professor lectured in a dull monotone. He droned away from the moment he walked in to the moment he walked out. There was no opportunity for questions. I soon found it impossible to stay awake. In desperation I chose a seat in the front row, right under his nose. I thought such proximity might stimulate adrenalin. But it was no use. My head was constantly drooping like some bobblehead duck. Foolishly I stuck it out, refusing to transfer to another course until it was too late.

Each student at Durham was assigned a moral tutor whose duty it was to monitor academic progress. Halfway through the year I received a summons to discuss my problems over a glass of sherry. Tony McDougall was a mild man who taught undergraduate courses in English literature with refreshing enthusiasm. He had a thin, white face and large round glasses that gave him an owlish look. He had rooms on the top floor of a mediaeval row house near the cathedral.

"Come in, Peter," he said as he opened the door to his study.

The walls were completely hidden by shelves crowded with books. Books were everywhere. The room was buried in books. Books balanced precariously on chairs. Books scattered in mounds over the floor.

Eventually McDougall freed up a chair for me by tilting its pile of books to join the heaps already covering the carpet. He apologized for the clutter with a vague wave of his hand. Reaching down into the bottom draw of a battered wooden desk, he retrieved a bottle of sherry and two glasses.

"I hear you are having some difficulty with climatology. Professor Gibson thinks you're suffering from sleep apnea. But you seem wide awake in my classes. What gives?"

"I made a mistake," I told him. I explained how I had followed Rinty's advice by taking a subject in which I had no background at all. "I just don't find geography interesting. No matter how hard I try, I can't seem to stay awake during the lectures."

"You seem to be doing well in all your other courses, including mine. So stick at it. You only need it for first year and then you can drop it. Have another sherry."

And that was the extent of my moral tutoring.

One evening, early in the spring term, Father Klapper called Rinty and me to his room on the second floor.

"Mill Hill wants you boys to spend the summer in America," he said as he lounged in his big, padded office chair. "As soon as exams are over you are to fly to Albany, New York. They have established a secretariat there to organize fundraising and promote vocations. You will be sent to do supply work in various parishes and to raise money for the missions."

"This sounds exciting," Rinty said with enthusiasm as we left the room. "I've always wanted to go to America, the land of Elvis, milkshakes, and Camelot!"

Like most young people in England in 1962, we had been captivated by the idealism of John F. Kennedy's speeches. America seemed to be bursting with youthful energy. Colleges and universities were beginning to fill with baby boomers eager to break out of the conservatism of the fifties. To spend the summer there was an opportunity not to be missed.

Chapter 48

Shortly after my birthday in May, Rinty and I left aboard a flight bound for Idlewild Airport, New York. From there we flew to Albany in a rather ancient Dakota belonging to Mohawk Airlines. We were met at the airport by Father Piet Dirven, who was the rector of Mill Hill's house in Albany. He was a young, tall, dark-haired Dutch priest who disliked his job as an administrator, but was very good at it. He had already arranged our work schedules.

"You must both learn to drive," he said, much to our delight. "You're no use to us unless you can drive. We have two older cars. You can choose whichever one you want and spend the rest of the week practising. I've arranged for you to take driving tests early next week."

The Albany house property was a farm that had been donated to Mill Hill. It had plenty of dirt trails for us to practise on. My car was a delight to behold. It was a bright red 1956 Dodge Custom Royal. With its elegant chrome tail fins and a push-button gear selector, it was a thing of beauty. The front grillwork was slightly rusted, but under the hood the V8 engine purred with effortless power. After a day or so I was ready to try the public roads, and the following week I passed the driving test without any problem.

"Your first assignment is to Holy Cross Parish in Providence, Rhode Island," Piet Dirven said as I walked into his office clutching my brand new driver's license. "It's about 200 miles from here, but it's a nice drive. See you on Monday."

I arrived at the Holy Cross Rectory shortly before seven o'clock on the Friday evening. Father Pietro, the effusive Italian pastor, welcomed me with open arms.

"You a Pietro too," he said, stepping back. "We fit together well! Here is Rosa, my cook. She has splendid meal for us. You like Italian food, yes? Sit down. We start with nice glass of wine."

It was a comfortable little house, spotlessly clean, with elegant Italian drapery and furniture. The dining room table was already set for the evening meal. Over supper Pietro told me about his parish; how he was by himself, but an old retired Augustinian priest usually helped him out on Sundays.

"He's sick, now. Can't come anymore. Please, you stay for long time, yes?"

"I'll have to check with my boss," I said cautiously. "He said I had to be back on Monday."

We spent a long time over supper getting to know each other. We were just enjoying our espressos when the phone rang. Pietro pushed his chair back and walked over to the sideboard. He picked up the receiver and almost immediately a shocked look crossed his face.

"I come at once," he said quickly and hung up. He turned to me. "Construction site cave-in; two little boys buried. I must go. You come too, no?"

"Of course," I said, getting up.

Pietro backed his car out of the driveway with a squeal of tires. He drove fast, skillfully negotiating the corners of darkened streets, our headlights briefly catching the startled faces of evening strollers. Then we drove into a darkened subdivision still under construction. A single, fierce, bright glow appeared ahead of us. Next to it, red and blue lights flashed across the silhouettes of fire trucks and police cars. As we got closer we could see a small crowd of people gathered around two stark, white lights. A roaring yellow excavator had been digging into a large pile of sand. While it paused briefly, two firemen cautiously probed around the hole it had made.

"A group of kids were digging tunnels in there," a policeman explained. "The whole pile collapsed on them. Two of them are trapped underneath. They're brothers. I'm afraid there's not much chance they'll still be alive. The parents are over there."

Pietro walked over to where the boys' parents were huddled close together, watching the firemen. He put his arms around them. They stood there, a still group, amid the roar of generators and machines. Then, someone yelled, "Stop! There's one."

In the sudden silence, the firemen dug frantically. The limp body of a small boy was pulled clear. A paramedic pushed down rhythmically on his chest. Another attached an oxygen mask. They lifted him onto a stretcher. Still working on him, they rushed over to an ambulance. They hoisted him in and immediately sped off into the black night, siren blaring, blue lights flashing.

"You wait here," Pietro said to me. "I go to hospital." He ran to his car and drove off after the ambulance.

A few minutes later, there was another shout. "There's the other one." A pale face, its eyes, nose and mouth smudged with sand, appeared under the glaring lights. Quickly, the firemen freed the rest of the body. They laid him on a stretcher and lifted him into the second ambulance. His parents climbed in after him.

"Ride with me in the front, Father," the driver said.

As we raced along unfamiliar streets, I stared out blankly into the darkness. Cars and trucks pulled out of our way, pushed aside by the shrieking siren. I felt the hopelessness and grief of the two people riding behind us. For them, all the normal cares of everyday life had suddenly fallen away, extinguished by this one terrible tsunami of sorrow.

In the hospital waiting room, Pietro and I sat with the boys' parents on hard plastic chairs. Everything felt artificial under the cold, harsh glare of the fluorescent lights. Then, a doctor came through the doors leading to the emergency ward. He shook his head.

"I'm so sorry," he said gently. "There was nothing we could do."

We stood up, while the boy's mother sat there sobbing, her arms held tight against her stomach to contain the pain. Her husband beside her looked utterly bewildered, unable to comprehend the finality of the blow that had been dealt them.

Pietro knelt down on the floor in front of them. He took both their hands in his, looking up into their grief-filled faces.

"It hurts so much when it's so unexpected," he said. "No chance to say goodbye. They are with God now. Just as we all will be one day. Do not blame yourselves. They were just being boys, wanting to play in the sand."

The front doors of the waiting room swung open and a small group of relatives came rushing in. Pietro got up to greet them.

"We go in now," Pietro said. "Father Peter and I will give the last rites."

We crowded into a curtained area where the two boys lay side by side. While Pietro read the prayers I helped with the anointing and together we said the final blessing. Then, we left so that the family and friends could say their farewells privately.

I must have looked as shaken as I felt. As we drove back to the rectory, Pietro actually apologized to me.

"Too bad this happened and on your first night," he said. "We priests act like we have all the answers. We don't. To the parents, God seems so arbitrary, so unfair."

The next day I was scheduled to preach at the evening Mass. Pietro was busy all morning with a parish council meeting, so I decided to go for a short drive. I could not get last night's tragedy out of my head. I drove south to Charlestown and found a secluded spot among the sand dunes by the sea.

The ocean was flat and calm, sparkling in the sunlight. I sat listening to the splash of the long, shallow swells as they broke and rippled along the beach. The sound was soothing after the numbing, nightmarish roar of machines the previous evening. I scooped up the warm sand and let it trickle between my fingers. Water and sand, how could they both be so smooth and yet so deadly?

It occurred to me that, perhaps more than for anyone else, a priest's life is constantly touched by the extremes of human experience. For a priest, the joy of birth and the grief of death are constantly repeated. It was something I was going to have to get used to.

In spite of Pietro's pleas, Father Dirven ordered me back to Albany after the weekend. He had just heard from Durham that I had failed my geography exam. Although the news was not unexpected, I was bitterly disappointed. I could no longer allow myself to be absorbed by my American adventure. I was confined to barracks in Albany for the next month, studying the science of global weather patterns. Supply work would be limited to local parishes on weekends. It was an effort to focus on geography while being distracted by Connie Francis' hit song that summer:

> "Put away the books, we're outta school!
> The weather's warm, but we'll play it cool!
> We're on vacation, havin' lots of fun!
> V-A-C-A-T-I-O-N! In the summer sun!"

In August I returned early to Durham, bleeding stress and anxiety from every pore. I had never felt such tension before an exam. It was only when I sat with the question paper open in front of me that I relaxed. All was well. I knew the answers. I could do it.

When I came out of the exam, the campus around me was strangely quiet. Most students were not yet back from the summer break. I walked alone down the narrow, cobbled street from St. Cuthbert's to the river. At this point, it loops around the great rock on which the massive Norman cathedral stands. The two majestic towers of the east facade rose high above the trees that clothed the riverbank in summer green. The water was broad and calm here, just before it tumbled over a weir downstream.

A long, sleek boat from a college rowing club slid past me, silent except for the stroke count from the cox. The oar blades flashed rhythmically, skimming the water before dipping again in perfect unison. There was such a feeling of harmony between those rowers and the river, between the trees and the cathedral. That harmony seemed to settle deep, deep down inside me, providing a profound feeling of peace. I felt confirmed in my calling as a priest.

Of course, it helped that I was done with geography forever.

CHAPTER 49

" B runo!" Rinty yelled from the bottom of the stairs, "Phone!"
I was sitting at my desk in Burn Hall, going over course selections for my second year at Durham.

"Coming." I pushed back the chair and went to the extension in the hallway outside my room. It was an ancient phone that originally had been installed as an intercom for summoning servants. Nowadays it rarely, if ever, produced a ringtone. When I picked up the receiver, the line hissed and crackled so badly I could barely make out the voice at the other end. It was my sister Elizabeth. She was calling from her new home in Crowborough, near the Ashdown Forest in Sussex.

"Peter, you have to come right away." She sounded desperate. "Mother and the three kids are here. They had to leave Fernhurst."

"What do you mean, they had to leave?" I was shocked.

"Mother called last week. Granny ran out of money. She couldn't pay the rent on their house anymore, so they had to leave. Kenneth drove down last week and brought them here."

"But you don't have enough space for them all. And what about all their stuff?"

"Gemma and Mother are sharing a room and the boys are in the baby's room. Their furniture is piled up in the garage. But once the baby arrives, I don't know what we'll do . . . we have to get Mother to contact Malcolm, whether she likes it or not."

I noticed how she was calling my father 'Malcolm' now.

"Mother has to start taking responsibility. Please come down and talk to her, Peter. She'll listen to you."

"Of course," I said. "I'll take the first train tomorrow. Somehow, we'll get this sorted out."

Kenneth was waiting for me at the station in Crowborough. To my surprise, he had a broad smile on his face. "Good to see you, Peter," he said, pumping my hand warmly. "Elizabeth will be happy you're here."

"How is she?" I asked. I had been worrying about her all the way down on the train.

"Coping," he said cheerfully. "The house is a bit crowded, but we manage."

He sounded so solidly reassuring that I immediately started to feel less anxious. I watched him as he skillfully steered the car through the sharp bends in the winding country road. Being a short man, he had to drive with his chin raised just to see over the steering wheel. But his broad shoulders swayed comfortably with the car, as if he was still rolling with the waves that rocked his wartime corvette. I could see how he would have won the complete confidence of his crew. They would never have doubted he would bring them all safely back to harbour.

We drove through the village and turned onto a gravel driveway. It curved down to a large, two-storied stone house with leaded, oak windows and a brown, ceramic-tiled roof. My pregnant sister came out the front door to meet us, her four-year-old twins clutching at her skirts.

"Welcome to Oak Lodge," she said, with a tired smile, and gave me a hug. "These two girls are a bit shy, but they'll soon get used to you. We've run out of bedrooms, so you'll have to sleep on a camp bed in the cloakroom. I hope you don't mind."

My mother was coming down the stairs to the front hall as we walked into the house. She had the apprehensive look of a small child about to be scolded. I gave her a hug to reassure her and we all moved into the living room. It was a bright room at the front of the house. Large windows looked onto a lawn, fringed with heather that ran down the length of the driveway. My mother and I settled onto a couch and Kenneth took an armchair close to the open fireplace.

"I'll make some tea," Elizabeth said, and disappeared into the kitchen across the hall. Once she got back and we were all settled, I asked where Gemma and the boys were.

"They're down the road playing on the golf course." Elizabeth said. "They'll be back in a minute. I've sent the twins to look for them."

"We need to figure out how we can give you your house back," I said. "Coming down here on the train, I thought about taking time off from university. I could find a job and rent a place for Mother and the kids."

"You can't do that," my mother said instantly. "You're a priest."

"There's such a thing as worker-priests," I told her. "There are lots of them in France and South America. I don't see why I couldn't be one in England. I'm sure Mill Hill would agree if they knew our situation."

Elizabeth looked doubtfully at Kenneth.

"That sounds a bit drastic," she said. "There are a few things we should try first, like tracking down Malcolm in Canada."

"You shouldn't give up university," Kenneth said firmly. "You have to finish your degree. We can take care of things here for the time being. I think our company lawyer can help find Malcolm. If he's practising law, he'll be registered with the Law Society in Toronto."

"But it's just not fair. You can't look after Mother and the kids with a baby on the way and the twins to think about."

My mother burst into tears. "This is all my fault," she wailed. "I wish I was dead. Then, at least I wouldn't be a bother to anyone."

"Don't be so ridiculous, Mother," Elizabeth said, her voice revealing her impatience. "You've always prayed to get back together with Malcolm. This is your chance to do something about it."

Just then Gemma, Dominic, and Barnabas came bursting into the room. They tumbled onto the couch and I was buried under an excited mound of arms and legs.

"We didn't know you were here." "How come nobody told us?" "How long can you stay?" They were all talking at once.

"I only just got here," I said, pleased at how glad they were to see me. "I've got a whole week before I have to get back to school. We've got lots of time."

Next morning Kenneth and Elizabeth drove my mother into Crowborough to meet with their lawyer. I stayed behind to baby-sit. It was a bright sunny day, surprisingly hot for late August. The twins begged me to blow up their little, plastic paddling pool. We set it up in the middle of the lawn and all five children spent the morning gleefully romping in and out of the water and spraying each other with the garden hose.

I sat watching them, their wet bodies glistening in the sunlight, their squeals and shrieks echoing around the garden. I envied them for their ability to be so completely absorbed in the moment, oblivious to any adult problems. Then I heard the crunch of tires on the gravel driveway. Kenneth's green Rover was just pulling up to the front door.

"We had some success," he said as he got out. "Our lawyer seems to think we can get in touch with Malcolm quite easily."

"That lawyer's such a nice man," my mother declared as we walked into the house.

"He's going to write an official letter," Elizabeth explained, "saying that unless Malcolm agrees to bring his family to Canada, legal proceedings will be started against him."

"Malcolm is registered with the Law Society in Canada," Kenneth added. He's a public trustee for the government of Ontario. He'd probably lose his job if it became known that he'd abandoned his wife and kids. I don't think it will be very long before we hear back from him."

Kenneth was quite right. A short time after I got back to Durham, Elizabeth called me again to say that the threat of legal action had produced results. My father hastily purchased plane tickets and, in the spring of 1963, my mother and the three children left for Canada. They settled into an apartment in Toronto.

I could only hope that at last they might have a more stable family life.

CHAPTER 50

I had found my first year of university life disappointing. I was surrounded by young students freed, for the first time, from the restrictive controls of family and school. They had moved into colleges or residences and were quickly making new friends. I shared their feeling of new-found freedom, but found it difficult relating to them. I was older by six years and aware that my clerical collar set me apart as some kind of freak.

One day, a few weeks before Easter, I was leaving the library on Palace Green when I heard a shout from behind me.

"Hey, Father Peter, wait up."

It was Wilfred Coates, one of the students from the Catholic chaplaincy. He ran to catch up with me, his college gown flapping behind him.

"Just came from practice in the cathedral," he panted as he reached me.

Wilfred was in the mediaeval music program, which allowed him to use the great cathedral organ.

"How would you like to join us for Student Cross?" he said between breaths. "We need a chaplain."

"Student Cross? What's that?"

"It's a walking pilgrimage to Walsingham. Students from all over England walk to Walsingham during Holy Week. Each group carries a big wooden cross. The idea is to pray for world peace."

It was such a coincidence. Exactly thirteen years earlier, outside my grandmother's house in Walsingham, I had first talked to a Mill Hill priest. He had been a chaplain to one of the university pilgrim groups at the time. I remembered how the students had sat around on the sidewalks in Friday Market tending to their sore feet.

"I'm not sure I could do it," I said. "I've never done any hiking before. I doubt that my feet would last. How far is it to Walsingham from here?"

"Oh, we don't start from here," Wilfred said. "It'd be too far to do in a week. No, we start just outside Nottingham. We walk about twenty miles each day. It really isn't that bad. We sleep in parish halls or schools. The parishioners prepare food for us. It's actually quite fun."

I hesitated. I wasn't sure I was comfortable with being part of such a public religious spectacle. I had always been uneasy at the way Catholics wallowed in the sufferings of Christ during Lent. On the other hand, it would be an opportunity to revisit my childhood haunts in Walsingham. And, as chaplain, I might get the students to focus on the more positive aspects of pilgrimage.

"All right," I agreed finally, still feeling a little doubtful.

A few days later I met with Wilf in the chaplaincy common room. We listened to a presentation by one of the students who had been on the walk the previous year. "Make sure you bring plenty of socks," he said. "Spend time walking around in bare feet to help thicken your skin. Some people say it helps to soak your feet in rubbing alcohol to prevent blisters. And if you have a new pair of hiking boots, break them in well beforehand."

Unfortunately Rinty could not join us. He had been asked to help in his home parish for Holy Week. But he supplied me with a decent-sized backpack and some camping gear and teased me mercilessly as I padded around Burn Hall in bare feet for two weeks.

On the Friday before Holy Week, our little group of fourteen pilgrims assembled at the university chaplaincy. We took the train down to Nottingham and spent the night on the floor of the parish hall in the village of Keyworth.

We started out early the following morning, dividing into groups of four to take turns carrying the heavy, oak cross. Sometimes, we would sing a familiar hymn, but mostly we walked silently, enjoying the crisp morning air. The fields and trees along the way were fresh and green with new spring growth.

Gradually I became a little more comfortable with what we were doing. We were on quiet country roads with very little traffic. As we passed through villages and hamlets, people would stop and silently watch us. No one shouted abuse. No one made mocking remarks. They were just curious.

At noon we stopped at a pub in the village of Willoughby-on-the-Wolds. There was a patch of grass next to the pub where we could eat our sandwiches and have a quiet beer while resting our feet. The cross had been placed upright against the wall of the pub.

"I think we should talk a bit about why we're here," I suggested, as we were finishing our lunches. "What's so significant about a pilgrimage that made you all want to come?"

My question seemed to take the students by surprise. For a while no one said anything. Finally Wilf volunteered.

"Well, I see this as a kind of last resort. Like when people are desperately sick. They go looking for miracles. World peace seems pretty hopeless right now. Russia's sending nuclear missiles to Cuba. We could use a miracle!"

"True," said Jim, a thoughtful looking biology student. "But I don't really believe in miracles. The odds against one happening are zero. We have to be realistic."

"Perhaps we should think about this as we're walking," I suggested. "Let's talk about it more tonight."

We struggled into our backpacks, picked up the wooden cross, and set off down the road once more. We were heading towards the little farming town of Melton Mowbray where we were to spend the night.

When we arrived we found supper waiting for us, provided by a group of kindly parishioners. There were bowls of stew and fresh bread and the town's famous Stilton cheese. Afterwards, we washed the dishes and unrolled sleeping bags. But before we settled down, I gathered everyone into a circle. I had borrowed a candle from the church and when it was lit, I turned off all the lights.

"This is our chance to begin exploring what this pilgrimage means to us," I said. "We don't really even know each other yet. So I want to pass this candle around. When it comes to you, tell us your name and why you chose to come on this walk."

The effect was amazing. The simple little ritual generated a whole new feeling of inclusiveness. Their faces were lit by the flame as they spoke. The sense of security from the surrounding shadows encouraged even the most reticent. They spoke about themselves, their hopes, fears, and longings.

When the candle came back to me, I spoke about my own feelings of isolation. I talked about how I wanted to be accepted simply as one of them; how I hated being treated as somehow different, just because

I was a priest. Afterwards, as we climbed into our sleeping bags, the chorus of goodnights felt encouraging.

We set off the next morning only to find that the weather had changed. Dark, grey rain clouds swept low across the fields from the fens. The wind whipped and flailed at the trees and hedgerows. It tugged at our ponchos and beat blasts of icy rain into our faces. Soon our pants and socks were soaked.

It became a struggle to keep the heavy cross from slipping from our wet shoulders. On being relieved by a fresh foursome, we retreated gratefully to the rear of the column, appreciating the slight protection afforded by the walkers in front. By the time we arrived at the village of Corby Glen that evening, we were an exhausted and bedraggled little group of pilgrims.

In the warmth of the parish hall, we slowly recovered. It was sheer bliss to pull off waterlogged boots from aching feet and change into dry clothes. The heating registers around the walls were soon festooned with wet gear. Mugs of steaming hot cocoa took the chill out of our bodies and before long we were feeling a little less like drowned ducks and more like human beings.

That night we repeated our talk circle. Jim, the biologist, impressed us. He was interested in Buddhism. He talked about how, for centuries, pilgrims had journeyed to a sacred mountain in Tibet, but that really it was not the destination that was important to them so much as the personal transformation they experienced on the way.

"There's not much that I, as an individual, can do about world peace," he said. "But today I was thinking about my girlfriend. When I'm angry I give her the silent treatment. I just don't talk to her. If it's that hard for me to make peace, it's no wonder whole countries can't. Perhaps that's what I need to work at, rather than joining peace marches and demonstrations."

Each evening after that others in the group began to open up. They were clearly looking for purpose in their lives. They shared goals and uncertainties and explored their own potential for initiating change. I was amazed. It was a literal fulfillment of what Jim had described as the goal of the Buddhist and Hindu pilgrims: a personal transformation.

On the last mile, from the Slipper Chapel to Walsingham, we were joined by student groups who had carried crosses from other universities. By the time we reached Friday Market, there were over a hundred of us. We sat at the wooden tables outside the Black Lion pub enjoying beer and sandwiches. I looked across at my grandmother's old house and told the story about the poltergeist. Later we walked down Walsingham High Street to the grounds where the priory had once stood.

We sat on the grass around an altar set up under the ruins of a huge Gothic arch. It was the only remnant of the mediaeval priory church. A Dominican priest celebrated the Mass of the Easter liturgy. The crosses that had been carried from all over England were set in a circle. I looked around at our small group from Durham. I thought about how much we had all gained from the experience of the past week.

I had started off feeling isolated and insecure, wondering how I could break down the barrier of priesthood that separated me from the other students. Each day I had become more relaxed with them and they with me. The physical discomfort of blistered feet, the chill of the rain, and the cold, hard floors at night all combined to pull us closer together.

Back at Durham, I felt a change. Other students, seeing me included by their friends, became more relaxed around me. We would get into intense discussions about student rights and freedoms and the protests against the USA that were taking place in Latin America. They challenged me about the Church's position on abortion and birth control. I was surprised to discover their views were often much more dogmatic than my own.

The student president heard that I would be in America again for the summer. He asked me to represent them at the World Catholic Student Convention that was to take place that year in Washington. I made a quick phone call to Mill Hill and was able to agree.

After being an outsider for so long, it was good to finally feel at home in the university.

CHAPTER 51

Rinty and I had both been assigned to return to the USA for the summer. We were to fly together on a Boeing 707. A few weeks earlier one of these planes had crashed on takeoff at Orly Airport. Then, just the day before we were to leave, another one had crashed in South America. As we boarded our flight at Manchester Airport, many of the passengers around us were clearly apprehensive.

The stewardess demonstrating the safety equipment was very aware of the tension in the cabin.

"It's extremely unlikely that God will allow this plane to crash," she announced confidently, "because we have two of God's special people on board with us today."

There was some nervous laughter from the passengers. Rinty looked at me with a grin.

"Whatever works," he said with a shrug.

Once we were in the air, a stewardess brought us some champagne. "Compliments of a grateful captain and crew," she said. "Just make sure you use your influence with the Almighty to get us safely back down."

Rinty and I did not see very much of each other that summer as we were sent to different parishes around New York State. In August, I travelled to Washington for the student convention. It was held at Georgetown University. Unfortunately I had not been officially registered as a delegate, so I was only allowed to attend as an observer.

Robert Kennedy was the keynote speaker. I was surprised at the lukewarm reception he was given. The students were clearly disillusioned by his overly cautious support for the civil rights movement. He had advised the Freedom Riders to get off their buses and leave the whole question to peaceful settlement by the courts. The students had neither forgiven nor forgotten that piece of advice. He was greeted with some boos and only scattered applause. I had an aisle seat and saw the annoyed expression in Kennedy's cold blue eyes as he swept past me with his entourage of G-men.

There was a large contingent of students from Latin America at the conference. They organized information workshops about the interference of the Central Intelligence Agency in their countries. I attended a seminar given by students from Chile. They described how CIA agents had bombed churches and right wing organizations to make it appear to be the work of leftists. They would infiltrate left wing parades, displaying signs and shouting slogans designed to antagonize the military government. It was all an attempt to prevent the election of the leftist candidate, Salvador Allende, to the presidency.

As an observer, I was unable to participate in drafting the final resolutions of the conference. However, the whole experience was an eye-opener for me. I was shocked at the anti-socialist policies that Jack Kennedy's supposedly liberal administration was prepared to endorse.

Right-wing paranoia about socialism seemed to be deeply embedded in the American national psyche.

On returning to Albany, I was assigned to help out at a resort parish in the Catskill Mountains. It was a favourite spot for many wealthy Catholics escaping the heat and humidity of New York City. The parish was financially dependent on these vacationers. It was my first real exposure to the incredibly skillful business practices of the Catholic Church in North America.

The parish was a well-oiled, fundraising machine. From the moment visitors arrived, they were trapped. A clanging electronic carillon atop the church tower belted out familiar hymns, shaking every cottage window in the valley.

The sound of the bells called the faithful to bingos, raffles, fetes, dances, corn roasts; every evening, there was a social activity of one kind or another. The Legion of Mary and Knights of St. Columbus operated the cash registers to ensure that everyone paid for admission and drinks. The amplified chimes bouncing around the surrounding mountains made it almost impossible to ignore the summons.

One night I was summoned from my room by Father Luigi, the parish priest. He was a tubby little man with Nixon-like dark stubble and a strong Italian accent.

"You must get dressed. We have formal dinner tonight. Miss Eva Gabor here. Every year she give donation. Every year we have fundraiser in her honour. Tonight, you will sit next to her."

"Eva Gabor?" I asked. "Who's Eva Gabor?"

Father Luigi's black eyebrows shot up in astonishment.

"You never hear of Eva Gabor? How come? Such a beautiful actress, in big musical on Broadway." He paused for a moment. "She married four times, but still good Catholic." He gave me a sideways look out of the corner of his eye. "She always come to church on Sunday; very generous, very generous. Tonight is $100-a-plate dinner. You will entertain her."

I looked at him in disbelief.

"What makes you think she'd be interested in someone like me?" I asked.

"Why not? You missionary. Ladies love missionaries. Very romantic."

He was wrong.

The lovely Eva Gabor ignored me the whole evening. She was much more interested in the silver-haired, older man with solid gold cufflinks who sat on her other side. He had seen her performance in *Tovarich* on Broadway. She was clearly enjoying his attention. At one point, however, she did turn to pat my hand.

"So darlink," she said in her trademark Hungarian accent, "you are a missionary, no? That is so . . . nice," and she turned with a little laugh back to Mr. Gold Cufflinks.

When I got back to Albany, I told Rinty the story. "Don't worry," he said. "Like all the jokes say, you have to be a bishop to make it with an actress."

Before flying back to England, I drove to Toronto to visit my newly reunited family. My father had bought a small bungalow close to Lake Ontario. It was in the village of Pickering, just east of Toronto.

I had mixed feelings about the trip. I was eager to see Gemma and the two boys again but worried how I would cope with meeting my father. It was almost exactly ten years since I had gone to see him in London. I still felt bitter that he had brushed me off by yelling, "Go visit the British Museum."

"Peter!" Gemma shrieked as she saw me getting out of the car. She came running down the driveway, jumped into my arms, and gave me a big hug. She was eight years old now, a pretty little girl in pigtails. The boys, Barnabas now nine and Dominic eleven, hung back a little, but with big grins on their faces. Then my mother was hugging me too.

I looked up to see my father leaning against the frame of the open front door. He had a stiff, fixed smile and his eyes were blank. "Hello, Peter," he said, as he turned to go back in the house.

"Hi," I said.

Pain suddenly ripped through me, unprotected by the anger that should have been there. What had happened to the dad who carried me in his arms in Ireland? The dad who made doing dishes so much fun in the middle of a Christmas snow storm?

The chatter of the children saved me.

"Come and see my room," Dominic said, grabbing my arm. "You have to see the bow I got for my birthday. I never thought Mum would let me have it."

"And you have to see the kitten," Gemma said, grabbing my other arm. "It lives next door but comes onto our lawn to play."

While my mother started to prepare supper, Dominic insisted we walk over to a nearby field. He was dying to demonstrate his prowess as an archer. The field, a long grassy corridor, was a right-of-way reserved for hydro lines. It was an ideal shooting range.

"There's a big, nuclear power station being built at the end," Dominic said. "That's why Dad could afford to buy the house. Not many people want to live this close to a nuclear reactor."

When we got back, the house was filled with the smell of roast beef. "In your honour," my mother said, stirring gravy in the roasting pan. She had always been very proud of her gravy. "The secret is to add flour very gradually so that it doesn't go lumpy," she would say.

Supper was early, as my father had to attend a meeting of the local Catholic school board. He had been co-opted as its legal advisor. The meal turned out to be an ordeal. From the moment we sat down, my father launched into a rant about the trustees.

"They're all nothing but a bunch of knaves and charlatans. They know nothing about education. They're only there to further their own political ambitions."

"What's a charlatan?" Dominic interjected.

"Someone who pretends to be what they're not," I said, hoping to defuse the topic.

"Exactly," my father declared. "These guys pretend to be more Catholic than the Pope. But they do nothing to enforce discipline in the schools. They let the teachers dress in casual clothes. The kids get away with chewing gum in class. There's no such thing as a school uniform. Catholic schools are no different from public schools."

"Mum sent us to school in our English uniforms when we first arrived," Dominic said to me. "All the kids laughed at us."

"Canadian children are all a bunch of ruffians," my father continued, ignoring the interruption. "They have little respect for their teachers and none for their parents. They're always blocking the street playing hockey. My car was dented by a hockey puck just the other day."

"That was an accident," Barnabas said. "The kids didn't mean it. Their dad offered to pay for it."

"I'll believe that when I see it."

Gemma sat very still throughout this tirade. Barnabas was obviously angry. My mother sat picking sporadically at her food. Finally, my father pushed back his chair.

"I don't know when I'll be back," he said. "These meetings always go on late. Don't wait up for me." He stomped out, banging the front door behind him.

It was only then I realized how tense I had been. The children came to life. They began talking excitedly about school. They were looking forward to being with their friends again. For them, coming to Canada was an adventure.

"I miss Doreen," my mother told me later. "I don't have anyone to talk to."

We were doing the dishes while the children watched television in the living room.

"Your father's hardly ever here. He says he can't stand driving to Toronto during rush hour. He leaves very early in the morning and comes back late at night."

She was scrubbing hard at a stubborn stain in the roasting pan.

"He spends his time in pubs after work. The children only see him on weekends. Then, he sleeps in while they're out playing."

"Was that spiel tonight just for my benefit, or is he always like that?" I asked.

"No, he's like that most of the time. If I disagree with him it ends up in a fight."

She stopped scrubbing, looking down at the soapy water.

"I don't know what to do. I wish we had never come here. I was much happier with just the children in Fernhurst." She brushed away a tear with the back of her hand.

"Well, you've only been here a few months," I said. "The children seem to have settled in just fine. Perhaps you should try making friends with some of the women at church, or . . . some of the school mothers. I'm sure you can find someone to talk to if you try."

I felt uncomfortable. Who was I to counsel my own mother? I suspected she was not making much effort to find friends. I knew she would be constantly critical of Canadian ways. Her British snobbishness would make it difficult for people to befriend her.

"You have to get past feeling different," I said. "Everyone needs friends. People will talk to you as long as they feel you are genuinely interested in them."

"I know that, Peter," she said, looking at me with a small smile. "You don't have to preach at me. I'll be alright."

I could only stay for a few days. Thankfully, the children were not upset when it was time for me to go. I told them I would be back the following summer. *Their lives are full enough without me,* I thought to myself as I drove to Albany. I tried not to think about them, but it was hard not to.

When I got back, Rinty told me he had just received a letter from Mill Hill. He had been appointed to teach at St. Peter's College where I had first met him as an eleven-year-old boy. He was bitterly disappointed. It had always been his dream, as it was mine, to work in a mission country.

I had to leave for England a few weeks before him, so he offered to drive me to the airport. As we stood at the departure gate, for the first time in our lives we gave each other a hug instead of a handshake.

"Take care of yourself, Bruno," he said.

"You, too."

241

I stepped back and looked away, feeling strangely upset. I didn't want him to notice. I walked towards the sliding glass doors, and then turned to give him a final wave. He was standing watching me. He had a forced grin on his face. He was upset too.

That was the last time I ever saw Rinty. After teaching for a few years at St. Peter's, he was sent to the Cameroon, in West Africa. He was put in charge of a seminary for training African priests. Then, while on leave in England, he suddenly fell ill. He died within a few days.

It was years later that I heard the news of his death. I was shocked and horrified. Why hadn't I been told? Why wouldn't Mill Hill have known we were friends? I was overcome with grief; a grief I still feel as I write this. And I was angry, too; angry that the Church had such an inhuman policy of preventing priests from developing friendships. That day I felt part of me had died too. In spite of all those seminary rules, Rinty and I had become close friends from just being together. Once separated, we had reverted to being distant colleagues, living on different continents, no longer communicating with each other.

CHAPTER 52

Burn Hall was dull without Rinty. I missed our morning chats over breakfast. Often, our discussions became so intense that we lost all sense of time. We would have to race madly down the long driveway to catch the bus. If our lectures coincided, we met afterwards for coffee at St. Cuthbert's and talked some more.

I tried to make up for Rinty's absence by focusing hard on my studies. I was determined to make sure I graduated successfully. I wanted to be ready for an appointment from Mill Hill, hopefully to some exotic foreign land.

Soon after getting back to the university, I delivered my report on the Washington conference. The students were as surprised as I by the ambivalent response to Robert Kennedy. Few young people in England appreciated the depth of the racial divide in America. There was also very little awareness of the extensive covert actions being carried out by the CIA in South America. Camelot was a thin veneer, concealing a deeply dysfunctional society.

The assassination of President Kennedy in November stunned everybody. As word spread throughout the campus, the whole university came to a halt. Classes were abandoned. Students rushed back to residences. Everyone watched the reports on television. It felt as if the familiar, predictable world we had all grown up with was slowly disintegrating.

But, strangely, the Catholic Church seemed unaffected. In fact it seemed to be changing for the better. The Vatican Council's liturgical reforms were officially promulgated in December. In practical terms, this meant that the Mass was no longer to be said in Latin, priests would face the people, and women could serve as assistant ministers.

These reforms might seem quite innocuous today, but at the time they represented a major break with tradition. In particular, they encouraged me to hope that more radical reforms, such as the ordination of women, a married clergy, and a more enlightened attitude to birth control, might soon follow.

In May, when it came time to write my final exams, I was reasonably confident. However, my Latin poetry exam caused me some anxiety. One section required the translation of a previously unseen poem from an anthology. The selection could be any one of hundreds.

On the morning of the exam, I got up early to do some last minute studying. Panic made it difficult to concentrate. In desperation, I took the anthology with me as I walked down the driveway to the bus stop.

It so happens that the buses into Durham alternate on two routes, a long one and a short one. Mistakenly, I boarded the bus that took the long route.

The bus was only halfway to the university when I heard the cathedral clock chiming the hour for the start of the exam. At that very moment, the students would be opening their exam papers. They would know which poem from the anthology had been selected.

"Okay," I thought, "I'll use the power of all those student psyches to tell me which poem they are looking at."

I opened my book and randomly chose a poem to study for the last ten minutes of my ride. When I finally arrived at the exam hall, I found my seat and opened the question paper. The poem assigned was the very one I had studied on the bus.

Perhaps it was just coincidence.

But I aced the exam.

"Congratulations on earning your degree, Peter," Father McLoughlin said when I travelled back to Mill Hill for my new appointment.

This time, Father McLoughlin was not the remote Superior General of my last visit. He stood up and reached out across his desk to shake my hand.

"You will be going to our mission in North Borneo."

I couldn't believe my ears. Borneo; the land of jungle adventure-stories Sister Vincent had read to me as a child.

"You will take over as vice-principal of a secondary school in Papar, Sabah. You must arrive for the beginning of the school year starting in January. You can choose how you get there, by plane or by boat. Just tell Father Duggan what you want to do. In the meantime, you are to go back to Albany to help out with fundraising. Good luck."

"Thank you," I said, completely thrilled.

I ran down the stairs, almost knocking over Father Duggan on his way up.

"So you've heard where you're going," he said, as I apologized. "Congratulations. Come and see me when you've calmed down. I'll fill you in on the details."

My final visit to America was a sobering experience. The summer of 1964 was full of hatred and violence. Race riots raged in Harlem and Philadelphia. Two black men and three civil rights workers were murdered in Mississippi. Anti-Vietnam War protests shook San Francisco, Boston, Seattle and New York. It felt like the social fabric of the nation was being torn apart. I was shocked when Barry Goldwater, the Republican nominee for president, declared that 'extremism in the defense of liberty was no vice, and moderation in the pursuit of justice was no virtue'.

Soon after I arrived, I was invited to give a talk to a local branch of the Knights of St. Columbus. The hall was full of grey-haired army veterans. Another guest was scheduled to speak ahead of me. He was a young helicopter pilot on leave from Vietnam.

I noticed how the old men's eyes brightened as the pilot talked about his missions. They leaned forward in their chairs, eager to enjoy vicariously the excitement of combat. Clearly they still missed the rush they had enjoyed from fighting their own wars. I realized it was unlikely they would be receptive to anything I might say about my mission. I quietly made my excuses and left. Sadly, it was support from men like these that helped make another war politically possible.

At the end of the summer, I flew to Toronto to say goodbye to my family. I would not be seeing them again for at least five years. My father was just as distant as ever, but my mother was much less anxious than she had appeared the previous year.

"I've made some good friends in the parish," she said. "We get together to play cards once a week. We talk about our kids and complain about our husbands. It's all very therapeutic."

The children were, as usual, excited to see me.

"How's the hunting?" I asked Dominic. Then I noticed the bandage around his hand.

I had an accident," he said with a rueful smile. "I shot at a muskrat in the creek. I didn't think I hit him. When I waded into the water to get my arrow, he was on the end of it. It had gone through his leg. When I tried to pull the arrow out, he turned around and bit my thumb."

Now that the pain was gone, thirteen-year-old Dominic was quite proud of his hunting wound. I told him about the Muruts in Borneo where I was going, and how they still used blow-pipes to hunt in the mountain jungles where they lived.

"Will you bring me a blow-pipe when you come back?" he begged.

"Of course," I said.

I stayed for a week. My father avoided me as much as he could. He was seldom home, leaving early in the morning and returning late at night. Gemma and the boys took time out from their friends to show me their favourite play areas. We explored Petticoat Creek and Frenchman's Bay, and ventured occasionally into the freezing waters of Lake Ontario.

On my last day my father drove us all to the airport. With three adults and three children, it was cramped in the little Volkswagen Beetle. I sat in the back with Gemma on my knee. She had been invited to a birthday party at a friend's house. We were to drop her off on the way.

Holding her, I suddenly began to feel enormously sad. Five years now seemed a very long time. I had not realized how deeply attached I was to the children, especially to Gemma. It was strange. I had been away from them so much. Yet I felt so close to them.

The boys were confident and carefree, but I was anxious about Gemma. She seemed particularly vulnerable. She was only ten years old. I worried how it was going to be for her having to live with a bullying, bombastic father.

"Who's your friend?" I asked her

"Theresa. She's in my class. It's her birthday party. A lot of my friends will be there. It's going to be fun."

It was good to realize that she was more preoccupied with her party than with the fact that I was leaving. She would not see me for another five years. As a child, the immediate present was much more important to her than a remote future. I wished I could feel the same way.

When we got to Theresa's house, other cars were pulling up. Gemma gave me a quick hug and jumped out. Two of her friends in party dresses joined her. They ran up the driveway together. She turned at the front door and gave a final wave. I kept my head turned away as we drove off, hoping Dominic and Barnabas would not see how upset I was.

"Well now," my father said, "that's good. We've got more room in the back without her."

DURHAM UNIVERSITY & WALSINGHAM

Durham University—Palace Green

Durham Cathedral

Oak cross carried on pilgrimage to Walsingham

Priory chapel ruins, Walsingham

Slipper Chapel, Walsingham

PART SEVEN

BORNEO, MISEREOR AND ROMANCE

1964-1970

CHAPTER 53

I gripped the ship's rail to steady myself. Through gaps in the grey fog, I watched for a final glimpse of the Cornish coast. Windblown sea spray stung my eyes, coating my glasses in a salty film. The little Scottish freighter doggedly reared and plunged, plowing its way through the dark November waters of the English Channel. A mournful warning bell clanged from beyond the bow. A red and white marine buoy tossed up and down in the waves. Its revolving light cast an eerie glow in the swirl of the surrounding fog. Slowly it faded behind us, the last link to England.

It was Father Duggan who had persuaded me to take the sea passage. "It will give you a chance to get acclimatized to the tropics," he had said. "You'll see a lot of interesting places. The Ben Line has been sailing to the Far East since the late 1800s. The boats only have room for a dozen passengers. You will be treated like a king. Their meals are amazing."

The one thing he forgot to mention was the possibility of sea sickness.

In the gathering darkness, I staggered along a narrow passageway to my tiny cabin. Collapsing onto the bunk, I wrapped a pillow around my ears to muffle the remorseless throb of the ship's engines. I pulled my knees up tight to my chest to still my roiling stomach. It was useless. Two minutes later I was on my knees in front of the toilet. After an endless series of gut-wrenching upheavals, I climbed back onto my bunk and fell into an exhausted sleep.

Waking early the next morning, I wondered how I had survived. My stomach felt as if it had been pounded with a baseball bat. I slowly swung my legs to the floor and managed to stand upright. Pulling on some clothes, I made my way out onto the heaving deck.

In the cold light of dawn, the ship was surging relentlessly through choppy seas. A stiff breeze blasted the wave crests into spray streamers. The fog from the night before had cleared, but the sky was blanketed with dull grey clouds stretching to the horizon. Above me, the ensign of the Ben Line, a blue anchor on a white background, snapped and flailed. And perched incongruously on the stern of the boat was the fuselage of a fighter jet, its silvery sides reflecting the overcast sky.

"You look a bit green around the gills, laddie."

The ship's captain was leaning on the rail next to me. With the noise of the wind in my ears, I hadn't heard him coming.

"I was pretty sick last night," I said.

"Most people are on their first day out. But you'll soon get over it. My name's Tom, by the way." He held out his hand and I shook it.

"Peter," I said.

Captain Tom McCloud was a broad-shouldered Scotsman in his late forties. His face was a permanent red, scrubbed raw by salty winds. Clear blue eyes matched the darker blue of his merchant navy uniform. His full, red beard made him look like the sailor on Player's cigarette packages.

"What's that jet plane doing on the back of the boat?" I asked.

"Oh that," he said, turning to look past me. "We have to drop it off at Aden. Apparently Arab nationalists in Yemen have started an insurgency. The British are building up their resources there."

He turned back, leaning his elbows on the rail and squinting out to sea.

"Let's just hope the Egyptians don't make a fuss about it when we go through the canal," he said. "Nasser supports the rebels."

He straightened up.

"Breakfast is being served in the saloon. That's if you're interested," he added with a grin.

I shivered. "I don't think I can handle food just yet. My stomach needs a little more time to recover."

Tom laughed. "As you wish," he said. "You'll be missing out on some really tasty kippers. We have a wonderful cook. He prides himself on his breakfasts. But you'll have plenty of time to find that out on this trip," he said, as he headed back along the deck.

During the course of the day, my insides gradually acclimatized to the boat's perpetual motion. By supper time I felt I could face the prospect of food without further fearful consequences. I found my way to the saloon.

Captain McCloud and a group of officers and passengers were already seated at a large mahogany table. I was surprised to see the passengers all dressed formally, the men in tuxes and the women in gowns. A Chinese steward, in a white coat and gloves, ushered me to my place, swiveled a chair for me and presented me with a napkin.

"This is Father Peter," Tom said, introducing me to the others. "He will be with us all the way to Borneo."

I was sitting next to an elderly lady, a Mrs. McDermott, who, it transpired, made regular trips on the Ben Line boats as a vacation. She was not interested in being a tourist; she just treated the ship as a floating boarding house for three months of every year.

The remaining passengers included two Chinese traders introduced as Ben and Charlie; Janet Pearson, who was writing a travelogue for a tourist agency; and Jim Baxter, an elderly businessman who owned a factory in Singapore and was terrified of flying. *By the end of six weeks,* I thought to myself, *we should all know each other very well indeed.*

The next day, as the ship turned south to sail along the coast of Portugal, the weather cleared. We stopped briefly at Gibraltar and then set out along the Mediterranean to Suez. During the long, lazy, sun-filled days that followed, I divided my time between learning to type on a small Olivetti portable and studying Malay from a cheap, teach-yourself handbook. I failed miserably at both these tasks, being distracted by a book on North Borneo that I found in the ship's library.

I learned that North Borneo had been a British protectorate from 1888 until 1942, when it was attacked and occupied by the Japanese. After the defeat of Japan in 1945, it became a British colony. I would be arriving just one year after it had gained independence. In 1963 it had adopted the name of Sabah and joined the Federation of Malaysia.

The total population of Sabah was only about 600,000 people. They lived mostly along the coast. In the interior, rugged, jungle-clad mountains made travel extremely difficult. The tribal people who lived there were isolated from each other in tiny, inaccessible villages. This possibly explains why there were some thirty different indigenous ethnic groups in Sabah, speaking eighty different dialects. Today Malay is the national language, promoted in order to unify the country.

I already knew some of the history of the first Mill Hill missionaries. They had been sent to Sabah in 1881. The British had been preoccupied with establishing profitable rubber plantations and timber exports. They left the task of building schools and medical clinics to the missionaries. During the Japanese occupation, most of the schools had been destroyed and the missionaries interned in prison camps. The years after the war were spent in a long struggle to rebuild.

As our little cargo boat steamed along the length of the Mediterranean, my life began to assume an established routine. On Sundays, I would celebrate Mass in the saloon for the few members of the crew who were Catholic. On weekdays, I said Mass alone in my cabin. I would create a makeshift altar by setting my suitcase over the sink, hoping that nothing would slide off as the ship rolled.

As day succeeded day, this lonely rite seemed more and more absurd. It felt like play-acting. Memories of Father Borelli's solitary sung Masses in Haslemere came flooding back. After a while I simply stopped performing my private little service. Something inside of me was missing. That something, I began to realize, was a respect for many of the irrational and outlandish rituals of the Church.

One afternoon, while I was relaxing in a deckchair, Mrs. McDermott came and sat herself down beside me. It took her a while to get settled. She had a pastel-coloured shawl that matched her powder-blue, pleated dress. Fastidiously, she arranged the shawl around her shoulders, picking at the folds to make sure they hung just right. Her wide-brimmed straw hat was firmly tied down with a white silk scarf to secure it from the wind. A pair of enormous sunglasses concealed most of her face. She clearly considered herself to be the dowager queen of the Ben Line.

Once everything was in order, she reached into a white crocheted bag and produced a book.

"Have you read this?" she asked, leaning over to show me the cover. "It's *The Cardinal*, by Henry Morton Robinson."

"Yes," I said. "Are you enjoying it?" I had read it ten years earlier when it had first come out.

"Well, I'm not a Catholic," she said, "but I don't see how a priest could let his sister die so needlessly. She could have had an abortion. What would you have told her if she was your sister?"

"I don't think it would have been up to me," I answered cautiously. "That would be something for my sister to decide."

"But doesn't the Catholic Church condemn abortion?" she said, taking off her sunglasses and giving me a stern look.

"It does," I said, beginning to feel uncomfortable. "But it also says you have a duty to form your own conscience. I do think the Church tends to be too dogmatic, especially when it talks about women and sexuality. It often treats people as if they don't have a mind of their own."

"Well that's fairly evident," Mrs. McDermott huffed. She replaced her sun glasses, settled back in her deck chair and returned to her book.

A pair of gulls, white wings gleaming in the morning sun, soared and hovered beside us. As I watched them, I noticed a tiny dot on the horizon. It gradually grew larger and larger until it became a huge ocean liner, proudly sailing past us. Then slowly, almost imperceptibly, it began to shrink into the distance, becoming just a tiny dot again until it finally vanished.

Mrs. McDermott was totally absorbed in her book. From what I remembered of the story, it was a kind of pious melodrama, full of implausible coincidences, where a Bing Crosby type priest rejects temptations to his celibacy and rises to the highest level of bureaucracy in the Church.

Unlike the hero-priest of the story, I was beginning to question some of the very doctrines I was supposed to promote. The details of the Church, like the cruise ship coming towards us, had become clearer as I got closer to ordination. When I started at St. Peter's College, I had seen the Church as simply a caring community. But now, as a priest, it seemed to be much more like a monolithic corporation, geared to protecting itself with arbitrary rules.

Strangely, I did not see this as a reason to question being a missionary. In fact it was Mill Hill that helped me see the Church for what it really was. Now I was simply being asked to pay my dues. I was being sent by Mill Hill to teach in a country where education was sorely needed. I could still do that, even if I no longer believed in all the corporate rules. While I watched the cruise ship diminish to a tiny dot, I did not stop to ask myself if ignoring my doubts was just a way to avoid giving up a secure, predictable future.

When we arrived at Port Said, the ship had to wait its turn to pass through the Suez Canal.

"You want feelthy pictures?"

A scruffy looking man stood in front of me. A ragged piece of cloth was wound around his head. His yellow eyes and toothless grin were an inch from my face. He tried to thrust a handful of pornographic postcards into my hand. He and a number of fellow hucksters had scrambled aboard while our boat lay at anchor.

When I pushed his cards away, he produced a dirty glass vial from a deep pocket in his baggy pants. "For your girl," he leered. "Make her horny as hell."

The vial contained an evil-looking, red liquid that frothed into pink foam as he shook it under my nose. Captain McCloud walked over and chased the man away. "He doesn't know you're a priest," he said, "although maybe he would have tried anyway."

I went to the rail and looked down at the flotilla of small dhows that were milling around in the water below. Women in grimy head scarves screamed at us, holding up fruit, clothing, and cheap jewelry for barter. This was my first contact with the culture of the East, far removed from the exotic romanticism of my imagination.

However, the passage through the Suez Canal proved to be spectacular. It was late afternoon. The sun behind us was already sinking to the horizon. Fascinated, I watched the dark shadow of our ship gliding over the bright yellow surface of the desert dunes beside us. At Timmi Island, a narrow strip of sand separated the canal into two lanes. A huge oil tanker passed us on the opposite side. From where we were, it looked as if it were sailing through solid sand. As the canal widened into the Red Sea, the shore was lined with clusters of white-walled Arab villages, each with its own minaret and domed mosque. The villages were fringed with feathery date palms, making them look much more like the East that I had imagined.

At Aden we anchored briefly while the fighter plane was unloaded onto a flat barge. Then we set out across the Indian Ocean to the island of Penang. The boat stopped there for a whole day to refuel and take on more cargo. It was an opportunity to go exploring. Captain McCloud urged me to go to Penang Hill to visit the Temple of the Jade Emperor.

Walking up the hill to the temple was a daunting experience. The gardens were swarming with monkeys, long-tailed macaques, who were not the least bit afraid of humans. Far from being cute, they became quite threatening if anyone got in their way, baring their fearsome looking fangs.

I climbed the granite steps to the temple entrance, marveling at the dragon heads, made from multi-coloured tiles, on the roof corners. The two guardian figures at the entrance, I learned, represented the God of Literature and the God of War. It was a juxtaposition that I found quite intriguing. But what impressed me most was seeing young people, just teenagers, kneeling and burning joss sticks in front of the Buddha statues. They were dressed just like any British teenagers riding the subway in London. But these teenagers had been raised with the Taoist tradition of prayer, laying their petitions at the feet of the Buddha.

When I got back to the boat, the last crane-loads of cargo were being hoisted onto the stern where the jet plane had been earlier. The new cargo consisted of bundles of live pigs, individually wrapped in rattan baskets and stacked on top of each other like so many cords of wood. They were destined for Brunei which, fortunately, was only two days away. The pigs were noisy and extremely pungent.

The sea around the tiny town of Miri, in Brunei, was too shallow and rocky for the boat to dock. We had to anchor half a mile offshore while the squealing pigs were unloaded onto a shallow-bottomed boat. I looked across to where the dense Borneo jungle poured down steep hillsides to the water's edge. It looked impenetrable, mysterious, exciting. Somewhere, hidden under those towering trees of rain forest, was the house where my former principal at Mill Hill, Bishop Anthony Galvin, was managing his Dayak mission.

We continued up the coast that night and early the next day I caught my first glimpse of Kota Kinabalu, the Capital of Sabah. As we got closer, the sea became a brilliant emerald green. The town stretched along four miles of white sandy beach. Behind the town, beyond the foothills, rose the majestic peak of Mount Kinabalu, the highest mountain in Southeast Asia.

Captain McCloud gently steered his ship alongside the dock. Deckhands heaved heavy cables over to the bollards on the jetty. A small knot of people was waiting for the ship to tie up. Among them were two of my Mill Hill classmates, Paddy Cahill and Jan Van Velzen. They looked up at me, waving and yelling, "Bruno, you made it!"

The Captain was standing next to me. "I thought your name was Peter."

"It's a long story," I said, turning to him. "Thank you for a great trip. I suppose for you it was routine, but for me it was an adventure."

"You're welcome. Good luck with your new school."

We shook hands and I headed for the gangplank.

Chapter 54

"I work in a Kadazan village called Limbahau," Jan Van Velzen said to me. "It's very close to where you will be in Papar."

"And I'm right here in Kota Kinabalu," said Paddy Cahill. "I'm an assistant in the Cathedral parish. I'm supposed to take you to meet the Bishop. His residence is up on the hill just behind the town."

While my luggage was being unloaded, Paddy, Jan, and I caught up with each other's stories. I was surprised to see they weren't dressed as priests. They wore casual open-necked shirts and slacks. "It's too hot to wear suits," Paddy said. "On Sundays we wear a white soutane with our red sashes, but otherwise we dress like this."

After piling my luggage into his car, a dusty yellow Volkswagen, Paddy drove us past rows of busy shops along the main street and up a winding dirt road to the Bishop's house. It was a small concrete building perched on the side of a hill, almost smothered by flowering shrubs and tall palm trees.

We climbed a set of stairs to the veranda, which overlooked the town and the harbour. Three people were sitting there in comfortable bamboo chairs, smoking cigars. One of them, a large, grey-haired Dutchman, got up and shook my hand.

"Father Frank van der Schoor," he said. "I'm just visiting from Sandakan. This is your boss, Bishop Buis." He gestured towards a rather pompous-looking prelate who sat sprawled in one of the chairs. Bishop Buis was short and round, and clearly not about to summon the energy required to stand up and greet me.

"This is Father Bekema, the pastor of the cathedral parish," Frank continued. Father Bekema, a heavyset Dutchman, lifted his hand with a slight wave. He made no move to get up either.

Without looking up at me, the Bishop took a long pull on his cigar and slowly exhaled. His eyes followed the cloud of grey smoke that drifted lazily over the bougainvillea blossoms spilling in glorious profusion along the veranda rail.

"You're going to have to leave for Papar right away," he said finally. "School starts in a few days' time. I don't know why Mill Hill let you take the boat. You should have been here a month ago. Van Velzen will go with you. Cahill can drive you to the station. Good luck."

Not knowing how to respond I looked over at Paddy, who simply shrugged. Without another word, the three of us turned and headed back to the car. As we were getting in, Frank van der Schoor ran down the steps from the veranda.

"Hold on," he said. "I'm coming with you. Let's find a cafe where we can chat for a bit. Peter deserves a better welcome than those two gave him, don't you think?"

"Absolutely," Paddy sniffed. "They were downright rude."

The next railcar to Papar was not scheduled to leave for another hour. We left my luggage on the platform and found a *kopitiam*, or coffee shop, nearby. It was open on two sides, allowing access to a cool sea breeze. Frank ordered cold Tiger Beer for us while we sat at a round marble-topped table. I was impressed by his fluent Chinese. "Most of the townsfolk in Sandakan are Hakka," Frank explained. "They really appreciate it if you talk to them in their own language."

"But I thought the national language was Malay."

"It is," Jan said. "But only since independence last year. Most people are still more comfortable in their original language. In my place at Penampang the people are Kadazan, so I have been learning their language as well as Malay."

"One of the first things you must do is to get some transportation," Frank said to me. "Otherwise, you'll go stir-crazy. I'd suggest buy yourself a motorbike. It will get you to many more places than a car."

"I don't think I could afford a car anyway," I said. I had been saving some money during my summer in the States, but it was certainly not enough to buy a car.

"Frank's right," Jan said. "Get a motorbike. It can go wherever there's a footpath."

"I can order one for you," said Paddy. "Anthony Fung at Harrison and Crossfield has them. A Matchless 350 would be ideal. They're virtually indestructible. Leave it to me. I'll have one sent down to you on the train."

After chatting for a little while longer, we walked back to the train station together.

"Nice to have met you," Frank said, shaking my hand. "You will enjoy working with Piet de Wit in Papar. He's been a buddy of mine since way back. We were in the same Japanese POW camp during the war. He was always getting beaten up because he insisted on teasing the guards. He's quite a character."

"See you soon," Paddy called out as Jan and I climbed into the railcar. "When you get your bike, come down for a visit. The road is not the greatest, but you won't have to depend on these railcars."

The railcar was a small, twelve passenger vehicle that looked as if it was a relic from pre-colonial days. "There's a steam train that leaves once a day," Jan told me, "but it's horrendously slow. It takes a whole day to go 134 kilometers. In spite of its age, this thing is much faster than the train."

The diesel motor of the railcar fired up with an ear-shattering roar. It shuddered and rattled for a moment and then, with a violent jerk, we were off. It tore southwards along a lovely bay bordered by mangrove swamps until it abruptly turned inland, pushing through dense, feathery branches of Nipa palms that immediately closed behind us as we passed.

"People use these palm fronds for everything," Jan shouted in my ear. "They make *attap* roofs and sleeping mats and all kinds of things. The water in the swamps is tidal, teeming with shrimp and small fish. No one needs to go hungry or homeless in Borneo."

Suddenly the railcar was rattling through the darkness of a short mountain tunnel. It burst into daylight on the far side to a completely different world. Placid, waterlogged paddy fields stretched towards distant hills, dotted with little bamboo houses on stilts. Farmers guided wooden ploughs behind lumbering water buffalos. Women in conical hats stooped to thrust bright green rice seedlings into the soggy ground. Small children waved at us, grinning from ear to ear.

"Papar is Sabah's rice bowl," Jan shouted above the roar of the motor. "There's always a grand celebration here after the harvest. Everyone drinks *tapai*, a fermented rice wine. Be careful if you try it, it's quite potent. You've been warned!"

Our railcar crossed a small trestle bridge and a moment later jerked to a stop in front of the railway station in Papar. It took a moment for my ears to adapt to the sudden silence.

A white-haired priest was standing on the platform waiting to greet us. A young boy stood shyly beside him.

"Piet de Wit," the priest said, reaching out to grasp my hand, "and this is Francis. He's going to be your right-hand man." He looked intently into my eyes for a moment, and then abruptly turned away. "Come along," he said, picking up a suitcase. He began to walk briskly down the platform ahead of us. At sixty-five he seemed sprightly enough but clearly still harboured the wariness of emotional attachment inculcated in our seminary training. I looked at Jan, who raised an eyebrow at me.

"Welcome to St. Joseph's," he said. "The school is just over there."

He pointed towards a large rectangular compound that bordered the railway track just a hundred yards south of the station. The school buildings were arranged in the form of an elongated semicircle. The centre was occupied by an old, wooden church, its weather-worn planks grey where the faded white paint had peeled away. In contrast, the two-story school buildings looked relatively new. They were built of solid concrete, painted a light yellow, with red pillared verandas running along their fronts. There were four buildings altogether, one being a boarding house for boys from the interior.

"We converted two of the upstairs classrooms at each end of the secondary school into living quarters," Piet said. "I live at one end and you'll be at the other. That way we can keep an eye on things. We have a cook who lives just behind the school. By the way, Jan, you're welcome to stay for supper."

"Thanks, but I can't," Jan said. "I have to get back to Penampang. But I'll see you next Sunday night for our weekly get-together."

His motorbike was parked under the stairs leading up to Piet's living room.

"Take care of this man," he said to Piet, clapping me on the shoulder. "He's been a good buddy of mine for years."

He threw his leg over the saddle, revved the motor, and took off in a cloud of red dust.

Piet walked me from his quarters, along the upper veranda of the school, to the end of the building.

"This is your room," he said, opening the door to what was once just another classroom. "Not quite the Ritz, but it's really all you will need. There's a shower and toilet outside at the bottom of the stairs.

Francis lives in the boarding house next to you. He will help you get settled. Supper's in forty-five minutes."

Piet left me alone with Francis to unpack. The boy shyly shook my hand.

"*Apa kabar?*" he said. I recognized it as the Malay greeting, 'What's the news?'

"*Kabar baik,*" I said. 'The news is good.'

He smiled. "You know Malay already."

"No. You will have to help me. Will you?"

"Of course," he said.

Francis Onung was eighteen years old, but he looked much younger. He was short, with the flat nose and wide-apart eyes of the Kadazan people. His dark black hair was cut in a straight fringe around his head. His parents had died when he was quite little, and he had been adopted by a Malay family. Their village was several miles away, so Piet had accepted him as a boarder. Because of his adopted parents, he had become fluent in Malay and his English was surprisingly good.

Later, at supper, Piet handed me a series of Malay school books. "You can work through these," he said. "We can take a half-hour each night before supper to review the exercises."

Piet de Wit already intimidated me. He had been living and working in Borneo long before I was even born. I wondered if I would ever be able to live up to his expectations.

Supper was a simple meal of chicken, rice, and boiled vegetables. It was prepared by an elderly Chinese lady whose house was just behind the school. Afterwards, as I walked to my room, I was astonished to hear the throbbing beat of the latest Beatles' song pounding out from behind the coconut palms surrounding the cook's house. She had three teenage children who seemed to have an endless supply of batteries for their transistor radio.

By the time I had unpacked my books and clothes and organized my room, all was quiet next door. Piet had provided me with a sarong to wear to bed. "Pajamas are just too uncomfortable in this climate," he had said. I climbed onto the bed and tucked the mosquito netting around me. For a while I lay there listening to the unfamiliar sounds of the Borneo night outside. The myriad brilliant stars of the southern night sky were reflected in the glass slats of the open, louvered windows.

It had been an eventful day. It was hard to absorb it all. My senses had been swamped by the novelty of everything. I felt totally unprepared for this exotic new world. It was good to know that I had a friend close by. Jan Van Velzen was only a twenty-minute ride away.

A kaleidoscope of images and impressions from the day swirled around in my head. Then, thankfully, they were smoothed away as I fell asleep.

CHAPTER 55

"Your first job is to prepare the master timetable. After breakfast, I'll give you a list of classes and teachers."

Piet wiped an errant drip of egg yolk from his chin.

"I've never done any school scheduling before," I said with some trepidation.

"You'll manage. It's not that difficult."

After Piet gave me the information I needed to work with, I went back to my room and began immediately. School was to start the next day. The timetable had to be ready. I divided a large sheet of Bristol board into squares for classrooms and days of the week. There were thirty-three teachers to be entered from Piet's list. I worked solidly the whole day, assigning rooms and teaching times.

By evening, everyone was slotted neatly into a space. I carried my work proudly to Piet for his approval. He surveyed it for a while and then gave it back to me.

"You forgot something," he said. "Each teacher is entitled to a preparation period. You've got them teaching the whole day without a break!"

Somewhat deflated, I took the board back to my room and started all over again. But the longer I worked the more mistakes I made. Determined not to let it get the better of me, I continued on through the night. By the time I finished, the grey light of morning was filtering through the louvered windows. Bleary eyed, I took the completed schedule back to Piet.

"Well done, Peter. I'll post this in the staff room."

By nine o'clock, the students had assembled in front of the school. They were smartly dressed in fresh, clean uniforms. The boys wore white shirts and grey pants, while the girls were in white blouses and blue gingham skirts. I was impressed, especially since Piet had said the girls all made their own uniforms at home.

"I'm pleased to introduce you to your new vice-principal, Father Peter Walther," Piet announced. "He's just arrived from England after earning a degree at a famous university. We are very proud to have him at St. Joseph's. He will enhance the academic excellence of our school."

There were a few more announcements, the national anthem was sung, and everyone filed into the classrooms.

Total chaos ensued.

My timetable was full of mistakes. Teachers showed up at the same classroom for the same class. Some classes had no teacher at all. Desperately, I tried to resolve the conflicts, assigning teachers randomly, just to get through the day. Finally, Piet sent the students home early and called a staff meeting.

"Clearly, there are some problems with the schedule," he said, giving me the evil eye. "I am asking the math department to sit down and draw up a new one for us."

Afterwards, the head of the math department, a young East Indian from Kerala, came up to me and put a sympathetic hand on my shoulder.

"It wasn't fair to give you that job without any experience," he said, "no matter how many degrees you have! Anyway, you earned the gratitude of the staff. They had an extra day to prepare."

After that singularly inauspicious start, the school settled into a comfortable routine. I taught English to the senior classes. To qualify for university they were required to take the Overseas Cambridge Examination, a hold-over from when Sabah was a British Colony. As this was their passport to escape from Papar, the students worked hard. They were a delight to teach, unfailingly cheerful and friendly.

The staff included a few graduate teachers who had been recruited from Kerala, India. The rest were untrained. But they were enthusiastic and seemed to have a natural talent for teaching.

My own teaching duties left little time to study Malay. With Francis' help I managed to learn enough to get by, but not enough to meet Piet's expectations. Over the years, he had become an expert in *sejarah melayu*, the language used by upper-class Malays.

A few weeks after school started, I got a call from the railway station. A brand new motorbike had arrived from Kota Kinabalu and was waiting to be picked up. It was a gleaming Matchless 350 with Norton shocks. Piet drove it from the station and gave me a quick lesson. In no time I was roaring around the school *padang* like a pro. It was a Saturday afternoon. There was no school. And Francis was watching admiringly from the boarding house. When I finally parked under the stairs to my room, he came running out.

"Let's go to Papar beach for a swim," he said, eyes shining. "I'll show you the way."

"OK," I said, "jump on," and off we went. I was twenty-seven-years old, revelling in the power of that machine between my legs. The roar of the exhaust shattered the afternoon stillness of Papar. Here comes the *orang putih*, the crazy white man, showing off his new toy.

Twenty minutes later Francis and I were splashing around in the crystal, clear waters of the South China Sea. Afterwards, we sat on the white sand to dry off. A few miles offshore, I could see a small, hazy, blue outline.

"Is that an island out there?" I asked Francis.

"Yes. It's called Pulau Tiga. It's not inhabited. A few fishermen use it occasionally. It has great beaches. We usually go over there for a picnic during the Easter break. It's a school tradition. You're expected to organize it."

When we got back I checked with Piet. "Yes," he said, "it's just the graduating class that gets to go. It's a chance for the boys and girls to socialize without parents chaperoning. Often there are not much more than a dozen. Many parents won't allow their children to go. I'll negotiate with a fisherman to take you out there."

On the morning of the trip, I was just as excited as the students. We gathered at a wooden jetty where the fishing boats tied up. There were twenty of us altogether, including three teachers and an equal number of boys and girls. Fully equipped with food, sunglasses, and transistor radios, they could easily have been mistaken for a bunch of western teenagers.

Our little fishing boat chugged smoothly down the Papar river and out to the open sea. Pulau Tiga lay straight ahead, about an hour away. A rough, wooden bench ran along the gunwales of the boat. Like the dance hall protocol in England, the girls squeezed together on one side of the boat, the boys facing them on the other. At first there was a lot of cheerful banter back and forth, but as the boat began to roll with the swells everyone quieted down. It didn't help that we were smothered by choking, noxious, diesel fumes from the sputtering motor. I was glad that I had two of the female teachers along to help when a number of girls started to retch over the side.

It was a relief when the boat finally ground onto the beach at Pulau Tiga and we splashed ashore. Towels were spread on the sand and everyone stripped down to shorts and swim suits. Feeling a bit like an outsider, I asked the teachers if they could keep an eye on things while I explored the island.

"Make sure you're back by four o'clock," they said. "The boat needs the tide to get back up the river to Papar."

"No problem," I said and headed off along the beach. It curved around to a point that opened out onto another beach on the far side. I took off my flip flops. The sand was soft and warm. It was slower walking than I had expected. As I rounded the last point at the end of the island, my watch told me it was only one o'clock. I felt confident that I could work my way along the ocean side and end up back at our beach well before four. I pushed on for another hour.

Then the island topography began to change. There were no longer any beaches, just a series of deep inlets. Fallen palm trees became obstacles that I had to climb over. By two o'clock, I figured I must be more than half way round the island. But the number of inlets seemed endless. I would arrive at the end of one only to find another in front of me. I started to speed up. I scrambled over tangled roots and sodden trunks. By four o'clock I still had not reached the far end of the island. I began to panic. It was five o'clock when I rounded the last inlet. Our sandy beach stretched out before me. The students were already on board the boat. The teachers were standing in the water waving at me to hurry.

"What kept you?" they asked as I panted up to them. "The fisherman is really worried. He doesn't know if we'll be able to make it back in time."

Fortunately, the tide was still with us. But I felt foolish and guilty. The kids were very quiet. The day in the hot sun had left them exhausted. The trip back seemed to be taking forever. The boat's diesel engine coughed and spluttered but kept going. As we approached the mouth of the Papar River, dusk was falling. Then we heard the throb of a louder engine. A huge army helicopter appeared out of the darkening sky. It hovered deafeningly above us before turning and swooping back towards the land.

Piet had called the army after getting phone calls from anxious parents. Apparently, the sea around Pulau Tiga was a favourite haunt of pirates. The army had decided to begin a search for us. Piet was not happy.

I was forced to listen to his lecture. I had acted like an immature greenhorn. I had besmirched the good name of the school. He would have to apologize to the village council. He would have to apologize to the police and the army. He might even have to pay for the helicopter.

I felt ashamed. It wasn't Piet who was lecturing me. It felt like my father. I was irresponsible. I was incompetent. I was untrustworthy. I couldn't even make a master timetable. What was I doing here at all?

Jan Van Velzen just laughed when I told him the story. I had driven to Penampang the next day feeling thoroughly sorry for myself.

"Don't worry. Piet will have forgotten about it by tomorrow. We all make mistakes. Besides, you *are* young and inexperienced. You can't expect to have the wisdom and foresight of a sixty-five-year-old veteran after being here just a few short months."

Jan was right. Piet soon forgot about the Pulau Tiga debacle. It was ironic that, thirty-five years later, I learned the island had been chosen as the site for the first episode of the television game show, *Survivor*.

Every Sunday evening Jan Van Velzen and his pastor, Father John Quinn, would drive over from Penampang for supper and a few beers. John Quinn was from Stockport in England and had been in Sabah as long as Piet. Like Piet, he had been interned by the Japanese during the war but had managed to escape the horrendous death marches. Over 6,000 soldiers and civilians died when they were forced to march from the coast to the interior.

John was fluent in the Kadazan-Dusun language. He was very popular with his parishioners because of the homeopathic medicines he successfully prescribed. His ability to absorb alcohol, however, was not great. He broke into sneezing fits after only a couple of beers. For us, that was the signal to hide any remaining bottles.

I always looked forward to these Sunday evenings. The two older men would reminisce about their early days. While interned by the

Japanese, Piet had written a Malay translation of the Bible and acquired a working knowledge of Hakka. Unfortunately, he had the kind of face that gave the impression he was always smiling, even when he was deadly serious. You had to look closely at his eyes to see what he was really feeling. Apparently the Japanese felt that he was constantly mocking them. In the prison camp he was viciously tortured, with sharp bamboos driven up his anus. As a result, using the toilet was now always a long and painful process for him. It was amazing to me that he harboured no ill feelings towards his captors. But he used very colourful language to describe the individual soldiers who had tortured him.

Both priests still suffered from the effects of their terrible ordeal. Their stories were always followed by long silences when they seemed to lose touch with what was going on around them. I felt their beer-fuelled banter still masked enormous depths of terror and pain. They protected themselves by keeping Jan and me at arm's length. They had no curiosity about us as fellow priests, or about how we were doing as we struggled to find our feet in this new, unfamiliar world.

CHAPTER 56

I taught for two years at St. Joseph's in Papar. Weeks and months passed quickly with the daily routine of teaching classes and marking assignments. My life seemed quite mundane compared to the expectations I had formed before coming to Borneo. However, school breaks provided an opportunity to do some exploring.

One of our more remote mission stations was Bundu Tuhan, a small village situated high in the foothills of Mount Kinabalu. Piet suggested I take some time off at the end of the school year to visit it. In order to get there I had to take the railcar to the capital, Kota Kinabalu, and then find transportation to the mission, some 80 kilometers away in the mountains.

Bundu Tuhan is 1,200 meters above sea level. The temperature there is significantly cooler than at the coast, making it possible to grow fruits and vegetables more suited to temperate climates. The mission had started a farm co-operative with the local people. The produce was shipped down to the city and sold to hotels and restaurants that catered to western tourists.

I arranged to visit Bundu Tuhan with an Austrian classmate, Josef Haas. Josef was a stocky, dark-haired young man who came from a farming family in the Austrian Tyrol. It was nostalgia for the mountains of his home that encouraged him to join me on the trip. "Perhaps we can climb to the top of Mount Kinabalu while we're there," he suggested.

The pastor at Bundu Tuhan was Jan Van Breemen, the brother of Piet Van Breemen, my classmate from Roosendaal and Mill Hill. Josef and I hitched a ride in his Land Rover as he was returning from the market in Kota Kinabalu.

It was a long, dangerous drive. The winding, muddy road clung precariously to the edges of steep mountains, providing spectacular panoramic views of valleys far below. Often we were only inches away from a vertical drop of hundreds of feet on either side.

"I had a scary experience on this road a few nights ago," Jan told us. "I was driving a little Volkswagen Beetle that belonged to the mission. It was late and very dark. Suddenly something huge and hard and heavy crashed down onto the hood in front of me. It was a buffalo. It had slipped over the edge of the cliff above me in the dark."

Jan looked across at me and grinned.

"The front of the car was completely smashed. There was blood all over the windscreen. But I was able to drive home. The engine of a Volkswagen Beetle is in the back. It was undamaged. With any other car I would have been stranded. And if the buffalo had fallen another second later, I would be dead now."

Jan's story did little to allay our terror as he negotiated hairpin bends and blind corners. There was very little room for two vehicles to pass each other on the narrow road. By the time we got to the mission, my knees and nerves were like jelly. But the cool air and the sight of the majestic slopes of Mount Kinabalu, rising from the valley opposite the mission, quickly erased the anxiety and tension of the trip. The front porch of the mission house provided a spectacular view of the mountain.

Jan told us that the name 'Kinabalu' came from the Kadazan words *aki nabalu*, meaning 'the revered place of the dead'.

"The Kadazan believe that when they die their spirits continue to live on the mountain top. Anyone who has been up there will tell you it's a very special place."

"Could we climb it?" Josef asked, "maybe tomorrow?"

"Of course. I'll take you. It's a two-day climb. Three quarters of the way up there's a hut where we can spend the night. After that, it's only a short way to the top. We can be back down here by the end of the second day. We'll need to pack some food and some warm clothes. It gets quite chilly up there at night."

That afternoon Jan gave us a quick tour of the farming co-op. It was started to help the local people get beyond subsistence farming. They now worked together to purchase seed and machinery and market the vegetables. It had been a struggle at first. Traditionally, the only crop had been hill rice.

Jan took us to a long building with a corrugated iron roof. Wooden crates were stacked along the walls.

"This is our lab and storage shed," he said. "We are constantly experimenting. Right now, we're trying to grow a variety of apples. We've already succeeded with strawberries."

That night's supper was a welcome change from the routine of chicken and rice at Papar. The fresh salad and vegetables made me realize how much I missed familiar, western food. The feeling of nostalgia was reinforced when I climbed into a bed without the need for a mosquito net. I snuggled down, relishing the cozy comfort of cool sheets and a warm blanket.

Next morning I stood on the front porch and watched the first rays of sun catch the jagged peaks of Mount Kinabalu. The valley below was still dark, hidden in the gloom of a cold damp mist. But up on the mountain top the sharp edges of the ancient granite shapes were clearly defined against the deep-blue sky. It wasn't hard to appreciate how that massive permanent presence, unchanged by the passage of centuries, inspired the belief that it was the home of departed ancestors.

"It's truly awe inspiring, isn't it?"

Jan had come onto the porch without my hearing him.

"I often come out here just to look at it. It's always there, solid, calm, and beautiful, no matter how chaotic life is down here. It's so ridiculous how climbers talk about conquering mountains. How can you conquer a mountain? Mountains are metaphors for eternity. Compared to the span of human life, they are timeless. Perhaps mountain climbers are just rebelling against their own mortality."

The sun rose higher, and we watched as its warm, bright light slowly moved down the granite slopes. It illuminated the first band of alpine scrub, then the conifers, and finally the brilliant emerald greens of the rainforest flowing down into the valleys below.

"Last year the government designated the mountain and valleys around here as a national park," Jan said, as we went back into the house to pack our gear. "I have asked a guide from the village to come with us. Two of his girls will help carry our stuff."

"But I have my own backpack," I said.

Jan looked at me in amusement. "These women earn their living as porters. They use a traditional carrying basket called a *wakid*. They will carry all the food and cooking pots we need, plus extra clothes and sleeping bags. It often gets close to freezing up there at night. You'll appreciate their help before we even get halfway up."

The *wakids* were cylindrical baskets, about two feet high, made of split bamboo. From a two-foot diameter circle at the bottom, they flared up to about three feet in diameter at the top. They were amazingly well designed for carrying heavy loads. They had two shoulder straps, like a regular backpack, and an additional strap that went around the forehead.

The six of us set off after an early breakfast. Soon, we were climbing up a trail through a forest of towering trees and trailing vines. Thomas Dalansu, our guide, pointed out exotic orchids and carnivorous pitcher plants. Once he stopped abruptly. "Look over there," he said. Through a tangle of ferns we saw an enormous red flower. It must have measured more than two feet across. "It's called a *rafflesia*," he said. "You're lucky to see it, as it blooms for only a day or two. It has a really bad smell, like rotting meat, to attract the insects that it feeds on."

Further up the trail we came across a series of concrete basins that contained steaming water from underground hot springs. "The mountain's not volcanic," Thomas said, "it's granite pushed up from below the surrounding sandstone hills. Right now it's about 13,400 feet high, but it is still growing, almost a quarter of an inch every year. We can stop here on the way down if you like. Then your leg muscles will appreciate the benefit of a good, hot soak."

By early evening we reached the hut where we were to spend the night. The women unpacked their *wakids* and prepared a supper of steamed rice and vegetables. Jan was right; I was grateful for the woolen jackets and blankets that the women had brought for us.

We sat around the cooking fire afterwards, our hands wrapped around mugs of hot cocoa. Thomas told us some of the stories about the mountain that he had heard from his grandparents. "Whenever they climbed," he said, "they carried charms with them and performed ceremonies at the summit, to honour the spirits of the ancestors." His brown, weathered face was solemn in the glow of the firelight. Becoming a Christian had obviously done nothing to alter his traditional beliefs.

Next morning Jan, Josef, and I set off again with Thomas. The women stayed behind at the hut with all our gear, as they had been to the top many times.

It was not a difficult climb. The trail led over sloping granite rocks and across gullies. Finally, we arrived at the summit, a rocky mound so narrow that only three or four people could stand on it together.

For a while we sat there in silence, just taking in the splendour of the peaks and valleys around us.

"This is an amazing country," Josef said at last, speaking quietly. "It has to be respected. We can't be like the old missionaries who came to promote the power and authority of the Church. We are only guests here. Our schools and co-ops can be enormously helpful, but we have to be so careful not to impose."

I looked at Josef thoughtfully. He sat with his arms around his knees, his eyes gazing out over the mountain range below us. He came from stolid farming stock and was not given to making long speeches.

"What makes you say that?" Jan asked. "Do you think we're not doing a good job here?"

"No. I just think it's important to realize, and accept, that Sabah has chosen to join Malaysia. It has chosen to be part of a Muslim nation. Some of the older priests worry that the government will force the Chinese and Kadazan Christians to convert to Islam for the sake of national unity. But as long as our students respect each other, what difference does it make if they are Muslim or Christian?"

Nobody said anything for a while. Somehow the spirits of the mountain top seemed to authenticate what Josef had said. Then Jan stood up.

"Perhaps we should carve your words on two tablets of stone and bring them down the mountain with us, a new commandment for missionaries." He was only half-joking.

We started back down, not talking much, each wrapped in our own thoughts. It was faster than the climb up, but I found it much harder on my knees. At the hut, we met the two women and continued on down. By the time we reached the hot springs, my legs were ready for a good soak, as Thomas had promised. Arriving at Bundu Tuhan, we discovered that our ride to Kota Kinabalu had been rescheduled; we would have to leave the next morning.

I was disappointed we had to leave so quickly. I would have liked more time to discuss Josef's ideas about our role as missionaries. He and Jan seemed to have a deep and genuine faith in their religion. Yet they both seemed quite open to acknowledging and respecting other beliefs. I, on the other hand, was already chafing under the strictures of Catholicism.

On the way back it was difficult to talk, between bouncing around in the open Land Rover and having to shout over the roar of the engine. When we got to the city we were immediately thrown back into the pressures and demands of our different jobs. But thankfully the calm solitude of the mountain remained with me as I rattled back to Papar in the railcar.

CHAPTER 57

My first real introduction to the culture and traditions of Sabah was the three-day *kaamatan,* or harvest festival. One day near the end of April, in my second year at Papar, Francis knocked at my door.

"My uncle wants you to come and visit his village for the festival," he said with his customary broad grin. "My uncle is the headman. The *Kaamatan* is our most important festival. It's how we honour the *Bambaazo,* the rice spirit. It's to make sure the spirit stays with us to provide a good harvest for next year."

"You have to go," Piet de Wit said when I told him. "Francis is right. *Kaamatan* is the most significant festival for the Kadazan. They are animists. They believe in five different sets of spirits. The spirit of rice is called *Bambaazon.* It is a part of the Creator Spirit, sustaining life. It protects the growing paddy plants to provide a good crop. For the Kadazan, the paddy plant is a sacred symbol of God's love for His people. The festival is an expression of their gratitude."

The festival began in May on the first day of the full moon. Francis rode behind me on my motorbike showing me the way. It was a tricky ride. There was no road, only narrow paths built up between the paddy fields.

At one point we came to a small river and I had to ferry the bike across on a bamboo raft. Then there were more paddy fields until we came to a stretch of higher ground with a cluster of huts built on stilts. Francis directed me to one of the larger ones in the centre of the village. As we pulled up we were surrounded by a crowd of bare-legged children, their eyes wide with admiration at seeing Francis perched on the back of the motorbike.

"Come and meet my Uncle Amir," Francis said to me as he scooped up one of the little ones.

We climbed up the veranda steps to be met by a large, jovial man who shook my hand vigorously. He looked very distinguished, wearing a black velvet jacket and long pants trimmed with gold braid. Around his head he wore a folded cloth called a *sigal*.

"*Selamat datang*," he said. "Welcome." This was followed by something I did not understand.

"*Selamat petang*," I answered, turning to Francis for help.

He laughed. "My uncle Amir is inviting you into his house. He is honoured to have you here."

After the bright sunlight, the inside of the house was very dark. Francis guided me to a spot against the bamboo wall and sat me down. Gradually, as my eyes adjusted to the gloom, I saw that I was surrounded by a crowd of villagers. They were hunkered around plastic containers full of *tapai*, the potent distilled rice wine that Jan Van Velzen had warned me about. They looked at me expectantly as Amir handed me a glass.

"You're supposed to drink it down in one go," Francis said to me with a grin.

Obediently, I tilted back my head and emptied the glass. The impact was immediate. It was like raw vodka. There was a chorus of cheers and handclapping and, before I could object, my glass was filled again.

"You don't have to drink this one all at once," Francis whispered in my ear.

I noticed an old man sitting behind a row of small brass gongs on top of two long bamboo poles. He started to beat the gongs with a stick in each hand, producing an almost hypnotic rhythm. The *tapai* jugs were moved to one side. Amir and his wife got to their feet and stood facing each other. They extended their arms out sideways and began a slow, elegant dance. Their feet made small movements as their heels moved up and down to the rhythm of the gongs.

"This dance is called the *sumazau*," Francis told me. "The movement of the arms represents the wings of birds preparing to fly."

After a few minutes, one of the women came across the floor. With a smile, she pulled me up to join in the dance. Like the other women in the hut, she was wearing an elaborate blouse made of black velvet, ornamented with gold buttons. A black velvet sarong covered with intricate embroidery hung to her knees. She wore a double belt of silver dollar coins and the whole outfit was completed by a conical woven hat with flowers at the peak. Later, Francis told me that the number of belts and hat decorations signaled whether the woman was married or single.

The *tapai* had given me the courage to overcome my normal shyness. I tried to copy the elegant, stately movements of my partner. Soon, other couples stood up to join us. The dance continued endlessly. Couples would break off occasionally to take a fresh glass of *tapai*.

When the dancers began to stumble and their arms to droop, the gong player finally stopped. Everyone sat down on the floor and food was served. There was buffalo meat, rice, and a kind of porridge made from chicken and egg. There were no vegetables, as they would be a sign of disrespect to the *Bambaazon*.

And then the serious *tapai* drinking resumed.

Through the alcoholic haze that was beginning to envelop me, I realized that perhaps Francis and I should be heading back. After a prolonged round of farewells, we staggered down the steps and fired up the motorbike.

I have little recollection of that long ride back through the night. How we managed to survive the raft trip across the river and along the dykes between the paddy fields, I will never know. The *Bambaazon* spirit must have been with us. All I remember is seeing the bright harvest moon reflected in the paddy fields beside us as we sped home.

At the end of my second year at Papar, a letter arrived from Bishop Buis.

"We are transferring you to the mission in Beaufort," he wrote, using the royal 'we'. "You are to join Father Tobias Chi there. He is in charge of the parish and the primary school. You are to be the new principal of St. John's Secondary School."

I took the letter to Piet de Wit.

"What do you make of this? Why do you think he's moving me so soon?"

"I have no idea," Piet growled as he stood up. "But I'm going to give him a piece of my mind. I'll phone him right away."

I only heard one side of the conversation but I got the gist of it.

". . . he is indispensable . . ."

". . . students and staff love him . . ."

". . . more students have passed their exams than ever before . . ."

". . . his Malay is improving . . ."

". . . his Sunday sermons are intelligible . . ."

". . . they are even instructive . . ."

". . . moving him right now will be disastrous for the school and the parish . . ."

I was astonished. I hadn't realized that Piet valued me so highly.

Finally, there was a long silence while he listened to the Bishop.

"Well, if that's what you really want," he snapped. "I am not pleased." He slapped the phone down and turned to me. "He won't change his mind. The man is an idiot. Apparently Beaufort needs you more than I do. You better start packing."

CHAPTER 58

W e had just finished supper. Father Tobias Chi leaned back in his chair, his face wreathed in tobacco smoke. He had been born in Yanji, Manchuria, and possessed the classic calmness of his Confucian culture. His placid disposition was a pleasant change from Piet de Wit's more volatile temperament.

Jenny Kong was helping her mother clear the dishes. Jenny was my Malay interpreter. It was she who had relayed the Timorese plantation workers' story of my bilocation that morning.

"So, Jenny," Father Chi said. "Now that you know your new principal has special powers, you better be careful. Make sure you don't skip your homework. He'll know if you do."

"I don't believe Father Peter really has special powers," she laughed, looking over her shoulder at me. "I think those Timorese people just mistook him for someone else. They were in a panic because of the fire."

"Nonsense, Jenny," I said. "I can be in two places at once, no problem. It's just that you don't know. You can't see me in both places at the same time."

"Maybe I can," she said laughing. "How do you know I can't?"

She walked out onto the veranda and down the steps with her mother, carrying a pile of plates.

"She's an amazing girl," Father Chi said. "There's no way she would skip her homework. She's one of the smartest students in the school."

We followed Jenny out and sat on the veranda to enjoy the cool of the evening. A tall papaya tree swayed slightly beside us, its dark fronds outlined against the thousand stars that lit the night sky. The sporadic flashes of fireflies and the scent of frangipani blossoms filled the air around us. The anxiety and stresses of the day began to slip away. I had been worrying why the Bishop had transferred me so suddenly to Beaufort.

Tobias interrupted my thoughts as if he had read them.

"I asked the Bishop to send you here because there are two big problems I need help with."

He paused to stoke his pipe.

"The first has to do with inter-Christian rivalry. The Anglican mission runs its own secondary school, St. Paul's, on the other side of Beaufort. When we opened our school, the Anglican pastor was quite upset. He was afraid that we'd be stealing his students away from him. An unhealthy rivalry has developed between the two schools. We have to deal with it before things get out of hand."

I couldn't believe what he was saying. It reminded me of what my father had told me in Uganda years ago. How rival Christian missions had started a civil war in Kampala.

"The other problem," Father Chi went on, "is potentially more serious. It's an ethnic one. Most Chinese parents in town view education as supremely important. They insist that their children commit to an intense work ethic. But Malay and Kadazan parents are more laid back. Their children often don't do as well at school. Now the federal government is putting pressure on the state education department to ensure that more Malay students pass the state exams, even if their work doesn't justify it. The Chinese are resentful when they see Malay students awarded higher marks while their own scores are downgraded."

I was glad Father Chi had brought this up while I was relaxed. It gave me a chance to think before saying anything.

"I don't imagine the ethnic problem is something we can resolve right away," I said. "It's something we can only tackle properly by developing better teaching strategies. But we should deal with the Anglican conflict immediately. Have you ever met the pastor over there?"

"No. I've only heard about him from the Chinese shopkeepers in town. They didn't want to say much. I don't think they want to take sides. But he's an Englishman like yourself, so maybe that will give you some common ground to work from."

"I'll phone him tomorrow," I said. "Hopefully we can sort things out together."

Colin Hurford, the Anglican pastor, sounded pleased when I called. He immediately invited me over to his house, greeting me warmly when I arrived. He looked to be in his late twenties, about the same age as myself. Like me, he was dressed casually, without a clerical collar or any symbol of his standing as a minister. He had an open, friendly face with a lopsided, self-deprecating smile.

"Come on in," he said. "My wife's just making a pot of tea."

He ushered me into a large front room that opened into a cozy kitchen. Unlike traditional Borneo houses built on stilts, his was a colonial-style bungalow. The floor was polished, rose-coloured concrete. It was practical as it helped keep bare feet comfortably cool. A fan, with long wooden blades, spun leisurely at the centre of the ceiling.

"This is my wife, Margaret," Colin said as we settled into a pair of wicker chairs. Colin's wife was setting a tea tray on a low table in front of us. She was an attractive young woman in a white cotton dress, her hair pulled back into a bun.

"Hello, Peter," she said, reaching out to shake my hand, "I'm going to leave you two to help yourselves. I have to prepare my classes for tomorrow. There's more hot water if you need it." She turned and walked over to a small room off the kitchen, closing the door behind her.

"Margaret teaches English to our senior classes," Colin said, pouring the tea. "So what brings you over to our neck of the woods?"

I told him what Father Chi had said about the hostility that had developed between the two missions.

"Father Chi's right," Colin said. "It began with his predecessor who built your secondary school about two years ago. Some of his high-powered business contacts in Kota Kinabalu did some arm twisting among the Chinese shopkeepers here to persuade them to transfer their kids to your school."

"Father Chi told me about that," I said. "I want to apologize, sincerely. It should never have happened. I was hoping you and I could start off on a fresh footing. It would be shameful if two Christian communities couldn't get along with each other in a small town like Beaufort."

"Absolutely," Colin said. "It's definitely time to mend fences. I'm willing to do whatever I can to get over this."

We discussed the possibility of us both jointly addressing an assembly at each school. I suggested that perhaps we could find a couple of teachers from each staff who might be willing to form a joint youth club for social activities. It could help break down the animosity between the students.

"This sounds promising," Colin said. "I'm meeting with my staff tomorrow morning. I can discuss it then."

I left feeling relieved. Colin seemed genuinely amenable to improving relations. I felt I had found a colleague who was not prepared to let the fog of dogma suffocate the spirit of Christianity.

The next morning, I walked along the railway line towards the school for my first meeting with the staff. I was a little nervous. I wondered how they were going to feel about a new, young principal taking over St. John's.

For the past year, the school had been run with one of the teachers serving as acting principal. He was now to be my vice-principal. His name was John Mui and he had taught for many years in the primary school at the mission. A confirmed bachelor, he lived alone in a little house next to the railway line. It was on my way to the school, so I arranged to drop in for a chat before the staff meeting.

"Welcome, come in," John said as he opened the door. His smile reassured me right away. He was, in fact, grateful that he was no longer acting principal. "I enjoy being a teacher much more than being an administrator," he said.

John was a self-effacing Chinese gentleman in his late forties. He had a quiet dignity that immediately won the respect of his students. He set clear boundaries for them in his classroom. He never referred anyone to my office the whole time I was at the school.

John filled me in on the routines for starting the new school year and I told him of my conversation with Colin Hurford. He agreed that bad feelings had been generated between the two schools unnecessarily, and that we needed to work together at breaking them down. He thought the younger teachers would be open to improving things, but that some of the older teachers hired by Father Yong might be more reluctant.

"We should try anyway," he said. "Just give everyone a chance to settle in. We can bring it up at a staff meeting in a week or so."

Together we set off along the train tracks to the school. Most of the teachers had already arrived. We chose a classroom and arranged the desks in a circle so that we could all see each other. I introduced myself and asked each of the teachers to do the same while I quickly wrote down their names. John then dealt with housekeeping details while I practised putting names to faces.

"You know much better than I how the school runs," I told them. "I'm not interested in making huge changes. I want you to carry on just as you did with John. And I want you to feel free to come to me if I tread on your toes by mistake."

The next day John introduced me at the school assembly. Afterwards I went around and visited each class for a few minutes so that the students could get to know me. Then I got down to teaching my first senior English class. The students were just as keen as the ones in Papar. It didn't take long for them to get over their natural shyness. I felt confident that we were set to have a good year.

After a week or so, with the school running smoothly, I called a staff meeting to raise the question of our relationship with St. Paul's School. I told them about my meeting with Colin and how we had both agreed to work on building a friendship between the two schools. There were a few uneasy glances, but most teachers seemed to support the idea of improving relations. Then Anthony Wong, a young gym teacher, spoke up.

"I would like to help form a youth club. I talked about it with a friend of mine at St. Paul's some time ago. We just didn't see how to get it started. But if you and Reverend Hurford hold joint assemblies, we could come too and make a presentation about it."

I was impressed.

"That sounds exactly like what we need," I said. "Let's get together afterwards and discuss details."

Over the next few weeks, Colin and I spoke at an assembly in each school. Then Anthony and his friend spoke about their new youth club.

"We could have joint basketball teams, one for boys and one for girls. If we picked the best players from both schools, we could represent Beaufort at the state championships."

This particular proposal was greeted with huge enthusiasm. Basketball, it turned out, was fast becoming one of the most popular sports in Sabah. We were off to a good start.

CHAPTER 59

As the school year progressed, I became more at ease in my role as principal. The staff seemed relaxed too. They were competent with their classes and comfortable enough to joke with me in the staff room. They always included me in their social get-togethers. But in spite of their friendliness, I often felt quite alone. I was still plagued by my poor grasp of Malay.

I enjoyed the classes I was teaching. Like the staff, the students worked hard and were consistently cheerful. I had started an art class to encourage the less academic students. But the demands of the Overseas Cambridge art curriculum smothered creativity. To establish uniformity for the exam we were restricted, almost exclusively, to developing the students' skills in a realistic rendering of local flowers. I felt torn if I devoted a period to more imaginative topics. The pressure on the students to succeed in the exam was just too acute.

In my English classes I began to notice the ethnic disparity Father Chi had talked about. The Malay and Kadazan students struggled, quickly becoming frustrated. The Chinese students, on the other hand, read voraciously and submitted lengthy essays until I was forced to limit the word count. I decided to raise the problem at a staff meeting and asked if anyone had suggestions for a solution. It was Anthony Wong, the gym teacher, who once again pointed us in the right direction.

"I don't have any problems in gym," he said, "because the students are all doing something physical. Perhaps we should have more hands-on courses in the school, such as drafting and wood-working."

He had a point. Our courses were overly academic. They were an inheritance from the colonial days. The British were interested only in basic literacy to ensure a supply of clerks for their government or for managing plantations. Whenever they needed to develop infrastructure they imported mechanics and engineers from abroad.

"That's it," I said to Anthony. "If Sabah is to be truly independent, we need to train people in the trades. Perhaps the less academically

288

inclined students would be more interested if we were to offer an industrial arts program in the school."

"True," John said, "but a program like that is expensive. We would need tools and machinery and a skilled instructor."

"I could explore possibilities for funding," I said, "as long as you all think the idea's worthwhile. There are lots of aid organizations that might help."

"Well, if you can find the money, I think it would be a great," John said. The others nodded in agreement.

I remembered Father Franz van den Schoor who had gone out of his way to welcome me when I first arrived in Sabah. He had a reputation in the diocese as a builder. I wrote to him about our ideas and asked if he had any suggestions about aid organizations that might help. Two weeks later, a package arrived with a letter.

"I like your idea," Father Van den Schoor wrote. "There's an organization called *Misereor*, set up by the German Catholic bishops. It is an agency for co-funding development projects with the German government. Its mandate is to 'seek and maintain partnerships with development organizations . . . irrespective of their religious convictions'. I think your project meets their objectives. I have enclosed the relevant application forms."

I was excited. When I read *Misereor's* guidelines for funding requests, I realized we had an excellent chance of being approved. One of the prerequisites was that we should provide evidence of our own contribution to the project. So I took the idea to Father Chi to see what he could come up with.

"We can contribute the costs of the classroom space and teacher's salary," he suggested. "I know an architect who would donate the cost of the construction drawings. We can also assign a cost to your supervision of the project. That should be sufficient to meet their requirements."

With this encouragement, I drafted a detailed proposal. I tried to anticipate any problems or objections that might be raised in the review process. I then took the railcar to Kota Kinabalu to present it to Bishop Buis. I requested an interview for the early afternoon when I knew he would be relaxing on the veranda with his cigar.

"So what's all this about?" he said, leafing through my proposal. "You youngsters are always coming up with new ideas to change the world. What is it this time?"

I explained that it was part of a solution that Father Chi and I had come up with to promote the success of indigenous peoples in our school. I felt that this approach would appeal to him because of the political pressure from the Department of Education.

"I hope you don't expect the diocese to come up with any money," he said, setting the file aside on his coffee table. "I'll take a look at it when I have time. I'll phone Father Chi in a few days to let him know what I decide."

He dismissed me with a wave of his cigar, and I went off to seek out my friend, Paddy Cahill.

I found him in the church hall, practising with a youth band. He had taken up the trumpet. "Herb Alpert's tunes are all the rage at the parish dances," he told me. "So I put together a band to play his music. We are very much in demand."

I listened for a while and had to admit that they were really quite good. Afterwards, he took me out to supper at his favourite restaurant. While we were waiting for our meal, I filled him in on my doings in Beaufort.

"I envy you," Paddy said, sipping his bowl of green tea. "It must be so satisfying to be doing something useful. I don't feel I'm really needed here. This town is as developed as any town in Europe. People here are not poor, sick, hungry, or disadvantaged. And I'm getting tired of trying to explain Catholic doctrines that make very little sense."

Nevertheless, Paddy was clearly popular among the youth of Kota Kinabalu. Our meal was constantly interrupted by young people coming over to talk to him. Paddy was a darkly handsome young Irishman whom the girls found very attractive. I felt quite jealous of the attention he was getting.

About a week after I got back from Kota Kinabalu, Father Chi called me into his office, which doubled as his bedroom.

"Sit down," he said, pulling up an extra chair. "I just got a call from the Bishop. He wants me to tell you that he didn't think much of your scheme. He says that offering a trade program in the school will make all the bright Chinese students transfer to St. Paul's. They'll think St. John's is just for dummies."

My heart sank. Father Chi paused to relight his pipe.

I gazed out his open window, wondering what I could do. Outside, a hummingbird hovered over a riot of red bougainvillea blossoms. The vivid colours contrasted sharply with the drab, grey wooden boards that framed the room. Clamped to the wall above the window, a sickly white gecko was poised to pounce on any unfortunate insect that might venture in. It was a bit like the Bishop, I thought, waiting to pounce on new initiatives.

Finally, Father Chi had the pipe drawing to his satisfaction.

"The Bishop said to tell you to go ahead anyway, that it will be a learning experience."

It took a moment to sink in. I leaped to my feet and knocked over my chair. Startled, the hummingbird fled. The gecko remained unmoved.

I wanted to hug Father Chi.

I began the very next day to complete the details of the application to *Misereor*. Father Chi's architect friend drew up plans for both an industrial arts room and a small house for the teacher. I went to Kota Kinabalu to consult with the principal of the only trade school in Sabah. He supplied me with an inventory of tools and machines that we would need and an outline of the courses we could teach. I then drafted a persuasive rationale for the project and sent everything off by registered mail to Germany.

At Mass I actually prayed that our proposal would be accepted.

CHAPTER 60

I was excited at the prospect of the *Misereor* project, not simply because of its intrinsic value. It promised to provide a new focus for my life. I was beginning my fourth year in Borneo and, increasingly, I was fighting loneliness.

Beaufort was a tiny little town, hemmed in by brooding jungle-clad hills. It had one ramshackle cinema that featured movies in Cantonese or Hindi. There was no television and very limited radio. To distract myself, I took long walks to neighbouring villages, visiting the homes of students for a bit of companionship. But language was always a problem. My Malay was not good enough for any real conversation.

But now, shortly after the new school year began, a letter arrived from Germany. *Misereor* had approved our project.

I was thrilled. Here was something I could pour my energies into. I immediately contacted the architect. We started to plan the layout of machines and workbenches, the ducts for the dust collector, the location of safety stations. Drafting tables and workbenches had to be ordered from a local carpenter. Advertisements had to be placed in the newspapers to recruit a qualified instructor. It was good to be so busy. The hollowness in my heart could be ignored.

It now became necessary to travel frequently to Kota Kinabalu for meetings with the architect. One day the railcar back to Beaufort was particularly crowded. At the last minute a young Eurasian woman climbed aboard. She asked if she could squeeze in beside me. As the railcar hurtled forward, lurching from side to side, her arm and thigh would press against mine. At a particularly sharp curve, she clasped my knee to steady herself. The sudden, intense jolt of pleasure took me by surprise.

"I'm so sorry," she said with a shy smile. "It's such a bumpy ride."

"No problem," I said, trying my best to be casual.

But the physical reaction to her touch unsettled me. It was a sharp reminder of the self-questioning I had gone through at the seminary. Priestly celibacy was like the biblical millstone hanging around my neck. As the railcar rattled on, I found myself envying Colin Hurford. As an Anglican priest he could legitimately share his life with a woman. I wanted to talk to this lovely lady sitting next to me. But I was too self-conscious to even begin a conversation.

Back in Beaufort, the next few weeks were hectic. Our annual Sports Day was coming up, and there was much to do in preparation.

The Sports Day was always a big event. The students were divided into houses, after the British boarding school model. Each house had its own flag and colours. On Sports Day the house teams competed against each other. The town *padang*, or playing field, became the venue. Running lanes were marked off and jumping pits filled with sand. Non-athletes in every house were co-opted to build *attap* shelters to provide shade for their athletes. The shelters were awarded points for creativity and these counted towards the final standings in the games.

The day began with the houses parading around the track. The townspeople gathered to cheer as they always did for any *ramai-ramai*, or crowded gathering. Under the hot sun runners raced, jumpers soared, javelins were hurled, and the winning athletes became heroes. The closing ceremonies were presided over by the district officer and local dignitaries. They handed out ribbons and awards from a raised platform at one end of the field. I stood on the platform with Anthony Wong, the gym teacher, organizing the various trophies.

One of the dignitaries was the town doctor, an anemic-looking British man whose nose seemed permanently tilted in an attitude of disdain. He had arrived in Beaufort just one year before me. After presenting his trophy he turned to me and said, "I have to introduce you to Elin Jones, my new district health nurse." He walked me over to where a young woman in a blue denim uniform was chatting with a group of students.

"Elin," he said, "this is Father Peter, the principal of St. John's."

She turned towards me and I recognized her at once.

"We've already met," she said, smiling. "Don't you remember? On the railcar?" Her soft, brown eyes shone with amusement.

"Oh, I'm sorry. Of course I remember," I said.

I shook her hand, and my body thrilled again.

This time it was as if she felt the electricity too. She withdrew her hand quickly, seeming slightly flustered. Then, recovering, she said with a laugh, "It was a very bumpy ride, wasn't it?"

"I'm afraid we have a favour to ask you," the doctor said to me. "We think the girls in your school could benefit from Elin's expertise. They can be quite ignorant about their own bodies. They don't get much information from their parents. What they do get is often a mixture of superstition and bad hygiene. I want Elin to do a series of presentations at the school. That way, the girls will get to know her. Then they won't be so shy about coming to the clinic when they need help."

"Sounds like a good idea," I said. "Let me talk to our family studies teacher. I'm sure she'll be grateful for the help."

"Good," the doctor said. "You can call Elin at the clinic to set up a schedule."

We were interrupted by District Officer Gordon Harris who wandered over to us while we were talking.

Gordon Harris was quite a character. A tall, wiry Englishman with skin like tanned leather, he had spent almost his entire life as an administrator in colonial Borneo. In his official capacity as a district officer, Gordon was capable and unpretentious. Fluent in most of the local languages, he had a reputation for being firm and fair. While most colonial officers had been let go after independence, he had been asked to stay on.

In private Gordon exercised a quirky sense of humour. He refused to take earnest young Peace Corps volunteers seriously, teasing them at any opportunity. A confirmed bachelor, he had an appreciative eye for pretty women but was always the perfect gentleman, considerate and courteous.

"I'm Gordon Harris," he said to Elin. "I don't know why the doctor hasn't introduced us." "Elin Jones," the doctor said hastily, "our new district health nurse."

"Pleasure to meet you, Miss Jones," Gordon said, while Elin flashed him a brilliant smile.

"Congratulations on a very smooth Sports Day, Father Peter," he continued, turning to me. "Your school always puts on a really good show, you know."

"Thank you," I said, hoping Elin would note the compliment. "I have an excellent staff."

"I'm having a reception tonight," Gordon said, "a farewell for some of the Peace Corps people. Hope you can come. It's in the government rest house. Eight o'clock tonight."

Normally I was hesitant to socialize with the *orang puthi*. Their parties were too reminiscent of the racial exclusiveness I had seen in Africa. But now Gordon had given me a golden opportunity to see Elin again and perhaps even to talk to her. I told myself that it was entirely necessary for me to get to know her. After all, she was coming to my Catholic school to speak with the female students about sexual concerns.

At supper that night I told Father Chi about the doctor's proposal.

"That's excellent," he said. "The girls are often confused at that age. We can use all the help we can get. The doctor should come too and talk to the boys. They can be even more ignorant than the girls."

I was a little late getting to the reception at the rest house that evening. By the time I arrived, the party was already in full swing. Gordon was engaged in a game of darts with an American forestry volunteer. They were surrounded by a group of boisterous, beer-drinking supporters who shouted comments at every shot. Elin was sitting at the bar looking gorgeous in an elegant blue sari. She wore her hair up, revealing tiny, turquoise earrings. With her was Rose D'Arrigo, an American Peace Corps girl who had been teaching at our elementary school. I walked over to them, relieved that Rose was there. Her presence would help keep me from being too overwhelmed by Elin's loveliness.

"Rose was just telling me about your *Misereor* project," Elin explained. "You must be so excited."

"I am," I said.

"I'm sad that I won't be here to see it," said Rose. "You must stay in touch. Let me know how things go."

"Did Elin tell you she's coming to talk to the girls at St. John's?" I asked.

"No, but it's a good idea. A couple of girls came to me the other day asking about contraceptives. They had heard somewhere, probably from Father Chi, that Catholics were not allowed to use them."

"That's why I think we should talk," I said to Elin. "It's important you give them all the information they need. You mustn't hold back just because we're a Catholic school."

Elin gave me a smile that threatened to melt the buttons on my shirt.

"It's good to hear you say that," she said. "I was afraid I'd be getting a list of things that I wouldn't be allowed to talk about."

"Not from me," I said.

A loud cheer came from the crowd at the dart board. Gordon had won his game. He came over to the bar with his empty scotch glass. "George, another double," he said to the bartender, "and one for Father Peter."

"Congratulations. I see you won," I said.

"Good to know I haven't lost my touch after all these years. What are you ladies drinking?"

Elin and Rose were nursing wine spritzers.

"George, get two more of those for the ladies."

"No, I'm fine with this," Rose said.

"Me too," said Elin.

"Well, we have to do something wild on your last night, Rose. Let's finish our drinks and go to the beach. Or better still, we can bring our drinks with us. We can use my Land Rover."

Rose looked a bit doubtful. "I have to catch the six o'clock railcar tomorrow morning," she said.

"What about you, Elin?"

"Only if Rose comes along."

"Come on, Rose. It's your last night. No more Borneo beaches after this."

"Oh, all right," Rose agreed. "As long as you get me back at a reasonable hour."

A few minutes later we were on the road to Kuala Penyu beach in Gordon's Land Rover. I sat in front; the two girls were in the back. The velvet warmth of the tropical night flowed around us as we drove. An hour later we pulled up onto the white sandy beach. Gordon cut the engine and we sat there in the stillness for a moment, listening to the gentle surge of the breaking waves. The beach was bathed in the faint glow of the million stars that litter the southern sky. Far out in the blackness of the water, tiny pinpricks of light flickered where invisible fishermen bobbed in their invisible boats.

"Let's go for a swim," Gordon suggested, breaking the spell.

He jumped out and sprinted towards the water, abandoning his shirt and shorts along the way. "Come on, Father Peter!" he yelled as he launched his long, lean body into the breaking waves. Not to be outdone, I stripped down to my boxer shorts and followed. When I surfaced, Gordon was calling the girls to come and join us. Soon the four of us were bouncing around in the water, splashing and yelling like teenagers. None of us had towels, and I began to worry how it would look to Father Chi if I returned to the house with my light tan trousers soaked. But the solution was simple. I would discreetly remove my boxers and wear only my dry pants.

When I sensed that everyone had about enough, I was the first one to leave the water. I ran up the beach and quickly changed behind the Land Rover. When Gordon and the girls arrived, they just threw their clothes on over their wet underwear and piled back into the car. I jumped in too, placing my wet briefs on the floor at my feet. Gordon drove us back to Beaufort, dropping the girls off at their houses and me at the mission. In my unaccustomed state of euphoria, I completely forgot to retrieve my sodden underwear.

Next morning Gordon drove up to the school in his Land Rover. My boxers were flying like a flag from his radio antenna for all to see.

Chapter 61

The day following my midnight swim I asked John Mui and the family studies teacher to come to my office. I told them about the doctor wanting Elin to talk to the students at the school. They had no objections and agreed to meet with her to review the topics she would be discussing. "I'll contact Miss Jones and find out when she can come," I said, trying to sound business-like. "I'll let you know."

As soon as they left, I called the clinic.

"Hello, Peter," Elin's voice answered. "I can't talk right now. I'm in the middle of delivering a baby. I'll call you tonight."

It was quite late when she called back.

"I'm just going to take a shower. Why don't you give me a few minutes and then come over to my house to talk about the program?"

"Sure," I said, with only a momentary pause. "I have some tentative dates that we can discuss."

When I put the receiver down, my whole body was trembling. I knew that by accepting Elin's invitation I was crossing a line. Catholic priests should not visit beautiful women in their homes late at night. I might have suggested we meet in my office the next day. But I didn't.

It was as dark as it ever gets on a clear night in Sabah. The stars provided enough light for me to see my way through the town to Elin's house. I climbed the stairs to her veranda and knocked. A minute passed and then the door opened. Elin stood there, framed by the light behind her, her hair wrapped in a towel, her body clearly outlined through the folds of a thin silk kimono. Sensing my confusion, she reached for my hand and drew me into the house.

"Forgive me. I had to work late," she said. "The baby refused to come easily. The poor mother had a long, hard labour. Sit yourself down while I finish drying my hair."

She disappeared into the bathroom, and I sat looking around at her living room. A single, delicate white orchid graced a glass coffee table. The bamboo armchairs and couch were covered with cushions embroidered with intricate Indian designs. An oval-shaped white rug broke the long lines of the polished, teak floor boards. There was a distinctly feminine feel to the room. I found it strangely exciting.

When Elin returned, I was examining a family photograph on top of a bookcase. It showed a tall, wiry white man with his arm around an Indian woman dressed in a blue and gold sari. In front of them were three young boys and a girl. The girl had a mass of dark, curly hair and was perhaps twelve years old.

"Yes, that's me," Elin said, frowning. "My father was Welsh and my mother was from India. He worked for the colonial government as a civil engineer. He died of tuberculosis shortly after that picture was taken."

"Oh, I'm so sorry," I said, seeing the sudden sadness in her eyes. "Where's your mother now?"

"She went back to India with my brothers when I was fifteen. I didn't want to go. All my friends were here. I was going to school at St. Francis in Kota Kinabalu. The nuns let me become a boarder. When I graduated, I went to the Queen Elizabeth Hospital to get my nursing certificate. And now here I am."

She led me over to the bamboo sofa and sat down next to me.

"How about you, Peter? What brought you to Beaufort?"

Her invitation opened the floodgates.

I had never talked as much about myself to anyone as I did that night. I told her how I had gone to a seminary for future priests at eleven years old; how I had been raised in an all-male environment most of my life; how, as a result, I always felt insecure and unsure of myself with women, especially with a woman as beautiful and attractive as herself.

"Even before I was ordained, I had doubts about the Catholic Church. Coming to Sabah on the boat, I realized I didn't believe in much of what I was supposed to be doing as a priest."

While I talked, she listened intently, her eyes full of encouragement and concern.

And then she told me about her own life; about feeling trapped in a tiny house with her three brothers; not having any privacy; desperately working hard at school as a way of escape. She had rebelled after her father died, refusing to leave for India with her mother. Still hurting from the loss of her dad, she couldn't bear to be uprooted from her friends and teachers. In the end, she had won the battle but was only now recovering from the pain it had cost her.

I couldn't take my eyes off her as she talked.

When she reached over and kissed me, it seemed the most natural thing in the world. I kissed her back, a long, long kiss. Then she stood up and gently led me into her bedroom. I was amazed. I could not believe she actually wanted me to lie with her, to hold her close in my arms. It was incredible, the feel of her body against mine, her legs wrapped around mine, inviting me in.

But I pulled away. I was terrified even while my body craved her.

"I'm scared," I said. "This is so new for me."

"I understand," she said.

"I was attracted to you the moment you sat down next to me on the railcar," I told her.

I held her close, not wanting to let go.

"Let's just lie here for a while and not think too much," Elin suggested.

Later, as I walked back to the mission in the semi-darkness, I was in a daze. I could not believe what had just happened. Suddenly there was a whole new dimension to my life. Everything around me seemed different. The silhouettes of rooftops and palms assumed strange, shadowy shapes against the starlit sky. The scent of Elin's perfume still clung to me. I was elated and frightened at the same time. Part of me felt like a guilty teenager. What if people found out? What if Father Chi found out? What would I do?

To my surprise, next morning the world was unchanged. As usual, streams of uniformed students made their way along the railway line to the school. Teachers appeared, classes resumed, and I sat in my office trying desperately to concentrate on the latest report for *Misereor*. The contractor was already bulldozing the site for the new staff house. Two boxcars of crushed limestone sat on the railway line opposite the school, waiting to be unloaded.

But I couldn't keep Elin out of my head.

When my phone at the mission rang that evening, I knew it was her.

"Peter, we didn't arrange a schedule for me to come to the school." She sounded all efficient and business-like. "Why don't you come over and we can set things up?"

"Of course," I said. "We need to talk."

This time I remembered to bring the notes from my meeting with John and the family studies teacher. But as soon as she opened the door, I was in her arms.

We kissed hungrily, stumbling awkwardly towards her bedroom. She unbuttoned my shirt. Her tongue was in my mouth. My fingers fumbled at the clasp of her bra. Then we tumbled on to her bed, our bodies urgent to make love.

But this time it was she who pulled away.

She half turned, raising herself up on her elbow and looking down at me, her incredible eyes starting to brim with tears. She collapsed onto my chest, one small fist beating away at me.

"It's not fair, it's not fair. How come you're a priest? How come I fell for a priest?"

"I don't know," I said, holding her close. "You're right. It isn't fair. I don't know what we can do. If Father Chi were to find out, I'd be on the next plane home. It would mean the end of us and the *Misereor* project."

She rolled off me, turning on to her back, staring up at the ceiling.

"How long will it take before the project is up and running?"

"Another year and a half at least," I said. "Perhaps we should stop seeing each other for the time being. It will be awful, but I don't know what else we can do."

She looked at me, horrified. "I don't know if I can do that," she said, and I could see a coldness creeping into her eyes.

"Well, let's at least try," I pleaded. I can't betray the confidence that the mission and *Misereor* have placed in me. Once everything is set, I can quit as a priest. But, until then I can't risk anyone finding out about us."

She lay there for a while, her head turned away from me. I tried to put my arm around her shoulders but I felt her stiffen. "You should go," she said, her voice muffled by the pillows. "I'll bring a schedule to school tomorrow."

I slowly got out of bed and dressed as she lay with her back to me. I leaned over and kissed her shoulder.

"Good night," I said.

I shut the door quietly behind me.

CHAPTER 62

I looked for Elin at school the next day, but I didn't see her. John Mui said she had been there and settled on a schedule. It was hard to concentrate on my work. I missed her intensely.

On Sunday I was astonished to see Elin sitting among the congregation at Mass. Her head was down and she did not look at me. I searched for her afterwards, but she had gone. I desperately wanted to talk to her. If she wanted to cut herself off from me completely, why had she shown up at the church?

The following two Sundays she was there again, but each time, she disappeared afterwards. I became more and more upset. I was obsessed. She was all I could think about. I would walk past the hospital hoping to bump into her. At night I would lie staring at the phone, wondering if I should call. Several times I started to dial, only to hang up. Then, late one night, she called me herself. She was crying.

"Peter, can you come over? Please. I can't stand it anymore. Please come over. The door's unlocked."

She hung up before I could say anything. I sat holding the phone thinking how much I wanted to go to her.

In the end, I did.

She was lying in bed, her face to the wall, exactly as she had been the last time when I left. I climbed in beside her and this time she turned and clung to me, her cheeks wet with tears.

"I'm sorry," she sobbed. "I missed you so much. I thought if I saw you at church it would be safe. No one would know. But it's no good. I want to be with you, and I know you want to be with me."

"You're right." I said. "It's been awful. I can't go on like this either. I keep looking out for you at school on the days when I know you're there. We've got to stop avoiding each other. We have to be able to meet and talk like normal people. I don't care what anyone thinks."

"But we can't risk you being sent away," Elin said, a touch of panic in her voice. "That would be even worse. Perhaps we can arrange to meet each other secretly. We could drive out of Beaufort and meet somewhere along one of the plantation roads. If you keep coming to my house, someone is sure to notice."

I cupped her face with my hands, looking into her eyes.

"Are you sure that's what you want?" I asked. "It's not going to be easy. Even talking to each other on the phone could be a problem."

Beaufort had a manual switchboard. An operator answered all the calls and plugged in the appropriate lines to make connections. The operator could, and probably would, listen in on our conversations.

"We could exchange messages when I'm at the school," Elin said. "We could leave notes in one of your books on the shelf in your office. It would be kind of fun, a clandestine cover-up."

It was good to see her eyes light up with a smile again.

"I have a copy of Tolstoy's *Anna Karenina*," I said. "I'll put it on the top shelf on the left hand side. It will be easy for you to find."

So that's what we did. Our communication system worked well. On the days that Elin was at the school, I would find a note from her suggesting a location to meet. My replies would be gone by the end of the day. It was fun, too, when we met accidentally outside a classroom or on the stairs. The girls would tease me. "You like Miss Jones, don't you, Sir?" they would say, holding their hands up to their mouths while they laughed.

Our secret meetings were made easier by the fact that I had recently moved out of the mission house. A volunteer teacher from New Zealand had been assigned to the school by Oxfam. I gave her my quarters at the mission and installed a bed in my office at the school. It was in full view of the boys' boarding house, so Elin could not visit me there. But it did mean I could come and go freely without Father Chi being aware of my movements.

Meanwhile, work continued all that year on the industrial arts project. In January of the following year Mr. Hoffman, the representative from *Misereor*, arrived to check on progress. He was impressed. The teacher's house was almost complete. The classroom was wired, water stations connected and the ducts for the dust collector installed. We were just awaiting the arrival of the machines being shipped from Germany.

I called a meeting to introduce Mr. Hoffman to the staff. I suppose I should not have been surprised when Anthony Wong stood up to make a request.

"Mr. Hoffman, Sir," he said, "you will have noticed that our playing field in front of the school is a sea of mud. It's constantly being flooded by the river. Would it be possible to extend your funds to include building two concrete basketball courts?"

Mr. Hoffman turned to me with a raised eyebrow.

"It's true," I said, impressed with Anthony's initiative. "We often have to cancel gym classes because we have nowhere to hold them. Our gym is the field."

Mr. Hoffman turned back to Anthony. "Very well, give Father Walther detailed plans and a cost estimate. I will see what we can do."

The staff rose as one and gave Mr. Hoffman an ovation. Anthony's face split in an enormous grin. He ran up and pumped Mr. Hoffman's hand.

It was a real coup. Basketball was one of the most popular sports in Sabah. After school the boys, and the girls too, played endlessly on the one court in town. Two new basketball courts would be ideal for the youth club.

Afterwards I took Mr. Hoffman to meet Father Chi, who opened a bottle of good Scotch for the occasion.

"How are things going with recruiting a teacher?" Mr. Hoffman asked.

"I posted advertisements in several Australian newspapers," I told him. "I also appealed to the Peace Corps and Oxfam. I've had several applications but only one that looks promising. He's a teacher from Sydney and he wants to bring his wife with him. I have sent a contract. I should be hearing back from him soon."

"Well, I think your project is well on track," Mr. Hoffman said. "If we can get the machines installed and a teacher over here, I think you should be ready to start by the beginning of the next school year. Once I send in my report, the final funding installment will be released. Let me know the cost of the basketball courts so that I can include them in the report."

Father Chi and I walked back together after seeing Mr. Hoffman off at the railway station.

"How's Miss Jones doing at the school?" he asked.

I hesitated. Was there something more to his question?

"She's been fine," I said. "The girls seem to like her and the family-studies teacher is happy to have her."

"That's good. I'm glad things are going so well."

I looked at him uneasily, but he gave no sign that there was anything behind his words.

Elin and I had been meeting fairly regularly late at night. We chose different isolated spots along the plantation roads. I would drive there on my motorbike. We would designate a clearing just off the road where we could park, hidden behind the curtain of vines that clung to the tall, rainforest trees. When she arrived in her Land Rover, I would climb onto the seat beside her.

We would sit close, holding each other quietly, aware of the jungle sounds all around us, the screeches of unseen animals, the clicking and clacking of insects, the call of night birds. Occasionally the sounds would be interrupted by the approaching roar of a truck on the road. We would instinctively duck down as its head lights briefly swept across the surrounding jungle.

"I can't wait for you to stop being a priest," Elin complained one night. "Having to keep everything secret is making me angry. Are you sure you can't talk to Father Chi and see if the Bishop would let you stay until the project is done?"

"There's no way he would do that," I said. "It would be a scandal for the parish. My friend, Paddy Cahill, tried. He fell in love with a Chinese girl in Kota Kinabalu. They shipped him off as soon as they found out." Paddy had phoned to tell me just before he left.

"Well, how can we get to know each other if we only snatch a few hours like this? It's really frustrating."

After that I found our trysts becoming more sporadic. It took longer for Elin to reply to my messages. Then one night she was over an hour late for our meeting. When I joined her in the Land Rover, she didn't want to snuggle like we usually did. She stayed far over on her side, holding on to the steering wheel. When I asked her what was wrong, she didn't answer immediately.

Finally she said, "I have asked for a transfer to Sandakan. I'm leaving Beaufort next week."

I sat there, shocked into silence, unable to absorb what she had just said.

"I just can't go on seeing you like this," she continued. "There's no future in it for us. You're a priest. You can't take me out on dates like a normal person. You're always afraid. Afraid of being found out. And I hate having to hide my feelings. I hate it when I see you at school or around town. I can't do this anymore. I just can't."

I felt completely numb. She was right. I had been unfair to her. How could I have expected her to stay while I skulked around hiding my feelings for her?

"I'm so sorry, Elin," I said. "It was mean of me to expect you to continue seeing me like this. I wish things were different . . . I wish I felt free . . ."

She turned suddenly. She was furious. She grabbed my shoulders, shaking me back and forth against the car seat.

"Peter," she yelled. "For goodness sake, wake up! Take charge of your life! Stop being so sorry for yourself! The women in my hospital are better than you. They know life only comes with pain and struggle . . ."

She let go of me, curling up tight in her seat, sobbing uncontrollably.

I sat beside her until the storm wracking her body began to subside. Gradually, her heaving shoulders relaxed. She was exhausted. Slowly she stretched one leg and then the other, the backs of her hands up against her forehead.

"I should go, Peter," she said. "I'll write to you when I get to Sandakan. Let me know how things go with the project."

I got out of the Land Rover and stood there, watching miserably, as it lurched back onto the road and disappeared into the night.

CHAPTER 63

After Elin left for Sandakan, I stopped using the railcar to go to Kota Kinabalu for the *Misereor* project. Instead I rode my motorbike down a road that had recently been carved through the jungle. Often I drove too fast, scattering stone chips and stray chickens, ignoring the danger of uncontrolled skids on the loose gravel. I missed Elin.

At one point, a river crossed the road. There was no bridge. Vehicles had to splash through a shallow ford. I knew enough to always throttle hard to prevent water from being sucked into the engine. But one day the water was so deep it came over my handlebars. The oil emulsified in the engine and the bike was ruined. Fortunately the friendly manager of a local plantation offered me his used Volkswagen Beetle. Now if the water was too deep the car would float.

By December 1968, our new industrial arts facility was complete. The Australian instructor, Mr. Atkinson, arrived with his wife. He was able to help organize the classrooms and check that all the machines were working properly. The first carpentry classes began in January 1969. Unfortunately Mr. Atkinson was unable to stay. He was succeeded by John Brady whose favourite phrase in the woodwork shop was 'cut it' which did not only apply to the lumber.

At the end of the year, in December 1969, I had to send an evaluation report for *Misereor*.

On the whole the project had gone well, but there was one recommendation I wanted to make. The policy of supplying German machines was problematic. It was an unfortunate attempt to combine foreign aid with business interests. The result was that spare parts were costly and difficult to obtain quickly when needed. Machinery manufactured in Asian countries would have been far more practical.

I was immensely pleased with our new instructor, John Brady. He had a relaxed way of teaching and an infectious enthusiasm for skilled work. The students responded well to him. As they began signing up for the next school year, I realized that our enrolment was going to increase. Many of the more academic Chinese students began to recognize the value of the program. They could see that Sabah was developing rapidly and that there would be a growing demand for architects and engineers.

"The students seem to be taking a lot of pride in the projects they are building," John Mui said to me one day. "I must admit I was a little doubtful about the program at first, but I was wrong. They seem really excited about what they're doing. I went into the shop just now and they all wanted to show me what they were working on. We were lucky to get John. He's doing a great job and the kids really like him."

"Perhaps we should have an Open House at the end of the year," I said, "and invite the town to come and tour the school. Then the students can really show off their work. I'll talk to John and see what he thinks."

John welcomed the idea. Students put up posters in town, and I sent invitations to the director of education and the principal of the trade school in Kota Kinabalu. On the big day parents and friends came from the surrounding villages. It became a *ramai ramai,* or gathering, something that the people of Sabah always enjoy.

In May 1970 the diocese arranged for me to go on home leave. I was booked to fly to Toronto, Canada, to visit my family. Normally I would return to Sabah after six months. But I already knew that leaving Sabah would be my first step to leaving the priesthood.

I had overstayed my appointment to Sabah by a year to make sure the *Misereor* project was sustainable. I felt my work in Beaufort had been really worthwhile and something I would always be proud of. Now I felt I could safely leave it in John Mui's capable hands. He agreed to take over from me as principal while I was away.

However I didn't want to leave Borneo without seeing Elin one last time. I felt I owed her a huge debt. She had awakened in me a longing for a loving relationship that could not be ignored. It confirmed for me that I had made a huge mistake in becoming a priest. Now I knew that the need for love lay at the very core of my being. So I arranged a quick flight to Sandakan.

Father Frank Van der Schoor greeted me warmly at the airport. It did not seem like four years since I had asked him for help to find funding for the industrial arts project.

"Peter! Welcome to Sandakan," he said. He took my overnight bag and stowed it in the trunk of his car.

"So how did things go with *Misereor*?" he asked as we drove to the mission.

"Very well indeed, thanks to you," I said. "You were right. It was the perfect organization for the project. Thanks for all your encouragement and help. And thanks too, for making me feel welcome when I first arrived in Sabah six years ago. I will always be grateful to you for that."

"My pleasure," Frank said. "Bishop Buis can be a terrible curmudgeon at times. By the way, one of my parishioners spoke highly of you the other day. Her name is Elin Jones. She thinks you did a great job in Beaufort."

I looked at Frank, wondering if Elin had added anything more. But he clapped me on the shoulder and told me that I must go and see her. At the mission, he found her phone number and address for me.

"I have to meet with a contractor about a community centre we're building. Why don't you give Elin a call now? I'll see you tonight for supper."

I looked at the number Frank had given me. All at once I felt ambivalent about making the call. But then, after some hesitation, I picked up the phone.

"This is Peter, Elin," I said when she answered. "I'm at the mission here in Sandakan. I'd like to come and see you."

There was a long silence.

"I don't think that's a good idea," she said at last.

"Please, Elin, just to talk. There are some things I need to tell you, and I'd rather do it in person."

There was another long silence.

"There's nothing to talk about. You have to forget what happened between us."

"That's impossible. You changed me. But I want to explain."

She let out a long breath. I knew her stomach was in a knot. Mine was too.

"Oh, very well, come over if you must. But just to talk. Do you know where I live?"

"Yes," I said, relieved. "Father Frank gave me your address. I'll take a cab."

She let me in as soon as I knocked on the door. The room felt somehow familiar. She had the same sofa, the same coffee table, the same little white rug.

But she was different. She stood in the middle of the room, cold and distant. I felt uncomfortable.

"Sit down," she said, a harsh edge to her voice. She didn't sit next to me, but chose a chair on the other side of the room.

She was just as beautiful as I remembered. But she wouldn't look at me.

I took a deep breath.

"I'm due to fly to Canada next week," I said. "And when I get there, I intend to start the process of leaving the priesthood."

I paused, struggling to find the words.

"I couldn't leave without coming to thank you," I said. "I don't know if you realize how much you gave me. You helped me see the longing I have for a loving relationship is not something trivial. It is an essential part of who I am."

I tried to explain to Elin how in the last year I had come to realize how deeply I wanted a family and a home. That it was something I knew I had missed when I was growing up. But that, until I met her, I had not really understood how incredibly important it was to me. In some ways, joining Mill Hill had been a kind of substitute. It had offered companionship and stability. But the constant struggle to meet the demands of celibacy had prevented me from recognizing what I so deeply wanted. Celibacy had required me to deny who I was.

"I can't do that anymore," I said.

For the first time since I arrived, she lifted her head to look at me.

"I also wanted to apologize," I continued. "I'm so sorry that I only came to realize all this by involving you. I know how much I hurt you. You didn't deserve that. But you helped me come to grips with who I am. You made me confront the pretense in my life. I will always be grateful to you for that."

I looked at her and saw the tension begin to ebb from her face.

For a few minutes she didn't say anything. Then she got up, walked across the room and took both my hands in hers.

"Thank you, Peter," she said.

I stood up and she gave me a hug.

"You're a good man," she said, standing back to look at me. "It's too bad that you were surrounded by nuns and priests growing up. Things might have been different for us. You have to know that I've found someone else here in Sandakan who loves me. He's a normal, ordinary person. We can go out anywhere, anytime. We don't have to hide."

She hugged me again.

"Goodbye, Peter. Thank you for coming to see me. Now I won't be sad when I think of you."

I decided to walk back to the mission. I needed the time to clear my head and my heart.

I was feeling resentful and angry. The resentment and anger had nothing to do with Elin. It was directed at the culture of the Church. The Catholic Church had so dominated my life that I was scarcely able to see myself as a separate person. Later I would come to recognize the good things the Church had given me. But at that moment, I could only feel the hurt.

Beyond the town, the Sulu Sea shimmered in the hot afternoon sun. Along the ocean front, I passed a group of huts perched precariously on poles above the water, forming a floating village. The peacefulness of the scene helped to soothe the turmoil in my heart.

I realized that becoming a priest had been a denial of what I needed most. Catholic culture had been so powerful. It had provided my mother with an excuse to hand me over to the care of strangers. It had promoted a feeling of guilt about my own sexuality. It had prevented me from forming a lasting friendship with Rinty. It had pushed me to create an unreal aura around women that masked their individuality as persons. And all this under the guise of an idealism that promoted self-sacrifice as a means of personal salvation.

When I got back to Beaufort to pack up my things, I found that the school staff and townspeople had decided to throw me a farewell party. They had co-opted the main room of the Government Rest House.

Speeches were made, toasts were drunk, and dancing continued well into the night.

The school children followed up the next day with a concert. It was performed outside on our new basketball courts. They teased me with skits, mocking my various attempts at speaking Kadazan, Hakka, and Malay. They brought tears to my eyes with a song they had composed in my honour, accompanied by a beautiful, elegant dance performed with lit candles and colourful bamboo umbrellas. At the end they presented me with a decorated gift box of locally made toys and puzzles. "For your young brothers and sister in Canada," they said.

Father Chi drove me to the station for my last ride to Kota Kinabalu on the railcar.

A small crowd had gathered to see me off. Jenny Kong was there with her mother. John Mui was there too, with the staff from the school and a crowd of students. Then I noticed that the students were not all wearing the same uniform. Mixed in among the browns of St. John's were the blues of St. Paul's. And in the background I saw my Anglican friend, Colin Hurford, with his lop-sided smile. There was even a delegation of Timorese workers from the rubber plantations.

As I climbed onto the railcar, I realized I couldn't leave without saying something. I stood up and turned to face them. I asked Jenny to stand up next to me and translate.

"Thank you," I said. "Thank you all for coming to say goodbye. Beaufort will always be special for me. Schools are places for people to grow, for teachers as well as students. I know I have grown here. It may well be that we will never see each other again. But you will always be in my heart. I will never forget you."

I nearly fell off as the railcar jerked to life and started to move. Jenny hopped down while I stood clinging to a window frame. Everyone was waving and I kept waving until Beaufort disappeared behind a bend in the railway line.

At Kota Kinabalu no one from the Bishop's house came to see me off. I took a cab directly to the airport.

As the plane lifted up into the deep blue of the Sabah sky, I looked down at the jungle below.

Off to my left Mount Kinabalu rose majestically above the surrounding foothills, trailing a long stream of white cloud from its peak.

There was so much I was going to miss about this beautiful country.

I was going to miss the *ramai-ramai* of harvest time, the elegant, dignified dancing of the *sumazau*, and the uninhibited joy of the *tapai*-drinking.

I was going to miss the generous, friendly people I had lived and worked with for so long.

But most of all, I was going to miss the laughing eyes and cheerful banter of the students who greeted me every morning at the school.

BORNEO

St. Joseph's Church, Papar, Sabah, 1965

St. Joseph's Secondary School, Sabah, 1965

Picnic on Pulau Tiga, Papar, 1965

Crossing the river to Harvest Festival, 1966

Kadazan men in traditional costume, 1966

Kadazan women in traditional costume; 1966

Mt. Kinabalu from Bundu Tuhan (Jan Van Breemen centre), 1967

Josef Haas and me at summit of Mt. Kinabalu, 1967

St. John's School, Beaufort, 1967

Downtown, Beaufort, 1967

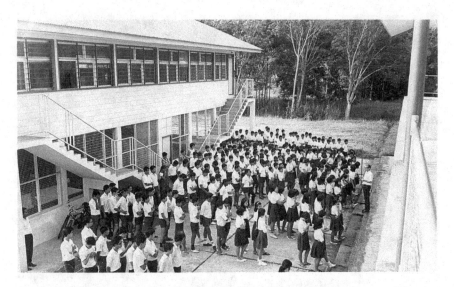

Begining the school day at St. John's School, Beaufort, 1968

Misereor Project: Drafting and Electronics, 1969

Misereor Project: Furniture and Building Construction, 1969

My farewell speech

Farewell Party, May 1970

EPILOGUE

I returned to Canada in the spring of 1970. My laicization was finally approved by Pope Paul II on January 8, 1982. It was Father Vince McCann who patiently persisted in pushing my application through innumerable layers of Vatican bureaucracy. In the meantime, I was hired by the Catholic School Board in Toronto and taught at several different high schools in the city. Very few of my colleagues ever knew of my former career as a missionary. I subsequently married and now have two children and one grandchild, all of whom I love dearly.

I must add that all but one of the characters described in this memoir were, or are, real people. The one exception is Mrs. Lily. She is a composite of several women who talked to me when I was on my way to the seminary. I have tried to represent all the other persons in the story as truly as I can. In a few instances I have changed their names to preserve privacy.

The happiest consequence that has occurred as a result of writing this memoir has been reuniting with many of my former students from Beaufort. They formed an alumni association on Facebook and have welcomed me to join them. Many have pursued interesting careers such as education and medicine, and all seem to remember their school days with nostalgia. It is a joy to see how they have maintained their friendship over the years. I am proud of them all.

ACKNOWLEDGEMENTS

There are very many people who provided me with support and encouragement in the writing of this book.

First and foremost was my great friend and mentor, Ted Tennant, who waded through the drafts of each chapter, blasting away at redundancy and inconsistency. He always challenged me if he felt I was becoming either too earnest or too superficial.

The other person who significantly influenced this book is Trevor Herriot, the distinguished author and naturalist. His guidance, offered at the Banff Centre Workshop for Writers, was particularly valuable. He emphasized the necessity of honouring truth in memoir writing, critical for someone like me who could so easily slip into imaginative fiction.

I was initially encouraged to write this memoir by a group of retired teachers with whom I continue to meet every Thursday evening at a Toronto pub. They all felt that my story was unusual enough to be worth recording. Michael Forster, Mary Slinn, Cecilia Ryan, and Marion McDonell took the time to read the first draft of my manuscript and provided valuable feedback.

Many other colleagues, friends and family have been enormously generous in offering editorial assistance, encouragement, and advice. Phil Small, Catherine Walther, Ruth Nicholls, Jennifer Dyer-Hayes, Anne Birks, Tina Flint, Dave Willekes, my daughter, Melanie, and my son, Michael—all have contributed in no small way to the successful completion of this book.

A big 'thank you' goes to Martin Eckart, who freely gave his time and expertise to create a very attractive web site, and to Dianne Brassolotto who cheerfully undertook the onerous task of copy-editing the manuscript.

I am also very grateful to John Notten at Mary Ward Catholic Secondary School. It was he who suggested I contact Mariah Llanes, one of his former students, currently at the Ontario College of Art and Design, to create the book cover. Mariah successfully captured the ambivalence I felt about being a missionary priest in Borneo. She is a very talented artist, whose web site at http://alongthelines.tumblr.com/ is definitely worth a visit.

And, finally, to my wife, Mary Anne, I owe an enormous debt of gratitude. She read through every page of this book, not just once but several times, searching for elusive typos and grammar mistakes. This was done in what little time she had, between teaching at the Faculty of Education in the University of Ontario Institute of Technology, doing volunteer work, and babysitting our new grandson in Hamilton.

I am forever in awe of this woman whom I was lucky enough to marry.

Peter Bruno Walther
October, 2012.